Marijuana Time

Also by Ken Lukowiak

A SOLDIER'S SONG

Marijuana Time

KEN LUKOWIAK

ORION

The right of Ken Lukowiak to be identified as the author
of this work has been asserted by him in accordance with
the Copyright, Designs and Patents Act 1988.

First published in Great Britain
in 2000 by Orion Media
An imprint of Orion Books Ltd
Orion House, 5 Upper St Martin's Lane,
London WC2H 9EA

A CIP catalogue record for this book is available
from the British Library

Typeset by Deltatype Ltd, Birkenhead, Merseyside

ISBN: 0 75282 127 X

Printed in Great Britain by
Clays Ltd, St Ives plc

For Jill Tweedie
In the name of love

Contents

The first seeds

If everything had gone the way it was planned to go, then I wouldn't even have been in Belize in 1983, and so maybe, just maybe, none of what happened to me there would have. I can only say 'just maybe', because the original plan had been for us to go to Belize the year before, so there's always the chance that it would all still have taken place, only earlier. In April of 1982, along with the rest of my battalion, I was, in fact, already packed for a tour of Belize and already wearing in my new jungle boots. But then (best-laid plans of mice and the general staff...) out of nowhere Argentina goes and invades the Falkland Islands.

'The where?'

Exactly.

Because we were destined for Belize at the time, none of us initially expected the Argentine invasion to affect us that much, and even as the first ships of the task force departed for the islands we were still all geared up to go to Belize. So when it suddenly became 'all change' and the happy news came through that we were to be in on the action after all, it could be said that our inclusion was very much an afterthought.

By the time we did eventually set sail, every other ship in the task force had already left, but we soon caught up. In fact, in the end we caught up so well that we became the first British battalion to land on the Falkland Islands, the first into battle for the attack on Goose Green, the only battalion to fight two battles when we took Wireless Ridge, and the first unit to march victorious into Port Stanley. All in all, we turned out to be an exceptionally good afterthought.

With the war won, we returned to England and the heroes' welcome that awaited us, and after a couple of days in barracks we were sent off on a long period of well-earned leave. Once that had all gone we headed back to Aldershot, where, as of hour one, the routine of normal military life soon kicked us right back into our place. War heroes or not, it was still going to be a left-right, left-right type of existence for us, because that's the way the army works. This also meant that twelve months on from when we were originally supposed to go to Belize, we found ourselves packing our kit once more for destination Central America.

As with anywhere the army might have sent us, with the exception of the Falklands, various pamphlets were made available to us about our destination, and these were backed up by a series of classroom lectures. The pamphlets covered a number of subjects, which ranged from the wonderful sun-drenched beaches we could spend our R&R on to what sort of nasties we could expect to pop out of the jungle and bite us. One piece of information that grabbed my attention early on – very early on, in fact – was that Belize was well known for its high-potency marijuana. Not surprisingly, though, the army approached this subject from a somewhat negative point of view and it was made more than clear to us, on several occasions, that any soldier caught smoking marijuana while in Belize would be discharged from the army via a very unpleasant few months in Colchester's military prison.

In case the importance of this information hadn't quite sunk in, one morning the battalion's junior NCOs (of which I was now a newly promoted member) were given a lecture on drugs by a plain-clothed sergeant of the Royal Military Police (booo!). The lecture's level of information – such as marijuana is also commonly known on the mean civvy streets as 'pot' or 'weed' and is rolled into cigarettes that are called 'reefers' – only made us wonder just where, exactly, the army thought we'd all been for the past twenty years or so. Not on the council estates on which most of us had been brought up and that was for sure.

At one point the plain-clothed MP lit a nice-sized piece of Moroccan hashish and passed it around the room for us all to have sniff. The idea of this was that should we ever be walking past the bike shed in Belize and smell such an aroma wafting through the air, we'd immediately recognise it and know what to do about it. In reality, of course, in Belize you have about as much chance of smelling a piece of burning hashish (which is quite different from the smell of burning 'weed') as you do of seeing an iceberg. And why-oh-why the MP sergeant didn't just burn a piece of grass instead I do not know. After all, it wasn't like he didn't have any. The little tinker had loads of the stuff, because he had brought along a large glass-faced cabinet containing, for identification purposes, a neatly labelled quantity of most types of dope.

Along with his case of samples he had also brought a 16mm projector and a film about military drug abuse to run through it. The film was a Joint Services production, which basically meant that the message contained within it was aimed at the complete military trinity of soldiers, sailors and airmen. To ensure that this message did get through to its full audience, the film told three separate parables of drug abuse in uniform. The first revolved around an army sergeant who became a dope-head while serving in Germany. The second was about an RAF mechanic who got forgetful with his spanners after a weekend of tooting speed, and a pilot who thankfully managed to eject. And the third told the far-out tale of a sailor who fell in with the wrong types while stationed in Hong Kong and ended up dropping acid tabs like they were Smarties, which, as you can imagine, soon led to a trip of the fatal man-overboard kind.

The parable that was aimed at us – and this I know, because as it came on the screen the sergeant said 'I'd like you to pay particular attention to this one, gentlemen' – was the army story about the dope-smoking sergeant. It not only warned us not to smoke dope ourselves, it also pointed out the folly of knowing that a fellow soldier was toking away but failing to report him. Plotwise, the story bore a remarkable resemblance to the early pages of the Bible: Adam and Eve in paradise, only this time with a young German girl taking the role of Satan's fruity temptress. The two main characters were a couple of bosom-buddy sergeants of the Royal Tank Corps who were stationed in the old NATO buffer zone of West Germany.

We first meet them as they're travelling into Berlin together for a boys' night out on the town. After a few drinks in a quiet bar they end up (the way you do when you're a squaddie away from home) at a nightclub, where their groovy-looking poly-ester shirts and flared trousers, not to mention their wallets overflowing with Overseas Allowance, soon attract the attention of a couple of short-skirted Fräuleins. After a bit of chat-up and some get-on-down disco dancing, the next scene has our sergeants back at the girls' flat, where they're drinking wine and all in all having a fine, and perfectly correct, time. This scene swayed between resembling the opening sequence of a Color Climax 8mm porno film and the middle of a Pearl & Dean advert for a high street 'Modern Man' shop. Surely at any moment one of the girls would start to unzip things? Alas, this did not come to pass, but as the wine flowed the two couples did partake of a bit of drunken heavy petting.

Then suddenly – da-dah! – one of the young German ladies breaks off from her moment of passion to take a ready-made 'reefer' from her purse. She lights it up, takes a couple of deep, done-it-before tokes and then passes it over to one of our brave boys. At first he quite rightly declines her offer, pointing out that drugs are not good for you. But German Eva's the persistent type, and as she strokes the inside of the sergeant's thigh and seductively holds the joint up to his lips, he gives in to her feminine wiles and has a toke on the forbidden fruit. The other sergeant, though, he's a very conscientious NCO and there's no budging him, no matter the amount of sexual bribes on offer. Long before Nancy Reagan's catchphrase, he just keeps saying no – and good for him (though we in the back row concluded that he must have been some kind of pansy).

If only his comrade had been as strong. Because before you

can say 'Don't Bogart that joint, my friend, 'cos I've got a tank to drive', Sergeant Spliffy's a total dope addict, desperate to light up whenever and wherever he can, and poor old Sergeant No-No's having to lug around the moral dilemma of what to do about it. After all, Sergeant Spliffy is his best army mucker, and if he turns him over to the Military Police for smoking marijuana, well, that'll destroy their male-type bonding thing, won't it? Oh, what to do?

After a fade to black we next find our two sergeants out in the woods on a NATO exercise. Sergeant No-No's taking the Warsaw Pact threat seriously and is charging around in an efficient manner, doing military-type things with his map and compass. Sergeant Spliffy, on the other hand, he's hiding away behind a tree having a quick puff on the old 'wacky baccy'.

But before he can get down to the roach, the command comes through to move out. Sergeant Spliffy grabs a last deep toke on his joint, then another quick one for luck, and leaps into his tank. At the same time Sergeant No-No climbs behind the wheel of his Land Rover and immediately starts issuing orders over his radio. In the notional battle that follows, dopehead Sergeant Spliffy is so off his face that he drives his tank right over his best friend's Land Rover, killing poor old Sergeant No-No instantly. The End.

Now, whether the makers of this film expected us at this point to start bleating aloud 'My, if only Sergeant Spliffy hadn't started smoking dope' and 'If only Sergeant No-No had [excuse the pun] grassed him up' I don't know. What I do know is that they would have been very disappointed with our group's reaction to it all. For our conclusion was that the German girls doing the tempting were such drop-dead shakeable babes that we'd have smoked heroin if we'd thought it would help us get into their knickers. Mind you, none of us drove tanks, did we?

After that, the only other discussion that day on the subject of drugs took place during the NAAFI break that followed the showing of the film, and once again I don't think it was quite the sort of thing the military were wanting from us. The discussion revolved around a plan to steal the MP sergeant's cabinet of drugs, which we'd just seen him put into the boot of his car on his way to the sergeants' mess for his elevenses. In our defence, I should point out that our reason for plotting to do this was based not so much on a desire to get our hands on a pile of illegal substances as on the very deep level of shit the sergeant would find himself in once he came out of his nervous breakdown. The paperwork alone.

If learning that there was marijuana in Belize was my first step on the road to what followed, then I guess I took my second on the morning I first walked into the army post room at Rideau Camp shortly after we arrived in Belize.

Waiting for me there that day was a lance corporal of the Royal Engineers, the corps responsible for the to-ing and fro-ing of mail within the British army, and the reason he was there was to give me a quick training session to prepare me for the job of running Rideau Camp's post office for the next six months. Now, in the army the explaining of 'how to' on every conceivable subject has been broken down to a level where hopefully even a soldier with a brain that's only two degrees short of becoming yogurt can take it all in. Therefore the lance corporal of the Royal Engineers had been allocated a whole day to pass on to me, the newly promoted lance corporal of the Parachute Regiment, what I'd have to know in order to take over as the new main man at Rideau Camp's post office.

Since I could already read and write, and so could my fellow lance corporal, all the information I needed had been passed on by him and understood by me within the first half-hour. So, with all of that learning out the way and a bit of time on our hands, we headed off to the NAAFI, where we could pass the time of day over a Coke or two and hopefully avoid anyone of higher rank who might just notice that we were doing what every soldier likes doing best, i.e. nothing.

In view of the fact that I had only been stationed in Belize since yesterday afternoon and my new friend from the Royal Engineers had been there for six months, he, naturally enough, did most of the talking and I, naturally enough, was very interested to hear what he'd got to say. At one point he went over the benefits of shopping in the camp's NAAFI, which, because it was a NAAFI abroad, was stocked with items that were all duty-free. Now, according to the lance corporal, if there was one item where the lack of tax really made a huge difference compared with the shop price back home, it was King Edward's cigars. Apparently, back in England King Edward's cigars retailed at one pound each, whereas here, in their state of Belizian duty-freeness, they cost less than a tenner for a box of fifty.

As he finished telling me all this, the lance corporal put on a very deliberate smile and then winked in a way that said there was a lot more to the tale of King Edward and his cigars. So I fed him the 'What?' that I felt he was fishing for, and sure enough, he leaned closer, looked around to make sure no one could overhear and told me his secret.

'I've been posting them home,' he whispered. 'One box a week for the past ten weeks or so.'

'But isn't that risky?' I asked.

'Nope,' he replied. And then he went on to explain why.

Rideau Camp's outgoing mail was bagged up early every morning, with the exception of Sundays, and taken by the postal clerk (which from now on meant me) to the local airstrip in the nearby town of Punta Gorda. It was then loaded on to the morning civilian flight to Belize City, where it was unloaded and passed over to the British Forces Post Office (BFPO) within the main military base at Air Port Camp (APC). And from there it was put aboard the next military flight back to Brize Norton in England.

Now, according to the lance corporal there was one military transport plane that left Belize City every Tuesday afternoon, flew via a base in Canada and arrived at Brize Norton in the very early hours of Wednesday morning. What this crucially meant was that on that particular day the mail was offloaded and picked up by a van that took it to the main BFPO in London before the officers of Her Majesty's Customs had even got out of bed in the morning, never mind clocked on for work.

'Of course I always wrap the box in a few clothes,' the lance corporal went on to explain, 'but every one I've posted has got through – no trouble.'

Whether I wondered right there and then, 'Well, what else could you post back then?' I don't now remember, but whatever, a significant part of the end plan had definitely been taken on board.

See the world and meet interesting people (the hard way)

Belize and the Falkland Islands held a certain similarity for me in that I hadn't heard of either of them until I joined the army. Unlike the Falklands, though, which didn't come to my attention until the Argentine invasion of 1982, Belize was pointed out to me during my very first week of army life.

Not that I'd joined up for the travel. To put it plainly and simply, my reason for joining up was that I wanted to become a 'real man'. A friend of my brother's had once been a sergeant in the Parachute Regiment, and it would be fair to say that it was his tales of battles past that influenced my decision more than anything else. And for top-up I had a friend in Bristol, called Bob, who had also been in the Paras. Just like my brother's mate, Bob would explain, as I sat there all wide-eyed and deeply interested, how the Paras were the army's toughest and bravest. If it was manhood I was looking for, they were the ones for me. They were the elite.

Having taken all this in, I became like a schoolboy sizing up the contents of a sweet shop whenever I considered anything to do with the Parachute Regiment. One of my main memories of my groupie-like hero worship of the Paras at that time is of Bob's old red beret, which he still kept on a hook in his bedroom. I would look at that beret and just think it was so wonderful.

Dear of me.

I eventually signed on the dotted line and took my king's shilling – which by then was up to a queen's six pounds – in

July of 1979, at the Army Careers Office in Bristol. From there I was given a rail warrant and dispatched to a camp at Sutton Coldfield near Birmingham, where, along with a whole bunch of other new recruits, I was to spend two days (or was it three?) being put through a series of mental and physical examinations and shown what the army had to offer careerwise.

At what point, during those early days, Belize first surfaced as a possible destination I'm not too sure, though I do remember that I first learned of its existence sitting on a plastic chair watching one of the many army travelogue-type films that we were shown. And like *The Holiday Show* they were, except that instead of being given the price of flights, food and accommodation at the end of each location, what we got was a breakdown of the extra money we would earn in the form of 'overseas allowance', plus the amounts we could save while serving abroad, because, unlike in the UK, all food and accommodation was free. And as for the air fares – don't even give them a thought. When a map showing where Belize was appeared on the screen, followed by footage of soldiers cutting their way through a jungle, I do remember finding it interesting. I'd never heard of the place before, but I guess I must have wondered even then if one day I might end up being posted there.

Initially, as a group of new intakes to the army, although we would eventually end up scattered around many different regiments and corps, we were all shown the same films and given the same lectures. But that all rapidly changed once we had completed the several written examinations. We were assured before the start of each exam that it was impossible to finish any of them in the time allowed, but that didn't matter, they said, because it was the quality of our answers that counted and not the width.

The only previous experience I'd had of an army exam was the one I'd been called in to take one morning at the Army Careers Office back in Bristol. That one had been of the multiple-choice answer type and was made up of a hundred questions, only one of which caused me to pause and re-read it before telling myself to stop being daft and tick what had to be the correct box. To give you an example of the difficulty of the questions (just so that you don't go around thinking I'm a bit of a brain), one of them went something like: Cat is to Kitten as Dog is to A. Giraffe, B. Puppy, C. Kangaroo. And yet when I'd finished the paper and was taking a smug look around the room, I saw that there were some amongst the twenty or so of us who ticked away that morning who struggled with it. And I don't know why, but that surprised me.

The exams at Sutton Coldfield turned out to be a completely different kettle of aquatic creatures. They all started off pretty much like the one in Bristol, but as they progressed they got harder and harder, and it wasn't too long before we all discovered that they hadn't been lying – it really was impossible to finish in the given time. In fact, it was probably impossible to finish in the whole of the rest of time. As my brain came to a grinding halt midway through the paper on maths, which I'd always considered to be my best subject at school, I couldn't resist sneaking a little look at what the questions were like on the last page, and believe me, they looked like they were written in Arabic. Soldier on.

When we had finished all the exams, our scores were totted up and, depending on our results, we were placed into five different groups. The top-scoring group (which, to my surprise, I was a member of) were given five sheets of paper on which were listed all the various jobs and trades within the army that were on offer to us. As this process of selection worked its way down to the none-too-bright within our ranks, the lowest-scoring group were given a single piece of paper, on which there were only three career options: the Royal Pioneer Corps, the Infantry, and last and by all means least, the Parachute Regiment.

Like most new recruits who eventually end up joining the Paras, I had arrived at Sutton Coldfield already knowing exactly which unit I wanted to join. For me it was the Parachute Regiment or nothing. But while I was at Sutton Coldfield, and even more so after my exam results, I found that I was being told time and time again by officers and NCOs, all of whom came from other regiments, that I did *not* want to join the Paras.

'You don't want to do that,' they'd say. 'You'd be wasted there. And anyway, you wouldn't get through the tough physical selection in the first place.'

The campaign to dissuade me from joining the Parachute Regiment reached its peak during my final interview and assessment at Sutton Coldfield, at which I got to sit down and have a cosy little 'Smoke if you like, son' careers chat with a major. At one point the major actually said that I couldn't join the Paras, that I wasn't allowed to (so there), and that I had to choose another unit or nothing at all. And when he went on to tell me all about the heroics of the army Commandos and the tradesmen therein who wore green berets and were attached to the Royal Marines, I did nearly waver.

But then I remembered, just in time, the words of a Parachute Regiment sergeant on the permanent staff at Sutton Coldfield, who the night before, in the NAAFI, had pulled aside the three or four of us who wanted to join the Paras and warned us not to believe any of the bullshit 'the hats' might feed us – especially the one about us not being allowed to join the regiment.

'Yes, sergeant.'

So I told the major that if I couldn't be a para, then I didn't want to join the army at all.

'Are you quite sure of that, lad?' he asked.

'Positive, sir,' I replied.

He then, seconds after telling me there was no way in the world that I could join my chosen regiment, did a complete about-turn by coming out with: 'All right, then. I'll send you to the Paras.' His white flag of submission to my wishes did, though, have a somewhat bitter and twisted sting to its pole. As I walked towards the door he called out after me: 'Believe me, you won't like it. And you won't make it through the selection either.'

Without a doubt, the major at Sutton Coldfield was my very first breathing example of what we paras called a 'crap-hat

Rupert wanker'. However, his words did help to drive me on by putting thoughts of eat, humble and pie into my head. I'd show him. I'd prove just how wrong he was about me and what I was capable of. (Which was all a load of bollocks, really. After all, what was I going to do? Invite him to my pass-out parade? Send him a postcard from sunny Northern Ireland when I got there?)

That evening, on display in the cookhouse at Sutton Coldfield was a print of a painting depicting a battle scene at Arnhem in Holland, where one of those glorious defeats for the British army, and specifically the Parachute Regiment, had taken place during World War Two. And bloody marvellous it was as well. Made you proud.

The print, though nicely framed, was not hanging on a wall but resting on a blackboard easel that you had to shuffle by as you queued for your food. The next morning at breakfast it was gone, and in its place had appeared another print of another battle fought by another regiment. As with nearly all the battle paintings of this genre that are commissioned by the British army, the print of the Paras in action at Arnhem showed the gallant last act of a medal-winning soldier, in this case one who had been awarded the Victoria Cross. Although the picture had dead bodies in it, and soldiers who were wounded and bleeding and wearing red-stained bandages, it still came across to me, keen as I was, looking like the cover of a box of Airfix toy soldiers.

When I first noticed it and read the label underneath – 'Soldier So-and-so VC, late [as in dead] of the Parachute Regiment' – I immediately flashed up a little fantasy that one day, chin up, chest out, I would do something equally as brave while wearing a red beret, and many years on others would look up to a similar painting of me. (However, in my version of future events I took it as read that I wouldn't get killed, and that my admirers would at least be able to remember my name.)

And wouldn't you know it? Just like some twat paratrooper that you might find in a Frederick Forsyth novel, nearly three years on from that cookhouse queue and its painting of paras from the past, I ended up taking part in two battles in the Falklands that led to the commissioning of four more army paintings. But do I appear in any of them? No I do not. Because what I was to find out, come reality time, about dead bodies and men who were wounded and bleeding and really wearing red-stained bandages (though by then I was referring to them as shell dressings) was that my one-time dream of 'chin up, chest out' didn't even enter my mind. All that did was 'look out' and 'head down'.

Looking back now, from cookhouse print to real-death battle – boy to man, if you like – it sometimes makes me feel like I was a perfect example of a human cliché.

Dear of me again.

After finally being granted my death wish to join the Paras, I was issued another rail warrant and from Sutton Coldfield I was sent to the Parachute Regiment Training Depot at Browning Barracks in Aldershot. As soon as I got to that wonderful place, with its real paratroopers, all in the faded red berets and Para smocks that I would one day wear, I was marched in front of the depot's adjutant to be welcomed into the family fold.

Once the formal greetings were over, the adjutant explained to me where I now stood, as a member of the Parachute Regiment, in the greater order of all units, army. He did this by first enquiring if I had been dissuaded in any way from joining the regiment by the 'crap-hats', as he referred to them, up at Sutton Coldfield. I confirmed that yes, I had, and I told him all about the major and his lie to me.

'Do you know *why* they didn't want you to come here?' the adjutant then asked.

'No, sir. I don't,' I replied.

'Because they hate us, that's why. And do you know why they hate us?'

'No, sir.'

'Because we're better than them. Never forget that.'

And I never have.

Another thing I never got to forget from my chat with the

adjutant that day was the moment when he looked at my file and commented on the marijuana-smoking that I'd confessed to at the Bristol careers office. As they knew I'd worked in a casino, and before that a television station in Australia, I reckoned they must have already figured out that I'd come into contact with drugs, so when I was asked if I'd ever smoked dope, I admitted that I had (though only at parties, you understand).

The adjutant asked me if I still smoked marijuana, which of course was a bit of a daft question, really. After all, what did he expect me to say? Sometimes, just at night, to help me relax? I don't think so. When I did hurriedly reply 'Oh no, sir,' he merely remarked 'I'm glad to hear it.' Then he wished me luck and sent me on my way.

From the adjutant's office I was told to go and report to the pay office, and, boy, was there a huge surprise waiting for me there. I was given yet another rail warrant (three in one week – I was never to match it) and about a hundred pounds in cash, and sent off on four weeks' leave.

It got better as well, because when I was actually on leave, halfway through it they sent me a fortnight's pay in postal orders. As my friends of the time pointed out, because I had a six-week pull-out clause, if I'd gone back to Aldershot and told them I'd changed my mind and didn't want to join the army after all I would have been well in front. Though the way I felt about becoming a paratrooper, there was as much chance of me doing that as there was of the Iranians putting a pig on the moon.

When I did eventually start my basic training, I did so along with sixty-two other new haircuts. On our first day we were marched on to the parade ground and lined up for a platoon photograph, which was later pinned up on the platoon's noticeboard. Six months later, of the original sixty-three only thirteen of us remained. Each time someone dropped out a cross was inked over their face on the photo, and we were told by our corporal instructors that the ones with the crosses hadn't been man enough to become paratroopers. As this was what

15

joining the Parachute Regiment had been all about for me, I was more than happy to believe them.

In a word, basic training was hard. So much so that all these years later it's become much like the experience of true fear – impossible to fully explain to others.

My first major shock (and shock was the word) came during our first period of something that went by the name of 'battle PT'. I had assumed that, as far as things of a physical nature went, we'd be built up slowly, day by day. As I bunny-hopped it across the gym floor, with the old 'muscles I never knew I had' firmly announcing their presence, I can distinctly remember thinking that I just could not believe how hard it was, and right from the off. Suckered again, as the weeks went by and life got harder and harder, I soon began to realise that they had of course been building us up slowly, day by day.

It wasn't only the exercise that I was a little innocent about, either. In our seventh week of training we moved from Aldershot to the Brecon Beacons in Wales, where for seven days we were to do something that was called 'basic Brecon' (and in this case basic was the word). We were camped, although there were no tents involved, in a forestry block, and on our second night we were timetabled to do what was known as a recce patrol. This involved covering about five miles across country in the dark, creeping up on an enemy position, spying on them, and then marching the five miles back home again. And all before dawn.

The weather that night was unbelievable. It rained and rained like I had never seen rain before. When I added the thunder and lightning and gale-force winds that came with it, I assumed that our patrol would be cancelled. After all, none of us had waterproofs. Well, dream on . . . and while you're at it, come and have a look at the little pink fairies that live at the end of my garden.

Once the two corporals to whom I had put this assumption managed to stop laughing and patting me on the head, we set off, and I soon found out that the rain was irrelevant, because they waded us through two rivers on the way out and another two on the way back. When we finally reached our patrol's destination, we lay down on the grass and stayed like that, with no movement and no sound, for hours. And they were hours that seemed to have thousands of seconds in each and every dark, windy minute. It was so cold and so wet that for the first time in my life I deliberately pissed myself in an attempt to warm my legs up. And I can recommend it, because it worked.

Another thing about the weather conditions that night was that they were a good example of something you hate while in training but are likely to pray out loud for in a real war. For when you're really attacking or creeping up on an enemy, then the louder and colder and wetter the weather, the better it is for you to hide behind and the more likely the enemy is to be all snuggled up and switched off. Then it's out with the knife and he's bleeding from the neck.

If I had one major problem during basic training – that is, besides the physical exercise and the weather conditions and the food you could never get enough of and the lack of sleep and the mornings before dawn and the late nights, oh, and the drill and the discipline and the constant cleaning and scrubbing, not to mention the persistent shouting – then I guess it was my aggression. Or should I say my lack of it? If I was to become one of our nation's elite killers, then this was obviously something they were going to have to change in me, and change it they did. And when they did . . . 'Oh yes, I remember it well.'

The day had begun, as it always did back then, with a quick two miles, in PT order, around Browning Barracks. Then it was breakfast and back to the block for an hour of kit and room inspections. At nine we paraded for a ten-mile battle march: 'T-shirt order', thirty pounds of sand in our webbing and no weapons. The weight we were carrying was always checked by the platoon corporals, who walked between our ranks with a set of butcher's scales. During this inspection we stood to attention with our webbing 'to our front' and our two water bottles, with caps removed, in our hands, held out so that the level of water could easily be seen and checked. It was a freezing morning, and when the corporal got to me, my offence on the bottle front was so terrible that he never got around to weighing my webbing.

One of my water bottles had room for at least another half-inch of water in it. He took the offending bottle from my hand and, while I stood rigidly to attention, slowly poured the ice-cold water over my head. Then he pushed the empty bottle into my stomach, leaned forward right into my face and yelled at me to 'go and fill the fucking thing up'.

I broke ranks and ran off to the platoon washrooms, and by the time I got there I was in tears. And make no mistake, they *were* sorry-for-myself tears. By this time a few weeks of basic training had passed and I just didn't think I could take any more. I didn't feel I 'belonged'.

The march that followed turned out to be the normal ten-mile nightmare over the tank tracks of Aldershot, and the last mile back into camp took us along the bank of the Basingstoke canal. As was normal during those early weeks of training, the previous nine miles had already strung most of the platoon out. But I was OK. By the time we reached the canal and broke from 'double march' to a slower 'quick march', I was up with the main group and trying to get my head together for the one where they run us right up to our barrack-room door and then turn round and say, 'Only joking. Not let's go for another five miles.'

The corporal who had poured the water over my head earlier appeared at my side as we marched and asked, 'How's my little mummy's boy, then?' And then he pushed me into the canal. As I hit the water I broke ice, screaming with the shock.

When I climbed out of the canal, shivering uncontrollably with the cold, the corporal was standing on the bank, hands on hips, laughing. On my knees, I looked up at him and – with no thought as to the consequences – shouted into his face that he was a 'fucking bastard'. This just made him laugh harder. Then he leaned forward until his face was about two inches from mine, smiled and whispered, 'Why don't you come and fucking kill me then.' Then he kicked me back into the canal.

As I hit the water for the second time I lost it completely. I didn't care who I was, I didn't care who he was. I was going to hurt him. I jumped out of the canal screaming with rage. The corporal, still laughing, ran off, but I ran screaming after him. I ran flat out for nearly a mile, and as I ran I pushed any platoon stragglers who were blocking my path into the canal.

I eventually caught up with the leading elements of the platoon just as they were slowing down once more to a 'quick march' to enter the barracks. By the time we came to a halt on the parade ground I was breathless and my raging temper had subsided to a mild hatred.

As we waited for the stragglers and the 'left-behinds' to catch up, the platoon sergeant told us all about them. We were now here where we had to be. They were not. We were now ready to fight the enemy. Those wankers, the ones still moaning and whining and hobbling along a mile back, were not. Because of them we were no longer at full strength. We had more chance of being killed when we faced the enemy because there were now fewer of us, and fewer men meant fewer weapons. They had risked our lives, they had let us down, they were weak-willed wankers . . .

While the sergeant continued his morning reading from the sacred book of Para, the corporal who had pushed me into the canal came over to me. I braced myself for at least a punch in the face for my earlier outburst, but it never came. Instead, he put an arm round my shoulder, playfully pushed his fist into my stomach, and said, 'That was better. Good man.' Then he gave me an all-boys-together punch on the shoulder and walked off.

I felt ten feet tall. I 'belonged' after all.

Two and a bit years later I was to run flat out again for another mile, but this time it wasn't into the training barracks but into the centre of Port Stanley on the Falkland Islands. And I was not alone. We were all there, two whole battalions of us, minus dead and injured – as one, together, ready to fight again. The training had paid off. In Argentina the families of the not-so-well-trained were preparing for the funerals.

The corporal who poured the water over me and pushed me into the canal that day later went on to become a sergeant in the battalion I served with in the Falklands – 2 Para. God bless Maggie, and don't fuck with us. At Goose Green he managed to keep his chin up and his chest out and was awarded a medal for bravery. I'm glad to say, because he was a good guy at heart, that he didn't get killed, and all these years later I can still remember his name. It was Meredith. Though I don't think he got a painting!

With the exception of the specialist training we received for tours of Northern Ireland, most of our basic training revolved around the assumption that one day all of those nasty Russian tanks that were based in East Germany would come screaming over the border. This, of course, proved to be a myth of the highest order, the truth being that the combined forces of the Warsaw Pact couldn't get an orange from an orchard in Georgia on to a barrow in Red Square, never mind move a hundred tank divisions across half of Europe without running out of petrol. We were taught to use and identify all of their weapons and enjoyed many a back-row chuckle as we watched Russian training films in darkened rooms. Whenever we were in an army corridor, somewhere on the walls there would be a poster identifying Russian military hardware, or photographs showing Russian ranks and insignia. Make no mistake, by the time the Parachute Regiment had finished with us, we were more than prepared for the Commie threat.

However, the next scene in the movie is that we're all up to our necks in blood, mud and sheep shit, fighting the Argentinians on a group of islands that not one of us (well, there was one guy in B Company, who had collected stamps as a kid) has ever heard of. Thankfully, though, come combat time it didn't really matter who they had trained us to fight against. As soon as the first bullet or shell comes your way, your head is zapped into what I can only describe as another dimension. Suddenly there are only two types of people in the world: the ones who want to kill you and the ones who don't.

As the weeks of training went by and we returned to Brecon and then went on to RAF Brize Norton for our parachute training, so more and more faces were crossed off the photograph. They just weren't man enough, we were told. By then, though, I knew, because I had shared a room and broken bread with them for months, that some of those who had dropped out had been more than fit enough and strong enough to make it through – if only they had believed.

And that was the big thing about making it through the Parachute Regiment's basic training. You had to believe. In yourself. And in the reputation of the regiment.

Downtown

Left out of the gate and then two miles down the straight dirt road that passed right outside Rideau Camp lay the town of Punta Gorda, or PG as it was known throughout Belize. Each and every night a duty Land Rover left camp at seven o'clock to take into PG any soldiers who felt like a limited night out on the town (and limited, or so they promised, was the word). At eleven o'clock the same Land Rover would return to pick up the hopefully by now pissed men and return them safely and quietly, with no harm done to any civilians, back to camp.

So, excitement-seekers that we were, come 1900 hours on our very first night at Rideau my pal Dave and myself paraded at the guardroom in our neatly pressed civvies and caught the duty vehicle to Excitementville, where we hoped to get to mingle with some civilisation, as in non-military personnel, preferably female.

The driver that first night was a soldier from the rear guard of the battalion we were replacing, and as he had driven into PG and back, as he put it, 'fuck knows how many cunting times', he gave us a quick rundown of the squaddie-type (and that's us, mate) pleasure spots the town had to offer. The place he advised us to visit first was the Mira Mar Hotel, which was apparently the best bar and restaurant in town by a long, long way.

When we got to Punta Gorda, sizewise at least it was pretty much how I had expected it to be: six or seven shabby but neat-looking blocks deep, eight or so equally shabby but neat-looking blocks wide. Most of the houses we passed were built out of wood, with roofs of corrugated iron, but as the driver took us on a five-minute recce through the backstreets, every now and then we would come across a house that did seem to have been built by the Third Little Piggy Construction Company. These brick-built houses were the homes of the rich people, we guessed. Mind you, what with the high walls surrounding them and their metal gates with nasty-looking spikes on top, you didn't need a commission and twelve months at Sandhurst to work that one out.

We came across only one and a half streets that were illuminated by street lamps and drove down many others with no electricity at all. In these the flickering light from hurricane lamps and candles that escaped into the night from the houses made me wonder what it would be like to be one of the people inside – and thankful that I wasn't.

We were finally dropped on a corner of PG's main drag and the only tarmacked road in town, which was known as Front Street (as in sea). From any point along this road you could throw a stone underarm into the warm waters of the Caribbean, though with two public lavatories that were no more than little jetties with cubicles hanging five or so yards out above the water, you wouldn't ever want to go swimming in it. It was really shitty. Literally.

The driver pointed down Front Street and asked us if we could see the place with the lighted sign where the music was coming from. Since it was the only place with a lighted sign, we replied yes, we could.

'Well, that's the Mira Mar,' he said. 'See you back here at eleven. And if you're not here, I go without you and you walk back. 'Cos there's no taxicabs in PG.'

We assured him we'd be there on time, thanked him for his little tour of the town, not to mention the lift into it, and set off to walk the hundred or so yards to the Mira Mar. And as we walked, I felt just great. The night around us was warm, there were thousands of bright stars scattered all over the black sky, and everyone we passed smiled a hello with a flash of perfect white teeth. Friendly place. It could just be me, but every time I walk down a street for the first time in a new country, I always get this very happy lift. Like I've achieved something just by being there.

The Mira Mar was Front Street's largest building and one of the few constructed completely from brick. At the front was a wide flight of concrete steps that led up to a narrow covered patio on which there were two doors. One of these was the entrance to the restaurant on the right, the other to the bar on the left. Since the bar was the place where the loud music was coming from, and where everybody else seemed to be going, we flipped a mental coin and took the left-hand door.

Inside, we instantly walked from warm into hot. The place was dimly lit and I would guess that we shared the room with maybe forty or fifty other people, most of whom were black, although there were some Latin-looking types and the odd white gathered around a jukebox at the far end of the room. Next to the jukebox were two more doorways, one leading to a room at the back that served as the disco, with a dance floor and chairs around the walls, the other a cut through to the restaurant next door.

Behind the bar was a mirrored wall that gave the room the illusion of being much bigger than it actually was. Most of the girls at the far end of the bar, who were mainly huddled in little groups sipping Cokes through straws and giggling amongst themselves, had brightly-coloured plastic curlers in their hair, covered by a hairnet. From the shoulders up they looked as though they were still getting ready to go out as opposed to already being out. It didn't take us long to work out that if you were a PG girl who was the proud owner of a set of plastic hair curlers, then number one on your positively must-do list was to flaunt 'em, baby! At the time, my young male mind couldn't help but wonder what those girls would be prepared to do for a set of heated rollers. And strangely enough, today my older male mind wonders the same thing.

Behind the bar a young kid appeared, who couldn't have been more than twelve years old and looked like he should really have been in bed by now in preparation for school the next day, and asked what he could get us. Thinking Rome and Romans, we held ourselves back from asking 'Does your daddy know you're here, son?' and ordered two cold beers.

Once the kid had expertly flipped the caps off the bottles and pocketed the 10 cents change we'd told him he could keep, we moved away from the bar and sat down at a wooden table. Two minutes later our first bar girl of Belize skipped over. Tall and thin, with skin as black as the plastic on stereo equipment, she was dressed in shorts and a T-shirt as if she was just off to the beach. Her name, it turned out, was Rosie, and over the next six months fate would have it that we were to get to know Rosie fairly well – though neither of us in the biblical sense of the word.

Rosie was also wearing a red baseball cap, the right way round, and was chewing gum. She did these things, and for some reason it was obvious right from the start, to help along her life's dream of becoming an American. In fact, she was by no means unique in having this dream, as nearly every other non-white we ever met in Belize also wished that they'd been born American and therefore been born rich. And this I could understand, as back in the days when I still wore short trousers and lived on a council estate in Swindon I would swap bubble-gum cards and read DC comics and have exactly the same dream, for exactly the same reasons. The comics carried advertisements for thousand-piece sets of toy soldiers that I wished so much that I could own. But I couldn't, because I didn't have a Zip code, whatever that was.

Five minutes into our first conversation with Rosie and her first rum and Coke (with no rum) on us, she asked, again a bit like Eve on page one of the Bible, if we'd like to score some 'weed'.

Well . . . we might. It depended how much for how much.

'Five dollars, and you give me one dollar for going,' she told us, smiling and tilting her head to one side.

How could we refuse? Six dollars was only two pounds sterling, which was hardly a huge risk, was it? So we said OK and handed over the money. Rosie then asked us if we'd like to go along with her, see the sights. Since this was not only our first night out in Punta Gorda but our first night out in Belize (as in new country) it did cross our minds that we might get led by Rosie-Posy here up a dark alley and get ourselves stabbed, or worse, and then robbed. And in a way, shame on us for that. Because, as we were soon to find out, PG was considerably safer than just about anywhere in England. In fact, now I come to think of it, the only aggression, either verbal or physical, that I ever witnessed in PG always had a British soldier on at least one end of it. But, as I said, we were new to the country, so what did we know?

We thought about it for a bit and then said, 'Oh, what the heck?' We were both British paratroopers, weren't we? We were fit and tough and could outrun anyone. So we let Rosie lead the way.

As we walked from the Mira Mar, taking what were to be our first of many steps through the unlit backstreets of Punta Gorda, our progress was annoyingly marked by the barking of dogs, which appeared to be a fixture in every home. It soon became apparent that these dogs were somewhat nasally racist, as they never barked at any of the locals we passed – only us whities.

After a few blocks we stopped at a T-junction, where Rosie asked as to wait on the track while she nipped off into the shadows to do the business.

From where we stood on the street-cum-dirt track, through the darkness we could just about make out Rosie tapping on what looked like a garden shed, and not a very sturdy one at that. After a few moments a sleepy, muffled reply could be heard from inside, which was followed by the sound of a door opening and a bit of whispering. Then Rosie handed our cash in through the doorway and the door was closed again. A minute or so later it reopened, there was a bit more whispering and something was passed back out.

When Rosie got back to where we were standing there was no need for us to ask how it had gone because we had seen, and it had gone just fine. A fuck sight easier than in Aldershot. In her hand she had five brown wraps that she had bought with our five dollars, and straight away I couldn't help but think: 'What a bargain.'

We broke our return journey to the Mira Mar at the next junction, taking a seat on what I think was the porch of the Belizian equivalent of a Spar shop (open from eight till it gets too hot to work, man). Not being Boy Scouts, we had unfortunately failed to come prepared for our first deal in Belize, and in no way was this failure more evident than in our combined lack of cigarette papers, which, when abroad, can sometimes be a constant problem. To make a joint, you really do kinda need them.

'Oh no you don't, man,' laughed Rosie as she opened one of the brown-paper wraps, spread its contents out a little with her finger, and then rolled it up again into a cone. Being gentlemen, we offered the lady a light, and our first joint in Belize was off and smoking. Rosie took a couple of tokes, which caused some popping of seeds, and then passed it over to me.

New boy on the block that I was, I took a long, deep pull just to show this bar girl what a man of the world I was. And then I coughed my guts up all over the street. Still bending over, coughing away like a cat that's just drunk petrol, I held out the joint for Dave, who was finding my bronchial discomfort highly amusing. Not half as daft as he looked, Dave, having taken silent heed of my violent reaction, did no more than dip his toe in with a quick, short drag on the joint. But it made no difference. The moment the smoke hit his lungs, try as he might to hold it in, he was bent double and coughing up in unison with me. Rosie just looked on and laughed, as though we were a couple of small children or kittens that had just done something funny. (All say 'aah'.)

When the joint got back to me for ding-ding, round two, I took a few smaller tokes of the once-bitten-twice-shy variety. This still resulted in a bit of coughing, but it got better the more I toked. And then bang! – like a truck hitting me – I was up and flying with the bats.

'Are those bats?' I asked.

'Well they ain't fucking penguins,' I answered.

'Good gear,' I said aloud.

'It certainly works, lance corporal,' agreed Dave.

'That's corporal to you, private,' I corrected.

When the joint was finished we thought about having a second but wisely decided against it. Instead, leaving a chorus of yapping dogs in our wake, we headed on back to the Mira Mar. But when we got there – hey, José! – was it a different place, in a flashing coloured lights and loud music sort of way. Bopping our way to the bar in tune with the Michael Jackson number that was blaring out on the jukebox, we once again ordered a couple of cold beers for ourselves and a nice rum and Coke, with no rum, for Rosie from the twelve-year-old working the bar.

We found an empty table and sat down. As I gazed around me, it was one of those rare moments when I could just sit back and feel that everything in life was fine. Look at it. A bar in a warm foreign country, money in our pockets, cold beer in our hands, plenty of girls (albeit ones who think plastic curlers are the height of fashion), and ultra-great gear floating around inside our heads. Couldn't get better.

And I was right.

Rosie got up from the table and disappeared off into the crowd. A few minutes later she returned, looking well pleased about something, and held out a hand for us to see what. She'd managed to scrounge some loose cigarette papers. Which was great. But then again, *was* it?

And then the happy stoned that I was suddenly turned into another thing. If she had gone and borrowed the papers off someone, the chances were they would have asked who they were for. And even if they hadn't, if they saw Rosie sitting with us it wouldn't take them long to come up with an answer of four. The more I turned it over, the more I felt that everyone in the bar, and I mean everyone, now knew that I was a British soldier and that I was sitting here stoned.

And could I reign in my brain? Pull it back a bit? No, I could not.

What if it had all been a trap? What if Rosie here had gone off and told the local police about the two British soldiers sitting in the Mira Mar stoned, and with more dope in their pockets? I scanned the room for clues and locked eyes with a young Spanish guy with a pencil-thin moustache and greased, combed-back hair who was sitting on a stool at the bar. He raised his beer bottle to me in a toast, and then gave a knowing wink. Maybe he was the one Rosie had got the papers from?

At that very moment (and you could never get away with putting this into a novel), into the Mira Mar walked two uniformed policemen. My heart went boom-ticky-boom, especially when they stopped at the bar and struck up a conversation with the Spanish guy.

At this point some kind of self-preservation kicked in. Who had the gear, I wondered? Did I have the gear, or did Dave have the gear? Stoned as I was, I had to think hard about this, even though we'd only been using the stuff about ten minutes ago. I had the gear, I decided. In that case, it was high time to get rid of it.

I got up from the table, not meeting eyes with anyone, and headed for where I hoped the toilets would be. Once through the doorway that led to the disco, I found another door that led to the toilets. And now we really were talking third world. I'd seen worse back home, mind you, but I'd never encountered anything quite so hot, or issuing such a stink, as this. I locked myself into one of the cubicles, trying my best to breathe in through the mouth only, and stuffed the grass behind the cistern.

Outside, the door to the toilets opened and footsteps entered. My first thought was police, but before I could really work myself over with that one I heard two men talking and joking in a way that didn't sound at all like policemen to me. I listened for more. This was the first time I'd had any real opportunity to eavesdrop on a couple of Belizians in full flow, and what I heard began to make me wonder if the grass was now tripping me out, because although I could understand near enough every word they were saying, I couldn't make out a whole sentence. They seemed to be speaking English, but it might as well have been Martian for all I was getting from it.

Eventually they zipped up and laughed their way out of the door (not washing their hands, I might add), and ten seconds later, leaving the grass where it was, I was right behind them (not having washed my hands either).

When I got back to the bar, the two policemen were now sitting at a table with the young Spanish guy, shooting the shit and downing a couple beers. And all right, maybe it wasn't me they were after, after all. Dave and Rosie had moved from our table to the bar, where Dave was busy ordering another round of drinks. When he passed me my new bottle of beer, I gestured with it that we should take a look next door in the restaurant part.

When we got in there and sat ourselves down in one of the booths that ran down the side wall, the buzzword was 'bright', as in fluorescent strip lighting. Although there were menus on the tables, none of the people sitting at them, or on the screwed-to-the-floor stools at the bar, were eating. It was plain to see that this place also doubled as a lounge bar to the 'public' one next door.

As we studied the menu, more to check out the prices than anything, a young waiter approached our table. He was older than the barman next door, but still only about fourteen. Once past his age, the second thing about him was that he was of Spanish origin, and the third was that he was obviously gay, in a very effeminate way. The boy shyly asked us, in good English but with a heavy accent, if we wanted to order anything.

He seemed to know Rosie of old, because while Dave and I ummed and aahed over the menu they struck up a conversation in the language I'd just overheard in the toilets. When I asked Rosie what they were speaking, she said it was Creole. At one point Rosie asked a question and the young waiter turned and began talking across the room, in Spanish, to a grey-haired man who was standing behind the bar drinking coffee and reading a newspaper. The man, who I would say was in his late fifties and could have been either Chinese or Latin, it was hard to tell at first, answered back in Spanish, but speaking directly to Rosie. She then carried on a conversation with him in fluent Spanish, but midway through their little chat they were interrupted by someone coming up to the bar and ordering something from the man – in Creole.

From all of this it soon became clear that everyone in this town spoke three languages fluently. And although English was the language taught in schools and printed in the newspapers and on the street signs, it was this Creole that was spoken the most in bars and shops. However, it bore no resemblance whatsoever to the way black people from the Caribbean talked in James Bond movies – except for the phrase 'Yeah, man', which seemed to act as the affirmative in every conversation.

In the end we decided against the food and chose instead to spend the rest of the night talking to Rosie and slowly getting pissed on beers and white rum and Cokes. Next door I'd guessed that Rosie was in her late teens/early twenties as she only seemed able to move anywhere by skipping, which gave the impression of youth. You've guessed it, though. Rosie wasn't that young, and the years she'd spent whoring had already begun to take their physical toll. Seeing her in the harsh bright light of the restaurant, when she wasn't skipping about, you could tell that she was unhappy inside. Lonely and old – mid-thirties at least. But then, Rosie was a bar girl.

She cut the majority of her living from us, the 'super-rich' British soldiers of Rideau Camp. However, as we were soon to learn, she wasn't alone in this respect. So did the shopkeepers, the bar-owners, the food-sellers, all the other bar girls, of course, and just about everyone else who had something to sell once the sun had gone down on PG. PG was a cutting type of town. So much so that it wasn't too long before we were out and about cutting a couple of things for ourselves.

Number one came our way that very first night, when the Spanish guy we'd seen next door talking to the policemen came into the restaurant and wandered over to where we were sitting. After he'd said hello to Rosie and they'd held a quick conversation that flipped back and forth from Creole to Spanish to English, he introduced himself to us. His name was Chico and he was the son of the owner of the Mira Mar, who (as we'd already guessed) was the half-Chinese, half-Spanish guy who had been reading his paper behind the bar.

Chico offered to buy us a drink and asked if he could join us, so we said 'Sure, man.' And why not? Nothing wrong with getting to know the owner's son. So he joined us and we indulged in a bit of small talk, explaining that we were with the British army and new to town, and that we'd be here for six months. We needn't have bothered. The Anglicans we were replacing at Rideau had already told the town all about us. And Chico had apparently been great, great mates with loads of them. *Great* mates. In fact, he even used to do some good business with them.

'Good business?' We pricked up our ears. 'Like what?'

Well, like things that were sold duty-free up at the NAAFI in Rideau Camp but weren't so readily available down town. For instance (since they had already popped up in the course of the night's proceedings), cigarette papers. Whatever we paid for them up at the camp, if we brought them to him, Chico would give us double. We weren't at all sure how much a packet of cigarette papers cost back at camp, but Chico knew. In fact, he knew the price of a whole range of items, from cigarettes and tobacco, through toiletries and chocolates, past electrical goods and batteries, right up to alcohol and soft drinks. And he knew them all to the cent.

The main thing we should be interested in, though, on which the profit was greatest, apparently, was English cigarettes. At the camp they cost $1 a pack and he'd pay us $2.25 for them, which sounded all right to us. The question was, of course, how many did he want? Although no one had ever specifically told us that buying things from the NAAFI and reselling them in town was wrong, we couldn't for one minute believe that it was permitted.

But hey! This was too good an opportunity to miss. Money

was money. So we told our new best mate that we'd bring him a couple of cartons tomorrow night – and from there we'd see how it went.

'Yeah, man,' said Chico. 'You see how it goes.'

When Chico was called away from the table by his dad and we'd sent Rosie off to the bar to get another round of drinks in, Dave and I got the opportunity to talk things over between ourselves. And we had to conclude that this was some kinda town. We'd only been in it five minutes, literally, before we'd scored some grass, and now we'd been given the opportunity (if it wasn't all bullshit) to financially cover our future nights out.

One observation we made was that we hadn't even been looking for these things in the first place. Rosie had offered us the dope and Chico had offered us the chance to make some money. I guess, as a pair, we were just easily led astray.

How does that noise go that sheep make?

Like the first morning...

As soon as I opened my eyes I straight away became a fully paid-up member of the Wide Awake Club. With that noted, my second thought of the new day was how warm and bright it was, although, when I looked at my watch, it was still only five-thirty. Remembering back to last night and our introduction to the delights of nighttime Punta Gorda, I figured that I couldn't have got to sleep until around three (and a fine state I had been in as well), so I was surprised to find myself feeling as 'jump out of bed now' as I did.

On the floor by my bed were the discarded clothes I had worn the night before. Searching through the pockets of my jeans, I came across the dollar wraps that good old Rosie had scored for us, and in amongst them I found a leftover half-smoked joint. The one we couldn't quite finish.

I hid the wraps inside the 'no-go zone' contents of my laundry bag and slipped the half-smoked joint into the map pocket of the trousers I was going to wear that day. With that all done and sorted, I grabbed my shaving bag and, in a smart, orderly and soldier-like fashion, set off to perform my morning ablutions. When I got outside it seemed as though every other man on camp was also up with the toucan. For zero five-thirty hours there was an awful lot of activity going on: the mentally unbalanced among us were already pounding their morning running circuits of the camp, and a ball game was up and arguing on the volleyball court.

When I reached the washrooms I had my morning shit, shave,

shower and shampoo and then headed back to my hut. By the time I got back there it was still only 6am, and as breakfast didn't start until seven, I wondered what I could get up to to fill in the time. I could go for a run (yeah, like really), but as Standing Orders had it that every soldier was to complete a three-mile battle fitness test under supervision each morning, there seemed absolutely no point in running down my batteries before having to go off and do that at eight. I could, of course, go over to the post room and familiarise myself some more with my new job . . . but hey! I had six months to get familiar with that.

But then I knew what I could do. I could go and find a nice quiet corner of the camp in which to smoke my remaining half-joint. So I got dressed (Now what shall I wear today? Let me see . . . jungle greens, perhaps?) and went for a stroll round the camp.

Along the way I struck up the spliff, and four or five puffs later I was taking it all in and thinking, 'Wow! It's a jungle, man!' And it was. All hot and sticky. All around me.

Yep. Stoned again. But it was all a laugh, eh?

It stopped being funny when I got to the cookhouse to have my breakfast. I queued to get my food, piling my plate to I've-got-the-munchies proportions, and found a nice lonely table all to myself. Sitting at the table I could look directly out of the open cookhouse door and all the way up the path that stretched to the far end of the camp.

Now, as I saw it, and you can quote me on this, I had reached the well-and-truly stoned stage a good half-hour or so ago, but as I stared up the path and watched the soldiers cutting across it and walking along it, everything started to look very different. The path suddenly appeared as though it was ten miles long, and the Nissen huts along its sides didn't seem big enough to hold four undersized retarded mice, never mind a dozen paratroopers.

It then turned into one of those moments (and be honest, we've all had them) when I thought: I *really* shouldn't have had that smoke. The next panic came when it dawned on me that at any second I could be joined at the table by another soldier. Although I could probably just about handle a conversation with a lepre-chaun right now . . . a brother soldier? Definitely not.

Time to leave.

So I legged it to the door and made the decision to go and have a little lie down. As my corporals in training always used to say: 'When in doubt in a battle situation – lie down.'

What little peace I did eventually find, spreadeagled on my mattress, was soon interrupted by a distant noise that sounded like someone trying to start up one of those little Japanese motorbikes, or a lawnmower maybe? Whatever it was, the thing coughed into life and the noise gradually levelled out into a whine. At first it definitely got louder, as if heading my way, then it faded before growing louder again a minute or so later. Yep, it was heading my way now all right.

But what could it be? As the noise faded away yet again, a riot suddenly broke out outside and I immediately felt a sense of danger. The noise then grew louder once more as whatever it was moved in even closer. This was out-the-building time.

Outside, once I'd crashed into the fresh air, I got the distinct impression that there must be a gas attack going on. The soldiers from the hut opposite were all out on the lawn, in various states of undress, cursing and coughing and evidently in need of medical care. And no wonder. There was smoke pumping out of every window of their hut.

When I took a look around the rest of the camp, things became even more surreal. Now, was this the smoke (as in what I'd inhaled earlier) or was this for real? Nope. This was for real. To my front all the huts were covered in this kind of mist. But was it a mist or was it smoke? It wasn't normal, that's for sure, and 'get away from it now' seemed like a good tactic. So I ran – or made a tactical retreat, as we in the army liked to put it.

At least, I started to. But I was frozen in my tracks by . . . I didn't know what really. Was it an alien? Or maybe a Guatemalan soldier in an NBC suit? Whatever it was, it was definitely wearing a gas mask and carrying a long *Star Wars*-type weapon that was definitely responsible for the mist-cum-smoke that was now enveloping the entire camp. Well, half of it anyway.

That was the thing, you see. As I looked around I could see that half the camp was in turmoil, covered by the strange mist, while in the other half everything was the same as usual. Soldiers going about their early morning business-type stuff.

Go on, then. Hit me with it.

It's not an alien is it? Nope. And that's not some kind of death-gas gun thing he's holding either, is it? Well . . . I'm still not sure about that one.

The 'alien' was, in fact, a soldier, who I'll just have to call Harry (because that wasn't his name), and what he actually had in his paws was a petrol-powered fumigating machine. And, as Harry pointed out, if I'd been familiar with yesterday's Part One Orders I would have known that fumigation was to be carried out every morning, on every building, on every camp in Belize. Furthermore, if you were still in bed when Harry arrived with his smoke machine, that was *your* problem.

'Tell me, Harry, is that smoky, dusty stuff that your whatsit throws out dangerous?'

'Oh no, not at all.'

'So why the gas mask?'

'Oh well, if you breathe it in, *then* it's dangerous. I mean, goes without saying, dunnit?'

Despite the fact that he was gradually gassing the whole camp, or certainly those inhabitants of it who, like me, were not fully *au fait* with last night's Part One Orders (and this sort of thing gets to happen a lot in the army), Harry was a private soldier who was in the right. And if Harry was in the right, it didn't matter if you were a field marshal mucker – at zero whatever-hundred hours it was, when your turn came, your space got fumigated. Sir!

In Harry the powers-that-be had chosen their man with care. He was the ideal type of guy for the task, largely because of his ability to address an officer as 'sir' but still make it sound like an insult. It could of course be argued, and in fact it often was, that Harry was basically just very thick. On the other hand, we were all of us paratroopers and there was a certain school of thought that reckoned we all had to be a little, shall we say, 'affected' to have wanted to join the Paras in the first place. It's a point.

But Harry was special. He couldn't read or write properly and had only managed to get into the regular army by joining the TA paras first and then coming in through the back door. As for his appearance, I wouldn't like to say that Harry looked thick, but he didn't look all that bright either, and I expect a creationist could have learnt a lot from Harry.

For some reason this allowed Harry to get away with saying things to officers that no other soldier would ever dream of saying – or if he did, he'd probably wake up and apologise. It was like Harry didn't care, and this tended to unnerve officers. You could see them thinking: 'Did he *really* just say to me what I thought he said? No, he couldn't have.' Chances were he had.

Once, way back in Northern Ireland, I was on a three-day border patrol with Harry, and on the way out to it we were helicoptered into Bessbroke Army Camp, where we were to wait for a pick-up vehicle to take us all back to Ballykinler. With time to spare, we found ourselves a spot in one of the camp's underground mortar-proof corridors (we liked them), got comfortable on our bergans and started to mind our own business until our transport arrived.

But then the swing doors at one end of the corridor flew open and through them walked a general, with the normal gaggle of 'chaps' in tow. Right away, everyone's radar was up and we were all hoping desperately to get away with just a fly-past (a quick salute and a 'carry on, men').

Well, did we fuck. The general stopped, and here we go . . .

'Do you find your tasks stimulating?' he asked. Which was a new one on us, and very good – 'tasks stimulating'. But then the general made the mistake of getting personal.

'And where are you from back home, corporal?' he enquired.

'Actually I'm a private, sir.'

'A private? Oh, well done. And where *are* you from?'

'I'm from Swindon, sir,' I replied.

And so it went on until the general got to Harry.

'And what's your name, private?'

'It's Jones, sir.'

'And do you like Northern Ireland, Jones?'

'No, sir, I fucking hate it here, sir.'

And right away we all knew more or less what was coming next.

Sure enough, Harry went off on one. His main gripe was that he'd been in battalion for nearly two years now and had never once gone on a course. As Harry pointed out in no uncertain terms, there were 'crows' in the battalion who had only been out of depot a month, and they were being sent on courses.

Behind the general's back our CO and the RSM were giving Harry looks that could kill, which they quickly flashed into wide grins whenever the general turned in their direction. As for the rest of us, all we wanted to do was put as much distance between ourselves and Harry as possible. You can take my word for it, they can be just like Pol Pot in the army. One of you does the wrong thing, and before you can say 'I'm not with him' they've got the whole fucking village out in the paddy fields. And I ain't talking the green, green grass of County Armagh.

Harry? We don't even know the man really. He just tags along with us on patrol. You know . . .

But do you know what? The very next time the courses came around, Harry got his wish and was sent off skiing.

No, we couldn't work that one out either.

After that first morning in Belize I never again smoked dope on camp, except on maybe thirty or forty occasions and one afternoon in particular when once again I got the opportunity to hopefully live and learn.

Now, right from the off the big drawback with smoking dope on camp (besides its being illegal, that is) was that grass smells to high heaven, which made it more than a little difficult to find a place that didn't bring the risk of discovery.

Well, I found one. The post room was a place that naturally generated a lot of paper rubbish. I was forever unwrapping things, screwing up odd bits of paper . . . chucking away all the officers' and sergeants' letters from home (joke) . . . and all this paper would mount up. To get rid of it I had to take it to the waste ground at the back of the cookhouse and burn it in the camp's incinerator – which was no more than an oil drum with some holes punched into it, but it did the trick nicely. As the paper burned away into the afternoon heat I would stand there in my shorts and flip-flops, poking the flames and toking a joint. If anyone ever approached, all I had to do was flip my smoke into the fire and it was 'Where's your evidence now, pal?'

I came unstuck one sunny afternoon when I went out paper-burning during the unofficial siesta period. When my rubbish was all burnt and my smoke finished, I headed back to the post room to chill out with the day-before-yesterday's newspapers, which was the best it ever got in Rideau Camp as far as keeping up to date with what was going on in the rest of the world was concerned.

So there I was, 'chilled out' (though we didn't call it that back then) in the post room – in fact, make that my post room – reading the papers and pondering important questions like what to wear down town that night, when, verily, there did come from yonder a knock at my post room door. In reply I did offer a friendly greeting.

'Fuck off. I'm closed.'

'Open the door Lukowiak!'

It was the unmistakable voice of the regimental sergeant major, who, to the best of my knowledge, should have been a hundred miles north of Rideau, all wrapped up in military spit and polish at Air Port Camp.

Oh shit.

When I jumped up from my chair and raced to open the top half of the stable door – surprise, surprise – I found myself eyeball to eyeball with the brigadier. Behind him, looking like a man it would be wise for me to avoid for the next century or two, was our RSM. Now, as a moderately experienced soldier I was able to work out in seconds what was going on here. And what was going on here was that the brigadier and the RSM had simply turned up unannounced on a surprise visit. Which was not very fair, because in the army you're supposed to be given warning of surprise visits.

Without so much as a 'How are you, soldier?' and even before I could apologise for the 'Fuck off, I'm closed', the brigadier asked: 'Has anyone been posting home pineapples?'

For a moment I did think (and you can hardly blame me – after all, we were in the army) that 'pineapple' might be the brigadier's combat-soldier banter for a hand grenade. But could I honestly see any of our blokes sending home hand grenades through the military mail? Someone from our lot: 2 Para? Well yes, I could, actually.

'I'm sorry, sir? Pineapples?'

'Yes, pineapples. You know . . . the fruit?'

He'd lost me. I didn't know what to think, so I fell back on the age-old soldier's safety net of looking blank and saying nothing. Fortunately this worked, as it forced some further explanation out of the brigadier. Apparently, what had been happening (although I only have his word for this) was that soldiers up at Air Port Camp had been buying pineapples and posting them home to their girlfriends back in Britain.

Predictably, perhaps, by the time these fruits of love reached the UK they were more like fruit juice than an essential ingredient for Hawaiian-style pizza. And that juice could spill out and be licked up by a mad, rabid dog . . . which might then bite a farmer's wife . . . and by nightfall the next day . . . everything growing in England would be wiped out by a withering-type dead leaf disease thingy.

Well, that's what the man said. Kind of.

I put the brig's mind at rest by confirming that no pineapples had left my post room, adding that now I knew that such illegal mailings were going on, I would be even more vigilant in future.

Mind you, if a bunch of fuckwits up at APC were posting home pineapples, what could an even bigger fuckwit like myself down here post home?

King Edward's cigars maybe?

Downtown (and at it) again

The thing with Rideau Camp was that once you got past the novelty of living on the edge of the jungle, the place could be quite boring. After the sun had gone down and the flag had been lowered on this quiet outpost of our once great empire (*Shut up, Lukowiak*), the only entertainment on offer was either a solo visit to the toilet block, girlie mag in hand, or an even lonelier pint in the NAAFI, girlie mag in hand. Personally, I could never work out which was the messier.

In the army, and I can't believe that the RAF or the navy is any different (building sites I've worked on certainly haven't been), you constantly come up against the presence of semen on lavatory walls, floors and seats. In Northern Ireland, at weekends, it could take a whole morning of running around the blocks just to find a cubicle that wasn't either spattered with sperm or littered with the stuck-together pages of self-abuse magazines. And in Belize it was hot as well – although at least there was no terrorist threat.

For some of the guys, in fact near enough all of them, serving at Rideau was like doing time behind bars. They ticked off the days and just could not wait to get out of the place and go home. As for Punta Gorda and the dubious pleasures to be found there, most of the troops just weren't interested. And why should they be? In the NAAFI a man could get pissed for £1.50 *and* there was ping-pong. There were also videos of last season's football matches and old episodes of British television soaps. (It was disturbing how many paras were addicted to that

Coronation Street.) In PG, on the other hand, it would cost a soldier more money to get pissed, he'd be surrounded by a load of the locals while he did so, and even if there was any TV to watch, it would be in Spanish and look like a snowstorm. Now where's the fun in that?

Boy, could Dave and me have shown 'em a thing or two.

On our second night out in Punta Gorda, ten seconds after stepping from the Land Rover we were once again walking the town's unlit backstreets, only this time having made sure we had a few packs of Rizlas on us. Once we had put these to good use (and how it does help to have the right tools), we let our legs lead us to the Mira Mar. By the time we climbed the stairs there and walked into the dimly-lit bar, which was nowhere near as busy as it had been the day before, we were both feeling well and truly pasted. Which, come to think about it, had been the whole idea. So, success.

As we sat on our stools (as in those things with four legs and a seat) drinking 20p rum and Cokes and thinking, then agreeing, that if we looked a quarter as out-of-it as we felt right now then maybe we should leave, the smoke really started to hit home.

'To be honest . . . I don't know if I could even stand, never mind walk.'

'Well then, we'll just have to drink lots to disguise the fact that we're stoned.'

Stoned soldiers? We can't have that, you know. Whereas pissed soldiers, that's fine. So we knocked 'em back. And, as the saying goes, time and alcohol can be great healers, so it wasn't too long before we'd forgotten how uncomfortable 'stoned' had been back there for a while and begun to consider scoring some more.

As those of you who read yesterday's episode will already know, in PG our only route to the sacred plant ('It's I & I's religion, sir') was via Rosie. However, we looked around the bar and checked the restaurant next door, but it seemed that Rosie wasn't in tonight. It was still earlyish, though, so maybe we should just wait an hour or so, be patient troops. Wouldn't kill us.

While we were sitting there trying our damnedest to remain patient, what was to turn out to be quite a major piece of the final puzzle was put into place. We figured, more or less simultaneously (proving that even not-so-great minds can think alike), that since we had already seen where Rosie got the gear from, we could go and tap on the shed for ourselves – cut out the middle-woman, so to speak. Now that did make sense.

'Reckon you can walk yet?'

'Dunno. I'll try.'

'You brave, brave man.'

When we did succeed in getting on our feet, we left the Mira Mar and traced over our steps of the previous night. Finding the shack exactly where we thought we had left it, we stumbled along what went for its garden path and tapped lightly on what we took to be its door. No response. We tapped a little harder, and with that something stirred. A voice mumbled something in Creole, and it was obvious that we had just woken someone up. That someone then came to the other side of the door and sleepily whispered another few words in Creole.

'What did he say?'

'Dunno.'

So we whispered back, name-dropping Rosie and reminding him of her little quest for us yesterday to explain what had led us to his door again tonight.

By now we were both feeling a little uneasy. After all, we had just woken the man up (if it was a man) and he/she/they might not like the idea of a couple of stoned squaddies on the doorstep trying to score blow at 8.15 at night.

'*What* time?'

'Quarter past eight.'

'That's not late.'

'It is when you ain't got electric.'

Inside, a match was struck and a paraffin lamp lit, and then the door opened. Standing there in a pair of knee-length shorts, a baggy T-shirt and bare feet (all of which could have done with a wash) was an old man. I guess we'd expected some mean-looking young black dope-dealer dude, but what we got was someone old enough to be our grandad.

Any worry we may have had about a hostile welcome from him turned out to be just that: a worry and nothing more. Straight away, all smiles, he asked us to come in and close the door behind us. If, from outside, the place had looked like a shack, then inside it was even worse. The walls were made of botched-together pieces of wood and the floor was no more than dry pressed dirt. In the middle of the room was a pole that supported the roof, and besides one chair and a small table, the furniture consisted of crates and wooden boxes. Nevertheless, it was home-sweet-home to him and, as I pulled up a box, it was off the streets and out of our minds for us.

The old man's name was Demas, and the very first thing he said to us that night was how happy he was that we'd come and knocked on his door. Rosie – and it would be good for us to remember this – had apparently told Demas that she was scoring the gear for a couple of British soldiers (even though we'd specifically instructed her not to) and he had been hoping to cut her out of the deal himself. Demas's second act of hospitality was to light up his pipe and pass it round. When I say pipe, I mean pipe as in the kind the Condor man would smoke his shag out of. Talk about cough. Talk about stoned.

If smoking Demas's grass with tobacco in joints had got us there, then smoking it neat, through a pipe, flew us express and kicked us out on arrival. When the pipe came around for the third time I didn't want any more, thank you all the same.

Then there was a knock on Demas's door. Without a blink, I freaked on the spot. And looking across at Dave, I could see that his pulse rate was no slower than mine. Who could it be? The local police? The military police? (Hold on a minute – there were no MPs at Rideau.) Whatever. With the old tickers going unlucky-for-some to the dozen, or 'shitting it', as we would have said, Dave and I got to our feet and tiptoed to the corner of the room furthest from the door.

The cavalry arrived when whoever it was who had knocked

answered Demas in Creole. No one likely to be of any trouble to us would speak in Creole. Demas and the voice exchanged a few words through the closed door and then Demas disappeared under the hanging blanket that led to his shack's 'other room'. He returned a few seconds later and opened the front door just wide enough to pass out whatever it was he had fetched (not that we couldn't guess). His hand came back into the room five dollars richer and the door was closed again.

Since we seemed to be on the subject, this looked like the perfect opportunity to enquire if we could buy some more of Demas's grass. Of course we could, but how much did we want?

'Dunno.'

We may not have been the smartest bunnies on the block, but even we could work out that the more we bought, then ounce for ounce, the cheaper it had to get. So we asked – though why I don't know, because we weren't seriously interested in buying that much (just acting big-time, I guess) – how much a pound would set us back. When the reply came, at first I thought I must have misheard.

'How much did he say?'

'Sixty dollars.'

'That's what I thought he said.'

Sixty dollars was roughly, nay, exactly, twenty pounds sterling, which had to make this grass the bargain of the century by anyone's standards, including our own.

'That *is* Belizian dollars, isn't it?'

Of course it was.

And just like that we were counting out the money and buying a pound of grass, a quantity which thirty seconds before hadn't even entered our minds. Demas once more disappeared under the hanging blanket, reappearing with a set of wrought-iron scales, just like the ones my mum used to weigh her flour on, and a cloth sack.

We did have some initial fears that he might rip us off, sell us a pound of dry seaweed or some such similar unnarcotic substance, but in reality that should have been the last of our worries. As we were to find out, a pound of dry seaweed in PG would probably have cost you more than a similar weight of grass. That is, if you could get hold of any. What was a worry, and a genuine one, was how we were going to walk the stuff back into camp. As Demas started to weigh it out, I would have been quite content if he'd stopped at the first handful. It looked plenty enough to me. And when he did finally bring it up to a pound's worth – well, like I said at the time, 'How we gonna get *that* back to camp?'

'Dunno.' (As you can tell, between us we knew very little.)

And then we had a thought: why bother to take it back to camp? We could bury it in town somewhere and pick at it as and when we needed it. The perfect plan. There again, where, exactly, were we going to bury it? And with what?

And then we had another, even better thought: why bother to bury it at all? As long as it was all right with Demas, we could leave it here with him. It stood to reason that we could trust him with it, and I'll tell you what, just to show what spot-on guys we were, we'd even pay him for minding it for us. Like rent.

How about that, then?

Cut to interior – daytime – next day

The old man Demas is sitting with two friends in a dusty PG bar. Between them on the floor is a crate of beer and each has an opened bottle in his hand. The men are playing dominoes and laughing. Something has struck them as very funny.

FIRST FRIEND: They *what*?

DEMAS: They bought a pound off me, man! And then they paid me some more money to keep it.

SECOND FRIEND: I tell you, those white boys, I just can't work 'em out. As it is, the stuff grows on trees . . .

Demas said it would be just fine for us to leave the grass with him and we could come over and pick it up whenever we liked.

When we finally left his place that night, we headed back to the Mira Mar (which seemed already to have become our home away from our home away), sat ourselves down with a couple of beers and couldn't help but start working out what we'd have had to pay for a whole pound of marijuana, buying it by the ounce, at UK prices.

'Tell you what,' I said, 'at only sixty Belizian dollars a pound, if you could get some of it back home . . .'

Say no more.

PG Saturday am (and friends)

Not all that much happened at Rideau Camp at weekends. In fact, come to write about it, after Battalion HQ was moved up to APC, not much happened at Rideau on weekdays either. On Saturdays I was still required to get the outgoing mail on to the plane in the morning and pick up the incoming in the afternoon, but in between, and afterwards, I didn't have to open my door or show my face until Monday morning. 'Stand down, that man.'

On one of my earlier Saturday morning trips to the airstrip, having safely waved the mail off to England I went into Punta Gorda to pay a visit to the post office. 'But you've got one of your own,' I hear you remark. Yes, but mine didn't sell the local stamps required by the philatelically minded soldiers amongst us, who felt a particular need for things Belizian on their love letters home (even though it added a fortnight to the trip). As mornings go, I can still remember that one as being bright and warm, the kind that lifted the old spirits just to be out and about in it. When I got dropped at the post office, I briefed the driver that I'd decided to stay in town for the morning and would see him in the afternoon when I went to meet the plane, at the airstrip.

'Well, you wouldn't meet it at the fucking jetty would you?'

I tell you, British army wit, it's some of the world's finest.

The post office, like everywhere else that mattered in PG, was situated on Front Street, about twenty yards up from the Mira Mar. A largish wooden building left over from the colonial years (veranda and all that), like most buildings in town it could have done with the odd nail and lick of paint. However, again like most places in the town, it was always clean and tidy.

I arrived with five minutes to kill before the nice granny who worked the counter had to get around to opening up (and why be early when you can be on time?), so I leant against the porch and took in the spectacle of Saturday morning Punta Gorda.

This was maybe my second or third trip into PG during daylight hours, and as I looked around me it was noticeable that this time the place was busier than I'd ever seen it before. Though hick by most people's standards (and even rabbits', come to that), it was nevertheless the largest urban area in Toledo District, and on Saturday mornings everyone from the surrounding villages either bussed, walked or hitched into town to stock up on those little luxury items that were unavailable back home, which meant anything that couldn't be grown.

Today there were a lot more 'Indians', as in Mayans, out on the streets, mostly gathered in loose family groups and all carrying things that were brightly coloured and made out of plastic. Although they made up the biggest ethnic group in Toledo District as a whole, the Mayans were normally only a small minority in PG itself, which was inhabited mainly by black Creoles. But not on Saturday mornings, when the town was packed with them.

To me, back then, the Indian people looked poor, but since serving in Belize I've seen towns and villages in Africa, burnt-out cities in Bosnia and even housing estates in England where, in many ways, the people were much poorer. And they didn't even have the pleasant climate and lack of street crime to compensate.

As I leant there idly people-watching, suddenly I saw this vision (at least, that's what she looked like from where I was standing) just passing the Mira Mar and heading my way. Long blonde hair and tanned skin. She was a white woman, and I hadn't seen one of those in . . . oh, hours. As she approached the steps of the post office I realised (and I'm only being honest here) that close up my vision of Caucasian beauty wasn't quite the stunner she had appeared from a distance. Still, she was better looking than anything I'd spoken to in days, so off I went.

'Hi! How are you? Lovely morning isn't it?'

I quickly discovered, master of the chat-up that I was, that the lady's name was Liz and that she was in Punta Gorda as a member of the American Peace Corps.

'The what, sorry?'

'The American Peace Corps.'

'Is that, like, military?'

I had noticed and made enquiries about a couple of Americans in the Mira Mar earlier in the week but had done no more than exchange a passing nod with them, and even though I'd been told they were 'peace corps' (I know I was) I couldn't have told you exactly what it was they did.

'We're the American equivalent of your British VSO,' Liz explained.

'Oh . . . right.' (The VS what? Never heard of it.)

'I'm a schoolteacher myself. But you know, some of us are doctors, engineers, agriculturists, that sort of thing.'

Right. Gotcha. They were charity-type people.

In the time it took for the post office to open and for me to purchase my good-deed-for-the-day stamps on behalf of my fellow soldiers (well, there was nothing in the job description that said I had to do it), Liz and I had arranged to go for a get-to-know-each-other Coke in the Mira Mar.

'Oh yes, the Mira Mar,' I smiled, all wide-eyed and innocent. 'Isn't that the place down there with the neon sign?'

When we got to my favourite haunt, the steps outside reminded me of the pub car parks in Swindon when I was a kid. Poor, we were. Wives and children sitting outside with soft drinks and crisps, while inside their husbands and dads were swilling beer and shooting the shit with the lads. The throng of people on the Mira Mar's steps were again mostly Mayan and had this look about them that told you they had just done some very heavy shopping, as in 100lb sacks of grain and lots of things that come in cans.

Like the streets and the steps outside, the restaurant half of the Mira Mar was busier than I'd ever seen it, and getting two stools at the bar in there was going to mean a long wait. But next door in the night bar it was empty, although the doors were open and the kid who worked the bar was dusting things behind it and raring to go. Being the soldier problem-solver type, to cut out the wait that would have come with ordering in the restaurant, I bought a couple of Cokes from junior and we wandered back into the restaurant with them.

Looking at all the other customers, it occurred to me that I'd never been in a place, with maybe the exception of a couple of airport terminals, that contained so many different races of people. There were the Mayan Indians, the black Creoles, white Americans, mixed-race Latins, a couple of Chinese, three old Germans (and what did *they* do in the war?), two English (counting me) and near enough every combination of all those.

Sharing one of the wall booths was a foursome of Mennonites, who, in case you didn't know (and I didn't until Liz told me all about them), are an old-fashioned European religious sect – of which the Amish, as portrayed in the Harrison Ford film *Witness*, are an even stricter branch – who ended up in Belize via a history of fleeing persecution. They all wear long beards (the men, at least) and plain, simple clothes, and they don't believe in anything too modern. Hence the horse and cart tied up down the road from the Mira Mar and the no tractors rule on their large farms.

The two Mennonite couples were joined at their table by two youths of maybe fourteen/fifteen years old, who I guessed must be their sons, and ... well, you know that Dusty Springfield song about 'the only man who could ever reach me'? It wasn't written about these boys. They were both dressed in clothes from the Tom Sawyer Spring Fishing Trip collection, right down to their straw hats. They even had bare feet and a local black kid tagging along behind. When they began talking to their parents, I noticed that the older Mennonites were speaking English with what sounded like a cross between a German and a South African accent. The youngsters, on the other hand, sounded exactly like Americans to me, but what was really strange was when they started to chat with a few of the local guys in fluent Creole. It just didn't sound right coming out of the mouth of a white person. It was like they were taking the piss or something, although of course they were not.

When Liz and I eventually managed to find a table to sit at, I soon discovered that she suffered from the common American infliction of answering 'Oh *really*?' in response to just about anything that was said to her. Now, if someone were to say to you that they'd seen this man with two heads, then all right, it's fair enough to come back with 'Oh *really*?' But with this girl . . .

'I got up at seven this morning, Liz.'

'Oh *really*?'

'Yeah, and once I was up I got dressed.'

'Oh *really*?'

'Yeah, and then I went off to breakfast.'

'Oh *really*?'

'No, not really. I'm making it all up.'

Like I said – British army wit, it's some of the world's finest.

What doubled the effect was that accompanying Liz's 'Oh really' there was always a nodding of the head, like one of those dogs you get in the back windows of cars, and a look of deep, sincere interest in whatever it was you were saying. You could tell that Liz was a caring person, a good listener.

'The paint had hardly dried at all, even though I'd been watching it for nearly five hours.'

'Oh *really*?' (nod – two, three; smile – two, three).

Over the months that followed that Saturday morning I got to know Liz and her fellow third-world botherers very well. My summing-up of Liz was that if you were to sit down and write an American sitcom, then she, with no need of a rewrite, would be your typical divorced late thirty-something who was walking around carrying the weight of the world on her shoulders. And yes, she was 'born again' – and Catholic to boot, although I didn't even know you could have born-again Catholics.

One time Dave and me found Liz sitting all alonesome in a

booth at the Mira Mar. Being a sharp pair of town bunnies by then, we could see that she was down about something, so over we went and asked if she'd like a drink. For once, she didn't have a snappy happy reply for us.

'What's up, Liz?'

'Well, you know, guys, I was at school this morning, right?' (Uh-oh, here we go.) 'And it was nine-thirty, OK? And I'm in my classroom and I look in my pencil case, and I've got six pencils, OK?'

'OK Liz.'

'Well, late morning, around eleven-thirty? The headmaster comes by and I leave the classroom to talk with him in the hall for a few minutes. So we talk, and when we're done I go back into the classroom and I send the kids off to go have their lunch. Then, over the lunch break, I take a look in my pencil case . . . and do you know what, guys?'

'No Liz. What, Liz?'

'There's only four pencils in it, guys!'

Earth-shattering, I know. *The X Files* years before TV ever thought of it.

'What do you think could have happened to them, guys?'

What could have happened? To us it was bloody obvious what could have happened, and did, while Liz was out the room. The kids nicked two of her pencils.

'Oh . . . my . . . God!' Liz gasped. 'You really think so?'

'Yes Liz, we really think so.'

'You know, that's what I thought. I didn't want to. I even prayed not to. But that is what I thought.'

It was at about this point, and with Liz was there was always an 'about this point', that I began to wonder if she might be having us on. (In fairness, we did have more than a slight tendency to be stoned when we were talking to her.) But no . . .

'I thought I was relating to these kids, and yet I leave the room for a few minutes and they steal from me. What am I doing wrong, guys? I mean, should I really *be* in Central America?'

Well, we could see that this particular slice of real life — namely the theft of a whole twenty cents' worth of pencils out of the Donald Duck pencil case that she'd 'actually' had in high school at the time she decided not to become a nun — was genuinely heartbreaking for our Liz. And you had to feel a little bit sorry for her, because she couldn't help but look on the serious side of everything. She took it all so personally.

In the end I decided there were three different ways you could look at the American Peace Corps 'volunteers' (well, they wouldn't do it for the money). Firstly, you could see them, and sometimes it was really difficult not to, as a bunch of college-educated, left-wing, pinko (though, as Americans, still slightly to the right of Attila the Hun) busybodies who should quit worrying about everyone else and let the world get on with it. I know Mr Reagan was in the White House and Nicaragua was wrong and fast food was covering the entire planet . . . but it wasn't their fault. Alternatively, you could view them as a group of good-natured souls who just couldn't help but care for their fellow 'person' and wanted — nay, needed — to put something back into life by helping the raped and robbed of the Third World. Or, finally, you could simply regard them as a bunch of very enjoyable white women — which tended to be the way I did mostly see them back in 1983. Especially when in the bath. (OK, that last bit was a lie. But only because I never once saw a bath in PG.)

Like most of the Americans in Belize, if not most of them in Latin America as a whole, Liz and her fellow Peace Corps workers had a big thing about the CIA. According to them, the CIA were here, they were there, they were busy corrupting things almost everywhere. Of course, having Ronnie in the White House didn't actually help Liz and her fellow intelligence-agency-paranoia sufferers, and many was the time you'd hear a member of the Peace Corps asserting, 'Oh yeah. Sure the CIA have infiltrated the Peace Corps. It wouldn't surprise me to find out that any one of us was really working for the CIA.'

To be honest, it would have fucking stunned me and Dave.

But then, as time went by and those Central American nights

began to seep in – the Latin music, the bar full of foreign faces, speech you couldn't understand a word of – you could get drawn into the conspiracy theory. Mind you, being stoned out your head nine and a half days a week did, I admit, probably help this process along a step or two.

'And don't you guys go thinking it's just the CIA. The Guatemalans have spies in Punta Gorda, too. They're bound to. As, of course, do you Brits.'

Our spy lived in a house on Main Street, drove a military Land Rover, spent most of his nights out on the town with local girls, and was about as undercover as a bacon sandwich-eating Pope at a Jewish wedding. Everyone knew who he was, where he lived, who he worked for and what he did. Or did they . . . ?

'A little *too* obvious, right, guys? You know, the way he's so open and all?'

'Well . . . maybe, Liz.'

And that was when the mind games could really start kicking in. One thing was for sure, though – no way did we ever want to meet 'our man in Punta Gorda', especially not while stoned. We intended to avoid that losing win double like the plague.

The bet went down one night in Suzie Wong's, a Chinese restaurant not far from the Mira Mar. Dave must have been on a rare camp duty, I think, because I was alone, stoned to high heaven, and had gone in there for a serious munchie session. As I sat down I noticed, at another table, a white man I'd never seen before. He wasn't army, I was sure, because his hair was just that bit too long, but I could tell by his clothes that he was British. When our eyes met first we smiled and nodded and then we started up a conversation. After a few minutes of the two of us talking across the room, he invited me to join him at his table.

'So what are you doing in Belize?' I asked.

'The same as you,' he replied.

He then leaned forward and whispered, though not in a dramatic way, that he was with the 'you know who'. Now me, I thought that by 'you know who' he meant the SAS, and even though he didn't look much like a mean killing machine, the more I studied him the more I could see that under his loose-fitting clothes he had a fit body, and that the face above it seemed to have seen the world. I had also met enough SAS men in my time to know that on average they tended not to resemble the Greek gods that all civvies expect them to look like. The more I thought about the man and his mild, laid-back mannerisms and speech, the more I could believe that he was SAS all right.

He wasn't, though. He was a sergeant major in the Intelligence Corps. This became apparent when he went on to explain what his role as the 'FINCO' in Punta Gorda was and what rank the job carried – after which I automatically started addressing him as 'Sir'.

'Don't call me that in here, mate,' he said quickly. 'If you see me up at the camp, then OK. But in town, always call me Clive.'

'What do the locals call you?' I asked.

'Oh, they all call me Clive, too. But sometimes they refer to me as Finco.'

'So it's no big secret that you're with the Intelligence Corps?'

'Hardly.'

And it wasn't, although by the time the likes of Liz and the rest of the Peace Corps contingent had worked their minds over Clive and back, they had him labelled as British Secret Service, working for the CIA, selling arms to the Contras, killing nuns in El Salvador and spending his holidays raping peasant children in Honduras.

My stoned self's reaction to discovering that the man before me was army, never mind the resident spook to boot, was one of wanting out of the place and away from him as soon as it was politic for my tactical retreat to take place. If anyone was going to realise that I was out of my right-said-Fred, it would be him. Unfortunately, by the time he'd invited me over to his table I'd already ordered a make-me-fat portion of Suzie's sweet and sour might-be pork, so I felt I had to eat my way through that lot before I could extract myself without arousing his suspicion.

In fairness, though, it wasn't like Clive was a total wanker. In fact he was interesting, in that he did seem to know near enough everything about near enough everyone in Punta Gorda. And if there's one thing I've found during my travels, it's that you can never learn too much too soon about a place.

Clive was good, as well, because he was army intelligence. Not that he'd tell you anything that was classified or wasn't openly known, but if, for example, you asked him 'Who's that good-looking girl over there?' instead of the usual 'Oh, that's Mary. She works as a barmaid at so-and-so's,' you tended to get 'Oh, that's Mary. She's from a village called Blue Creek and has been in PG for thirteen months. Her mother's local but her father originally came from . . .' and so on.

Now, being a squaddie and one who had lived through the diplomatic fuck-up that was the Falklands War, the thing I wanted to make no mistake about was the Guatemalan threat to Belize. Like was it real? So I quizzed my new acquaintance about it.

'. . . because I'd never heard of those Falkland Islands. I really did believe they were off Scotland somewhere.'

Apparently (and I was sure I'd read mention of this in one of those pamphlets they'd kindly given us back in Aldershot), in the 'seventies the Guatemalan army had mobilised twice to invade Belize, but what stopped them on both occasions was the Harrier Jump Jets. They didn't like them up them, they didn't, 'cos they didn't have any fighter jets of their own and could do nothing about them. (Hurrah!) As for the current situation, according to our man from the Intelligence Corps here – and who better to tell you? – the chances of a Guatemalan military invasion of Belize were almost zero, zilch, non-existent. Which was double major good news, as far I was concerned.

However, that didn't mean we could let our guard down. There may never be a combat war, but there is, was and always will be a war of intelligence.

'Right, sir.'

'I told you. Don't call me sir.'

Another useful thing about Clive was that he knew a lot of the local women. He even employed a couple of them – and boy, did he know a thing or two when it came to employing. His 'housekeepers' were two sisters, who I'd guess were both in their early twenties and were both real lookers. Without wanting to make them sound like racehorses, their breeding, if that's the word, was a mix of Creole and Spanish, which meant that they had a combination of dark skin and European features. Between them they took turns to cook and clean for Clive and, judging by the way they could strop and moody about with him and the amount of drinks and meals he was always buying them, probably a few other things besides.

One night the two sisters found Dave and me drinking with Clive in the Mira Mar and insisted, in their sulky, girlie way, that he escort them to what sounded to us (because we didn't quite understand) like some sort of late-night party that was going on in town. Well, you know us . . . never say no to a party.

The venue was only a couple of streets back from the Mira Mar and when we reached it the place turned out to be no more than a large straw-roofed hut illuminated with oil lamps and candles. Just as we got to the door, drums, like you might get in a Tarzan movie when there's a jungle newsflash, started to thump out a fast, repetitive beat. When we got inside I couldn't quite work out what it was that we'd walked into. It was nothing like any party I'd ever crashed before. For aperitifs, the majority of the hut's occupants were either hanging from the ceiling beams in hammocks or lying on the dirt floor making out like Nelson after he'd been shot on the deck of the *Victory*. And for starters, around the room various people were burning Lord-know's-what both over and in little fires, leaving a breath of the room's air equivalent to smoking about two hundred a day.

My first thought was that we must have walked into some weird form of Belizian hospital, say a bit like Lourdes in France. But that chain of thought was soon broken when this bloke, who until then had been doing nothing more harmless than bouncing up and down on the spot in rhythm with the drums, picked up a chicken (and that's not as in a piece of KFC deep-fried), got hold of it by its legs and started smashing its brains out on a conveniently placed slab of stone.

You *are* fucking joking? Nope.

And over in one of the corners of the hut, in stacks of wooden cages, were plenty more chickens where that one came from. In the end, the guy swung the chicken's head so hard and so many times into the slab that it parted from its neck. The head was then kicked around what went for the dance floor for a while before it was picked up by an old woman, who promptly (and where are the food hygiene inspectors when you really need them?) dropped it into a cauldron that she had boiling over a wood fire.

Now you *really* are fucking joking. Nope.

With the head gone, the loony then breaks into his impression of a water-sprinkler like the ones you see on rich people's lawns and golf courses. He starts running around in small circles and swinging the headless chicken carcass above his head while hollering some mumbo-jumbo up to the roof. And what a 'difficult stains' detergent commercial they could have made using this guy.

And then the wholesale chicken slaughter was on. Like some form of local karaoke, one by one people came forward and dispatched another chicken to meet its maker. A lot of the night's contestants were obviously sick (so I had been right – this was a bit like Lourdes), in fact so much so that quite a few of them didn't have the energy to head-smash a chook to death, never mind make like a sprinkler with it afterwards. The Lord does provide, though, because on hand was a chap with a sacred machete to lop the heads off for them. And in case you've never seen anything like this . . . yes, it *is* true. Headless chickens do run around like headless chickens.

Just as I was coming round to thinking that I'd quite like to leave now, I realised that, along with Dave, Clive and the party sisters, I was bouncing up and down on the spot in rhythm with the drums. It was definitely time to leave.

When we got outside and set off in the direction of the Mira Mar again, it was naturally enough time for us to reflect on the 'healing service' we had just attended. (Oh dear, I think I missed the collection.) I remember to this day that as we walked along I related my famous tale of the great world leader I had once met in the Western Australian desert. Since this man was, and perhaps still is, one the most widely recognised human beings ever to have walked our planet, neither Dave, Clive, nor the sisters (who knew of him even though he had no churches in Belize) believed I'd really met him. Accused me of making it all up, they did. But it's absolutely true.

In 1974 (though it may have been '75) in Kalgoorlie, Western Australia, while working at the local television station, I met . . . Colonel Sanders! And to this day I can remember all the words to all the hymns that we used to play on our station in praise of his chicken. All be upstanding:

> *99 cents is all you need*
> *for the Colonel's great new feed.*
> *You get two bits of chicken*
> *and that's finger-lickin'*
> *– and a bag of french fries too!*

Amen.

The bestest stoned I've ever been

Late one Sunday morning, on a nothing-much-to-do weekend at Rideau, Dave managed to borrow a motorbike from the camp REME sergeant (who was not a homosexual), and we set off on it to have a swim in a not-too-far-away river.

When we got to the river we changed into our trunks and Dave lit up a little 'spliffy' which he'd knocked together earlier. Surrounded by the every-shade-of-green stereo jungle, we then got a little stoned and had a splash around in the water. After half an hour or so Dave decided he was thirsty and suggested popping into Punta Gorda to score a couple of Cokes. The idea of a nice cool Coke appealed to me no end, but Dave drove far too fast for my liking and I wanted to limit my rides on the back of the motorbike to the bare minimum. So I stayed there by the river while Dave set off on his own to fetch us some soft drinks.

From where we were in the jungle a trip into town and back on a motorbike should have taken no more than thirty minutes, so when forty-five had passed and Dave failed to return I was starting to get slightly annoyed – the way you do when you're waiting for someone or something that should have been here by now. Another three-quarters of an hour later Dave still hadn't arrived back, and by now my slightly annoyed had grown into a highly pissed off. I could just fucking picture him boozing away with some tart down at the Mira Mar while I was left standing around in the jungle twiddling my thumbs.

After a further half-hour had gone by and there was still no sign of Dave, I did finally begin to wonder whether something bad might have happened to him. After all, with Dave the scope was endless. But just as I was about to give up on waiting and start making my own way back to camp on foot, I heard him calling my name through the trees. He was also (wisely, since I was all ready to punch him in the teeth as soon as I set eyes on him) shouting out the reason why he was back so late. He had run out of petrol.

If my memory served me right, we had put half a gallon in the tank before leaving Rideau Camp, so there was no way he should have run out, even with the extra trip to PG and back. Although he hadn't yet come into view, I passed this observation on to him and politely enquired how such a thing could have happened.

'So how come you fucking ran out of fucking petrol then?' I yelled into the jungle.

'Don't fucking start on me,' he snapped back. 'I've had to push this fucking thing for miles.'

'Oh yeah? And I've been standing here for fucking hours not knowing where the fuck you were. So I'll ask it again – how come you fucking ran out of fucking petrol?'

'I gave someone a lift somewhere, didn't I?' he admitted.

'Oh, you gave someone a lift somewhere, did you? And fuck *me*, I suppose?'

From that point our out-of-sight shouted conversation escalated into all-out verbal jungle warfare. But this meant, looking on the bright side, that by the time Dave did at last trudge into view we were both more or less ready to call a truce.

His excuse, when I finally allowed him to get it out, was that while on the way back from town he had come across a girl we knew from the Mira Mar bar. (So I was right. There was some tart involved.)

The lady in question was on her way to visit her parents' house, which was out in the hooley somewhere, so Dave, ever the gentleman, had offered her a lift. But before letting her climb aboard, or so he told me, he got an assurance out of her that her parents' village was not too far away. And as she seemed to have been planning to walk there, Dave took her word for it when she said that it wasn't. It turned out, however, that 'not too far away' was a good fifteen miles along and over narrow jungle paths.

When Dave and his ladyfriend finally reached her parents' house, which was apparently no more than a wooden hut in a one-and-a-half-goat village, as a thankyou the girl's father gave Dave a handful of his home-grown back-garden marijuana.

I leapt in at this point. 'Oh, so that's it? You stood around smoking dope all afternoon and fuck me.'

'I fucking didn't. I told you. I came straight back, but I ran out of petrol on the way.'

If it had been me that had run out of petrol, rather than push the bike for miles through temperatures in the thirties I would have hidden it in some undergrowth and gone back for it later with a can of petrol. So why hadn't he thought to do that?

'Oh yeah,' Dave sneered. 'And if some fuckwit came across it and nicked it, where would we be then, eh? In the fucking shit, that's where we'd be.'

As the motorbike didn't belong to us, I had to admit that he had a point.

Once he had rested the bike against a tree and given it one last kick, Dave reached into his jeans pocket and pulled out the grass that the girl's father had given him. My first reaction when I saw it was that he'd been ripped off. It didn't look like any herbal cannabis I'd ever seen before. For a start, it was a much lighter green in colour than the usual stuff, and it also had a fair amount of red in it, which was something new to me. What's more, it was 'stringy' in appearance and didn't seem to have any seeds. As Dave held it out in the palm of his hand, he said 'Look at this' and then turned his hand upside down. The grass remained stuck to it. He passed it over for me to do the same, and I could immediately feel why it had stuck – it was sticky. I held it up to my nose to have a sniff and found that it had a strong, perfumed smell, again unlike any grass I'd ever handled before. As far I was concerned, this could be any one of a range of organic substances, but marijuana wasn't one of them.

Dave had serious doubts about its quality too, but then he reckoned what did it matter? He hadn't parted with any money for it, and he would still have run out of petrol even if he hadn't been given it. All the same, if it had been good dope it might at least have made it all seem worthwhile.

The only way we could really find out if it was kosher dope was to skin one up and have a puff or two. So we got the papers out and knocked one together. The first joint we rolled, we rolled too tight, and it wouldn't even get warm, never mind light. So we broke it down and rolled it up again, though a bit looser this time and with an added pinch of cigarette tobacco to help it on its way.

When we finally got it up and burning, my first thought was how mild on the throat it was. I passed it over to Dave, and after he'd taken a puff or two he thought the same.

'Very mild on the throat,' he said.

My second observation was how stoned I was feeling already.

'This is grass all right,' I confirmed.

'Yeah,' Dave agreed, 'and it don't hang around either.'

Then we both burst out laughing. And could we stop? I don't think so.

We laughed first about Dave running out of petrol and then about him having to push the bike back in the really amusing mid-afternoon heat. Next, I started to explain all about my hilarious wait for him in the jungle, and the even funnier bit about how angry I'd got hanging around not knowing where he was. By then we had reached the point where all we could see was the humour in everything, and that in itself soon became funnier still.

By this time we had completely forgotten the reason why we were acting like a couple of victims of laughing gas and had let the still unfinished joint go out on us – which, as far as quality is concerned, is always a good benchmark. So when we remembered it again, we relit it, deciding that the best thing we could do about our motorbike problem was nothing. We would just remain in our little riverside paradise and hope that some other soldiers would turn up to have a swim, then we could bribe whoever it was who was driving to run one of us back to the camp to fetch some petrol.

When we finally decided that we shouldn't smoke any more, even though we still hadn't managed to get through the first joint, we went and had another dip in the river.

Sticking out of the water about ten feet away from the bank was an old and rusted metal ladder that was part of an equally old and long ago scrapped river barge. The ladder was protruding out of the water about five feet, and if you climbed up and stood on its top rung you could use it as a diving platform. During our earlier swim I had dived off the ladder several times, so once again I swam towards it and climbed to the top.

When I peered down into the water it looked as though it was miles away from me, which at first I found hilariously funny. But then, below the waterline, I noticed for the first time the sunken remains of the barge that the ladder was welded to, and straight away this conjured up the image of me diving off the ladder and scraping my chest against something sharp on the way through the water. Suddenly I really didn't want to dive any more.

Dave, who was floating nearby, noticed my discomfort on top of the ladder and started to laugh at me. And boy, did he think it was a hoot. I was this, I was that, I was something else, and all of them were yellow to the core. I turned around and told him to piss off (which only made him laugh all the louder), then I prepared myself to dive off just to shut him up. I bent my knees to dive, but, looking down again, I just couldn't do it. I was left bouncing up and down on the spot, meaning to dive but stopping myself at the last moment. I just couldn't do it. Dave, by this time, was laughing so uncontrollably that if he didn't stop he risked drowning, which just made things even worse for me.

Still laughing all the way, Dave swam over to the ladder and climbed up alongside me. He was going to demonstrate how it was done. But just as he was about to dive I couldn't resist whispering into his ear: 'Make sure you dive over all that sharp metal down there.' And with that he hesitated, looked down and immediately became as stuck as I was. We looked at each other and both began laughing again. After all it *was* funny: two combat-hardened paratroopers scared to jump into the water from a height of five feet. Boy, we were stoned.

We then got a very nasty and very unwelcome reminder of just exactly where we were on the planet when a fifty-foot river snake (which was maybe a metre long) swam by doing the wriggle stroke. We both began to scan our minds for information about long swimming things in the water. I was sure that one of those army pamphlets on Belize that I'd looked at the pictures in had mentioned something about rivers and the dangers therein. In fact, when we thought about it, we both now seemed to remember reading somewhere that we weren't even allowed to swim in the rivers in Belize. They were out of bounds. And shit, could we now see why.

If we had seen a snake on the surface of the water, then what other nasties might there be below the waterline? We ran through a list of what we thought were possibilities and both came up with the same three things: piranha fish, piranha fish and piranha fish. Then I remembered a James Bond film I'd seen when I was a kid, in which 007 had been on an alligator farm somewhere in America. If they could have alligators there, it more than figured that they might well have them here.

And what about sharks? This river flowed into the sea, so it must be possible for a shark to swim into it and then up it. After all, there were sharks in the Yangtze River in China. Or was that dolphins? Neither of us was sure, but so as to be better safe than sorry we worried about sharks as well.

By now the distance between us, hanging on to the ladder, and the safety of the riverbank seemed to have grown from ten feet to long enough to be attacked by something with lots of teeth before you made it across. But across we had to go at some point, so we tried to think along more reassuring lines.

'How many times have we come swimming here?'

'Loads of times.'

'And how many times have we been bitten by anything?'

'No times?'

We also reminded ourselves that soldiers had been swimming in this spot for as long as soldiers had been stationed at Rideau Camp.

'So why don't we just stop poncing about and jump in?'

We finally psyched ourselves up to set off on the epic journey ashore by shouting aloud together the paras' mantra: 'Red on. Green on. Go!'

For the three or four metres that it was, we ran on water. But once we were back on dry land and relaxing on our towels, life soon turn into a full-length comedy again, and we agreed that we'd smoked some dope in our time, but shit, were we stoned this time. Really stoned. Really, really, really, really, really really . . .

We had a camera with us that day, and when we had finally managed to figure out again how the thing worked we took some photographs. I still have one of them, a small black and white close-up of me in which I'm grinning away like an extremely contented with life, thank you for asking, mental patient.

Finally, after we'd sat there on our towels for some time just staring across the water at the wonder of the jungle beyond it, reality returned and at the same time the light began to fade. For the last however long it had been since we put out the smoke, we had forgotten all about the motorbike and its lack of petrol.

With the day coming to an end, it was obvious that no other soldiers were going to turn up for a swim now, so we got dressed and took it in turns to push the bike along the track that led to the dirt road. By the time we reached the road it was dusk and we were beginning to wonder if we should hide the bike under cover of darkness and come back for it later. But there again, since we were now only a mile or so from camp and would have to walk the rest of the way even if we left the bike behind (which would anyway mean going through the hassle of getting some petrol before walking back yet again), we might as well press on.

Along the road we passed the odd shack lit by oil lamps and a couple of times we stopped to ask people sitting on porches if they had any petrol to sell us, but no one had. Eventually a set of headlights appeared behind us, and we hoped, almost prayed, that the vehicle would be an army Land Rover. As the lights got nearer and became sharper, though, we could tell that it wasn't. What the hell – we stuck out our thumbs anyway.

The vehicle turned out, blessing upon blessings, to be a small open-back truck, which came to a halt when it drew level with us. Sitting in the cab of the truck were three people, and when one of them reached up and turned on a small interior light I could see that they were all male and all of Spanish extraction. Something else I could see was that the one in the middle had a rifle resting between his legs. This quickly made me realise just how stoned I still was and it began to feel really weird standing on a jungle road at night confronted by three Spanish guys with a gun.

Not at all sure what to do, I decided to smile. To my great relief, they all smiled back (and I swear I caught a glimpse of gold teeth). Saying to myself right, get your head together, I then told the three occupants of the truck our story about running out of petrol.

Great guys that they turned out to be, they were on their way into Punta Gorda and so would be going right past the front gate of Rideau Camp. Two of them climbed out of the cab on to the back of the truck and gave us a hand to lift the bike over the tailboard. Once the bike was in, Dave and I grabbed hold and pulled ourselves up after it. But when we landed on the other side we both saw what was in the back and we both froze. Lying right under our noses was an enormous cat. And I don't mean cat as in the ginger tom from next door (mee-ow), but cat as in fucking huge lion-looking-type-thing with big teeth and even bigger claws. What was going on here? River snakes in the afternoon and now lions at night!

Was it dead, I wondered? It certainly looked dead. There

again, it could just be sleeping. Either way, I didn't intend to hang around long enough to find out, and neither did Dave, so we quickly jumped back out on to the road. Seeing our moment of panic, the three Spanish guys began to laugh almost as hard as we two had been laughing when we were out of our trees back at the river. Eventually, to put our minds at ease, one of them gave the cat a kick to prove that it was, indeed, very deaded.

The 'lion', as it turned out, was in fact a jaguar, like as in E-type, and in life it had been feeding itself on the livestock of a nearby village, which was why the three guys had hunted it down and killed it. Dead it might have been, but just in case of any miracle of resurrection we didn't take our eyes off it for one momento on the (whee-whee-whee) all the way home.

When we finally reached Rideau we offloaded the bike and then called the guard out to come and take a look at the dead pussycat. The jaguar was pulled off the back of the truck and placed under a light outside the guardroom. It looked almost purple in colour, and you could see that it had been shot once in the stomach and once in the head – though which came first was anybody's guess.

Once everyone had had a good geek, and we'd managed to convince the three hunters that we didn't actually want to buy their feline corpse, we offered the guys ten Belizian dollars as a thankyou for giving us a lift. Being from Belize, though, they had already worked out a better deal. If we gave them five packets of English cigarettes, which would only cost us five dollars in the NAAFI, they could then sell them on in town for fifteen dollars and everybody would be double-bunce-time happy. Since Dave had been the one who ran out of petrol, he graciously went off to the NAAFI to get the cigarettes while I helped the guys load the cat back on to the back of the truck. And bloody heavy it was, I can tell you.

When Dave returned with the fags, we bade a grateful farewell to the Spaniards and went off in search of the REME sergeant to let him know that his bike was back in one piece. It was only after we found him that I learned that Dave had promised to get the bike back before dark. Luckily, the sergeant was a good guy and, even though he tried, he couldn't quite manage to give us both the bollocking that Dave deserved.

Once we'd got back to our Nissen hut, Dave went through his pockets to have another look at the dynamite smoke . . . but could he find it? No, he could not. Short of both bending over and taking it in turn to pull each other's cheeks apart, we looked everywhere for it – twice. In the end we concluded that we (meaning Dave, as usual) must have left it down by the river, along with a few thousand of our brain cells. The only way we could think of to console ourselves was to agree that its departure from our lives was probably not such a bad thing, because otherwise we would only have banged up another one by now, and a right state we'd have been in then. But we mourned its loss, all the same.

The next afternoon, without telling me about it, Dave borrowed the bike again, on the excuse that he had left his watch by the river, and went in search of the lost marijuana. I caught up with him again just as he returned and, joy upon joy, he had actually managed to find it.

'So where exactly did you find it?'

'Where we left it.'

'Yes Dave. And where was that?'

'Under the rock where we'd put it specially so that we wouldn't lose it.'

Like I said, we were really, really stoned.

At a guess, the girl's father must only have given Dave about a quarter of an ounce of his grass, but it lasted us the rest of the week, which as far as we were concerned was some kind of low dope consumption record. The beauty of this stuff was not only the strength of the hit, but how long it lasted. Two minutes after the first toke you knew you were stoned, and three hours after that you realised that that had been only pretend. Today I'm a little better informed about marijuana and I now know that what we were given that day, with its wonderful smell and its colourful appearance, was grade A 'sinsemilla'.

One night, just for a change, we took a smoke of it round to

Demas for him to have a hit. As soon as we lit it up he knew what it was we'd got hold of, and after we'd had more than enough and Demas had smoked a little bit more of it in his pipe, he passed on to us a few words of Caribbean marijuana wisdom. He told us that true sinsemilla could only be grown by old people and children, and even they had to love the plant.

Since then I've got to read many more words about sinsemilla and have come to learn that what's so special about it is that it's the unpollinated flowers of a female plant – hence its name (the Spanish term *sin semillas* means 'seedless'). I've also smoked a fair amount of the indoor variety, which is now cultivated in hydroponic gardens and under grow-lights all over Europe. For all I know, it may still be great smoke, and scientifically it may even contain more THC than anything else, but none of the Rastas I met in Belize (and that's as in genuine followers of the Rastafarian religion, not Afro-Caribbean fashion victims) would touch it with a bargepole. It would be too interfered-with for their liking – not enough God involved and grown too often for money and without love.

Food, films and the Chinese connection

Most of the food in Belize was grown by the Mennonites, although surprisingly, because it was all good, wholesome Old Testament stuff, nothing they produced was ever consumed on camp by any of us fine men of the British army. All of our food, right down to the cardboard cartons of milk and the plastic-wrapped loaves of sliced white (they knew what the troops wanted all right) was flown in from the US of A. At Rideau the milkman only called four times a week, and he arrived by helicopter.

Apparently this was all to do with health and safety regulations. NAAFI rumour had it that any local produce purchased abroad by the British military had to be sent back to the UK and tested by ICI before it could be passed as fit for consumption by the troops. It was also rumoured that one of the local rums in Belize (which shall remain nameless) had been shown to contain five chemical substances previously unknown to man. Whether or not this was true I don't know, but one thing was for sure – they didn't sell that rum in any of the NAAFIs in Belize. Mind you, we all still bought and drank it when we were down town, and we all lived to tell the tale.

But that's the army for you. And in case I thought it might have changed over the years, in 1995, when I visited an army kitchen in the Falklands, I discovered that it certainly had not. Outside, just over the other side of the camp's fence, were approximately 720,000 sheep. Inside, however, in one of the cold storage rooms, were various frozen bits and pieces of baa-lambs that had once upon a time munched grass in New Zealand before flying deceased class to the UK and finally on to the Falklands. Meanwhile, down town, soldiers and civilians alike were happily spreading mint sauce on the local sheep, of course. And yet still they live.

If we did eat out in Punta Gorda, then it tended to be either at the Mira Mar or at Suzie Wong's, one of PG's answers to a Chinese restaurant (and yes, there were two). Suzie – late-fortyish, slim, Chinese ('No!') and not at all bad-looking – ran the place with her husband, who seemed perfectly happy to play second fiddle, banging and flaming his wok out back while Suzie sat up front working the till and counting the cents. (By the way, if you don't know what a wok is, it's something you fwow at a wabbit.) In view of this set-up we not unnaturally got the impression that in the Wong household it was Suzie who wore the Mao suit-bottoms, but in fact Mr Wong's lack of communication with his customers, bar the odd smile, might have had more to do with his poor command of English (and as for his Creole . . . huh!). As well as the restaurant the couple owned the grocery-cum-hardware store next door, and about town it was rumoured that Mr Wong also had interests in a local logging company, so by PG standards they got by better than most.

In fact, Wong wasn't their name at all, and what their real name was I don't now recall. Come to think about it, I'm not even sure that I knew it back then. Suzie, though, *was* called Suzie, and because of the famous film/play/book (five words, last word sounds like 'song'), calling her by the name of a Hong Kong prostitute seemed the obvious thing to do. Whether this was racist and/or sexist, once again, today I'm not too sure, though it had to be an 'ist' of some kind. Isting all day we were, back then.

Suzie's restaurant was situated on Front Street, some four or five doors up from the Mira Mar, and as our days at Rideau and our nights out in PG lazily passed, it rapidly became one of our regular haunts. Its menu, oddly, featured curried goat, knee-jerk chicken and a couple of dishes containing fish that anyone back home would have expected to still be in an aquarium. Apart from these rare culinary delights, however, a quick glance at Suzie's menu showed that high street Chinese food in Belize and high street Chinese food in Britain were pretty much one and the same. That being the case, I couldn't help but wonder how it was that Suzie and her family had ended up in Punta Gorda in Berize as opposed to, say, Reeds in Yorkshire. Was there some sort of lottery back in Hong Kong that decided which part of the globe you ended up sweet-and-souring in?

It didn't take too many visits to Suzie's before she came out with what sounded to us like a soundbite from a Vietnam war movie. And the 'real' Suzie Wong would have been proud of her.

'You boys likee makee some business?'

Unfortunately (I think), Suzie's idea of business had nothing to do with suckee fuckee but (and you've probably guessed it) had just about everything to do with products from our NAAFI shop. The deal she offered us on cigarettes, which at first were all she appeared to be interested in, was no better or worse than the one offered by Chico up the road: the going rate. But there again, we didn't have to choose between the two of them, did we? We could sell goodies to both. After all, that is/was/always has been free enterprise, and we *were* supposed to be Maggie's boys. And PG may have been cheap by English standards, but going out near enough every night was beginning to add up.

On maybe our third or fourth visit to Suzie's we couldn't help but notice, for it was loud, that there was a television on somewhere upstairs. (Was there an upstairs?) Lots of explosions and bangs and screams. It was definitely a war movie – and we should know. A barefoot kid came into the restaurant and walked up to Suzie, who was sitting on her normal high stool at the bar next to the till (which only she and Mr Wong ever got to touch). Suzie and the boy swapped a few words in Creole and the lad handed Suzie a dollar bill. She rang her till, gave the kid some change, tore him off a ticket from a raffle book and then the kid disappeared up the stairs. Well, what was that all about then?

Only one way to find out . . . 'Hey, Suzie! What was that all about then?'

'Film show upstairs. You want see? Fifty cents.'

Well, anything for something new. But could we have a quick peep before we committed ourselves to paying 16.6p recurring?

The top of the stairs opened on to a doorless room that held maybe six or seven rows of wooden fold-away chairs. Facing these was a twenty-six-inch colour television connected to a video recorder, and seated on the chairs, with their eyes glued to the screen, were twenty or so locals.

The film they were all fixed to was *Zulu* (Michael Caine commanding the vastly outnumbered Welsh at Rourke's Drift), which I'd first seen as a ten-year-old, on a somewhat bigger screen, at the ABC cinema in Swindon. My dad took me one Saturday afternoon, and great it was. Colourful and loud and exciting. To the ten-year-old me, *Zulu* was basically just another version of my favourite play theme of cowboys and Indians. And you can guess who I had playing the cowboys, i.e. the good guys.

Now for some reason, and I wouldn't like you to think that I'm exaggerating here, but really, every time a red-coated Welshman got a spear through his chest, the audience at Suzie's (which was 100% black apart from us) hooted and cheered with delight. White men getting stabbed and bleeding all over the place? Bloody marvellous. And of course, I soon realised the patently obvious: that in Belize the British army were cast as the Indians, i.e. the bad guys.

(Luckily there was nothing racist about this – the local population's delight in the Brits' defeat was all good-natured stuff really. In fact, just as Dave and me were starting to wonder if we should leg it or not, considering our similarity in skin tone to the 'Indians', people started grinning in our direction, the way a football fan might grin to an opposing fan when his team gets away with an outrageously offside goal.)

We sat and watched *Zulu* for no more than five minutes anyway, as the Wongs' upstairs cinema was crowded and hot, and besides, we'd both seen the film before on many occasions. Back downstairs we returned to our table and beckoned Suzie over to order another couple of beers. No sooner had we done so than, with exactly the same manner and tone of voice she might have used if asking us whether we wanted our rice boiled or fried, she enquired of us:

'You boys, you like watch porno movies?'

('Well, actually, no. We find them somewhat offensive.')

'We might do. Why do you ask?'

(A bit more like it.)

'You maybe like make some money?'

We could have guessed. We should have guessed. Come on then, out with it. How can we make some money this time? And what do porno movies have to do with it?

Well, Suzie's film rights, that's what. And here's the deal. If we could get together a crowd of, say, twenty soldiers or so and bring them to Suzie's one night, preferably a Monday or Tuesday, to watch porno videos and drink beer at inflated prices, then she'd charge them, say, five dollars each and split the proceeds fifty/fifty with us.

Now, the first calculation here was to work out whether or not our guys would be willing to part with some of their hard-earned Maggie dollars just to watch moving pornography. Mmm . . . what do you reckon? Too bloody right they would. Though of course, there's porn and there's porn, and if the men were to be enticed into town and made to pay for the privilege, then the films would have to be of the hot Danish porno lust variety (or 'hard core', as I believe it's referred to).

When the Zulus had called it a day with their slaughter of the Welsh, Suzie summoned Mr Wong from the kitchen and, after giving us a polite little bow, he led us up the stairs to view some sample tapes. In case there are any minors reading this, I'd better not go into any great detail on the material that was in the said tapes. Suffice it to say that after watching them for two seconds we knew that we'd have no trouble at all pitching the contents to the boys up at Rideau. So, let's have a little think about this . . .

The problem here, we decided, was that if we were going to bring twenty-plus men into town one night, we'd have to get the duty Land Rover to do four separate trips, which wouldn't make the driver very happy, even though I think technically he'd have to comply. After all, there was nothing in Part One Orders that said transport into town was only for the first six soldiers who showed. Nevertheless, he'd be bound to complain, and it wouldn't be too long before every sordid detail was passed up the chain of command and we got called up in front of the stewards.

'And what were you doing in town last night, Lukowiak?'

'We were running a video night, sir. You know, sir, a few beers, get the troops out of the camp for a bit?'

'Oh, well done! And what type of videos, exactly, were you all watching?'

'Foreign-language films, sir. From Scandinavia, mostly.'

Alternatively – and you've got to hand it to me, I'm quick, for the idea flashed right into my brain – rather than taking the mountain to Mohammed, we could bring Mohammed to the mountain.

'You fucking *what*?'

'What about if we were to hire the tapes from Mr and Mrs Wong and show them up at Rideau on one of the camp's videos?'

Great idea. And it got better, because if we did that we could not only show the tapes in the NAAFI, we could then hire them out to the sergeants' mess, and, I dare say, if we picked our moment and our man with care, even the officers' mess as well.

'Yeah but hold on, you know what those sergeants are like. Hand a pile of porn over to that lot and we might never see it again. And where would that leave us with the Wongs? In the shit, that's where.'

Dave had a good point. We probably would have to fight, literally, to get the sergeants' mess to hand the films back. So, not such a good idea after all.

'There again, who needs the sergeants' mess anyway? Showing them in the NAAFI would be enough, wouldn't it?'

Halfway through our deliberations on how best to take financial advantage of the female exploitation on offer, Suzie interrupted and settled the matter for us. The porno films were apparently from America, and, in case we weren't aware of it, they had a different system of television there, so the US tapes wouldn't work on our English video equipment anyway. Was she sure? Of course she was. Because, at the end of the day, what we were being invited to do here was simply pick up the trade she used to carry on with the unit that had been at Rideau before us. This was not the first time that British soldiers had wondered if they could play her porno tapes up at the camp.

So that did settle it. We'd have to bring the troops into town.

The next day we set to work, taking care over choosing who to issue our twenty invites to and plumping for the machine-gun platoon who lived next door to us. We then paid a visit to one of the drivers over at Motor Transport (just like in *Bilko* only with everyone dressed in shorts). Under the pretence of organising a birthday party in town – well, the guy said he had to tell the MTO something, and by the way, *he* wouldn't have to pay to get in, would he? – we booked a four-ton truck to act as the duty vehicle for the night, thus enabling the driver to get our audience there and back in only a single trip each way.

When the night came, if I say so myself, the whole thing went off with military precision. And why wouldn't it? On-the-truck-off-the-truck was a game we had all played a hundred times, even when pissed. So Dave and me made a few dollars, the boys got to watch some nice porn movies, and Suzie sold a load of beers that she wouldn't have otherwise.

And what's wrong with that then, eh?

In Suzie Wong's one night, one of the Peace Corps workers asked Dave and me if we'd ever been to PG's other Chinese restaurant.

'You mean there are two?'

'Sure, buddy.'

'We didn't know that.'

'Oh *really*?'

It seemed that we must have passed the other one on numerous occasions while out and about on our nightly smoking tours of PG's backstreets, but we'd never noticed it. So, feeling bored and with nothing better to do, we left Suzie's to go take a look at something we hadn't looked at before.

Had it not been for the Chinese girl sitting on the doorstep (which was a major clue), we probably wouldn't have spotted the place even though we had been told where it was. It sat a few yards back from the street and looked no different from any other run-of-the-mill PG 'brick' (which, for any soldiers reading this, in Belize meant a building constructed from brick and *not* a four-man patrol hard-targeting in the Ardoyne).

Inside, the restaurant resembled the front room of a bunga-low which the builders hadn't quite finished yet. Its large window had no glass in it and the room's concrete floor had no lino or carpet (though come to think of it – and this is deeply interesting – I don't think I ever once saw a piece of carpet on a floor in Punta Gorda).

Right from stepping into the place we couldn't help but feel that we had moved somewhat downmarket from Suzie Wong's. (Oh *really*? It was deeply contagious.) Which was strange, because we had never before looked upon Suzie's as being upmarket. We did wonder, when we took our seats, if we shouldn't just order a beer and go. And to be honest, the menu, hand-written in misspelt English, didn't inspire much culinary confidence either.

'What do you reckon?'

'Dunno.'

'Shall we just leave?'

'Dunno.'

But do you know what? We stuck with it and ordered the day's special, and when the food finally arrived and we each took our first mouthful, it turned out to be:

a. The best Chinese food we'd ever eaten
b. Quite nice really, but we'd chopsticked better
c. Something we wouldn't have fed to a dog
d. It *was* dog

Well, actually, it was none of the above, smarty, so there. The food was no different than it was in Suzie Wong's, or, come to that, in the Hong Fu Happy Opium Garden in Leeds. What was different, though, and this is something I'll one day tell my grandchildren about, was that it was without doubt the slowest restaurant in the world. I thought I'd seen slow in Mexico and Kenya, and in the NAAFI up at Rideau, but not this slow I hadn't. From the time the young girl, who was the only member of the family who could speak either English, Spanish or Creole, wrote out your order to the time the food was placed under your by now starving nose: an hour and a half minimum.

The first time we partook of one these marathon waits for our meal, I went up to the door that led to the kitchen in the mistaken belief that, because our meal was taking so long, they must have forgotten all about us being there. (As you know, we do all look alike to them.) The door, by the way, was a stable-type double one not dissimilar to the door of my post room, but if I say it myself, my post room was definitely tidier, definitely cooler and definitely didn't contain as many Chinese.

And that was the thing . . . over the months during which we used this restaurant and got on at least nodding terms with the family that ran it, every time we poked our heads into the kitchen there were always a good five or six adults working in it, plus their various children. By the amount of activity that was going on, you'd have thought they were cooking a meal for the hundred and forty four thousand, and yet most times there was only me and Dave in the whole place.

Eventually, even we learned that the thing to do in this establishment was to order your food and then go off for a stroll. And we got really good at it, to the point of arriving back just as the food was ready to be served.

By taking these little walks we also learned that grass and Chinese food go great together. Mind you, wrecked? Most nights I could have eaten a dog.

Don't even think it . . .

Prostitutes, sinners, Jehovah God and me

I was raised as a Jehovah's Witness, which meant that until I left the family fold at the age of fifteen to join my elder brother in Australia, I got to attend thrice-weekly bible meetings at the Kingdom Hall of Jehovah's Witnesses. At weekends I also got to spend many a boring hour following in my father's footsteps as he went knocking from door to door in the greater Swindon area. Now, you can say many things about the faith of the Jehovah's Witnesses, and chances are most of them are true, but credit where credit's due, provided you swallow it all hook, line and sinker, as a Jehovah's Witness at least you know precisely what is a sin in the eyes of the Lord and what is not. There are none of those grey areas that you get with the good old C of E, where one dog-collar says one thing and another tells you the exact opposite.

For example, and I mention this because I remember it well, if you're a Jehovah's Witness you know not to go around celebrating birthdays. There are to be no cards, no candles, no making wishes, not even any popping over to your friend's house to throw up large quantities of chocolate cake and lemonade. And why? Because John the Baptist got separated from his head on King Herod's birthday (tart called Salome does a get-hard dance for Herod, he grants her a fairy-tale wish, she plumps for the head of John the Bap). So birthdays are a sin.

Another sin, which probably won't stun you into conversion

83

either, is that it's a very big no-no within the faith of the Jehovah's Witnesses to go partake of the services of prostitutes.

So, with all that said and prayed for, it would be no falsehood before Jehovah to admit that on my sixteenth birthday I was really running up the sin points on double when I handed over the twenty Australian dollars it cost for straight sex in Kalgoorlie, Western Australia, and the lady set her alarm clock for twenty minutes.

Kalgoorlie, being a mining town in the middle of the Australian bush, was, naturally enough, one of those unnatural places where the men outnumbered the girls by far too many to one. To help even out this sexual imbalance, running parallel to and only two blocks away from Kalgoorlie's main thoroughfare was Hay Street, infamous throughout Australia for its 'tolerated' brothels and its tin shed of an 8mm porno theatre.

By the time of my sweet sixteen I had been in Kalgoorlie for five months or so, and during that time I'd given up on high school and got myself a job on the bottom rung of the ladder at the local television station: 'VEW. Channel 8, Kalgoorlie. Channel 3, Kambalda. G'day!'

On the night of my sixteenth I went cruising up and down Hay Street, as I so often did, with some of the guys from work. The others were all much older than me and therefore knew more about the ways of the world, and until then I'd really only tagged along as they went from girl to girl negotiating and bullshitting and making out all grown-up.

But this time – da-dah! – one of the guys asked if I was going to go in, as it was my birthday, and 'sort out' one of the girls.

'I'd love to,' I told him mournfully, but I couldn't. Shame, but I didn't have enough money.

'Don't you worry about that, mate,' said the guys. 'It's your birthday! We'll have a whip-round for you.'

Gulp.

Well, me, right there and then I could have died. I may have made out like I'd been shagging since I was ten, but the truth was I was still very much a virgin. With the boys alongside, though, this wasn't something I wanted to let on about, and so . . . what could I do but take the cash and face the lonely walk up to the metal gate illuminated by one of Hay Street's many red lights?

As soon as I reached it a woman appeared: short blonde hair, wearing a bikini and a shirt, about thirty years old (or maybe younger – everyone over eighteen looked thirty to me back then), and all smiles. Without so much as a squeak, I nervously held up the twenty dollars and in through the gate I was ushered. I was led along a short path and in through a door, which led to another door, which creaked into a dimly lit room. The room was home-sweet-home to a double bed, a dressing table, a pink washbasin with matching pink taps, and not a lot else. Once I was inside with the girl, the door was closed behind me, I handed her the money and she set her alarm clock for twenty dollars.

She beckoned me to the sink – gulp again – and when I got there I was asked to drop my pants, which I did. She took hold of my boyhood, leaned over and then carefully inspected it for 'marks' (no, *not* the out-of-ten variety). After pulling back my foreskin and lifting my balls, she wondered aloud if I'd ever had any sexually transmitted diseases? I was pretty sure that I hadn't, so I shook my head. She then proceeded to wash me, and if my poor Wee Willy Winkie had been a soft one-and-a-half inches and stable when I was led in, by now it was a very soft one-and-a-half centimetres and shrinking in the breeze.

When all the bits of me that mattered had been sanitised and dried off to the lady's satisfaction, just like that she took off her shirt and bikini. And for the first time in my life I was taking in an eyeful of a real, in the flesh, grown-up, naked woman. Hairs between her legs and everything.

If only I could have appreciated it.

I was instructed to lie on the bed and, as soon as I did, she took control. The lady did stuff that I still think about to this day. But, for all her efforts, poor little scared, innocent me just could not rise to the occasion. After a few minutes of hard labour she stopped, looked up, smiled and said:

'You don't really want to do this, do you?'

'No!' I squeaked.

'Then why did you come in?'

The big boys made me do it, I bleated, and I explained that they would have laughed at me for ever more if I hadn't. I also confessed in full to my lack of past sins. Looking at me kind of different and blessedly changing the subject, she then asked me if my name was Ken. I said yes, that was me, but how did she know that?

'I've seen you on TV,' the girl replied.

And she had, because one of my duties at the television station, in addition to making the tea and cutting the lawns on Saturdays, was the co-hosting of *Tele-club*, our fifteen-minute daily output of children's programming.

We shared a joke about a tabloid headline reading 'Kiddies' TV Presenter in Prostitute Shock' and then my new friend told me about the time when she'd been on television herself, dancing in a show that had been filmed in Singapore. From there we went on to talk about this and about that, and we laughed and we joked, until finally the alarm went off and my time was up.

To my joy, for I was having young men's fun, she leaned over and hit the clock to stop it ringing and we carried on talking for nearly an hour. When I did finally leave she followed me out and, in front of all the guys (Jehovah bless her), told me what a great lay I was and said that if ever I wanted to come back, then next time it was on her. I walked away, best mates by my side, feeling ten feet tall.

Oh yes, those were the days.

Eight years later – and, incidentally, only one year on from the Falklands conflict and my crossing-off of 'Thou shalt not kill' from the Jehovah's Witnesses' top ten of never-do's – I recalled my teenage innocence on that warm, so-long-ago-now night in Kalgoorlie. And when I did, I found myself looking back on it with a sense of loss.

I was in a brothel in Belize City at the time, so it's no great surprise that I was thinking about whores past, but on this occasion the dollars involved were American and the girl El Salvadorian, if that's the right word.

We were in Belize City, believe it or not, to do a parachute jump.

A fucking what?

I know. It's fucking outrageous.

Before going to Belize we had taken it as read that we'd be safe from all that jumping out of aeroplanes business. But no. Someone, somewhere behind a desk in England, just *had* to show someone else behind a desk in Guatemala what we were capable of. So we were all off to the not so big or bright city to lob ourselves out of aeroplanes. And we could shut the fuck up with the moaning, because it was a great honour for us to be involved.

If the truth be told, nine out of ten paratroopers who express a preference hate military parachuting. It's a hard and heavy haul that means hours of low-level flying and people throwing up, and it's all very different from what those death-defying civilians so much like doing as a sport.

'. . . and do you know what, troops?'

'No. What, sergeant major?'

'Those civvies actually pay money to do what the army lets you do for free!'

(Oh, what quick-witted men those senior NCOs were.)

Through bribes and favours, Dave and me managed to hike a helicopter flight up to Air Port Camp, whereas everybody else from Rideau below the rank of brigadier had to travel up by sea.

I got to do this myself one time, and believe me, the twelve-hour journey was a total nightmare. For a start, this wasn't no cross-channel passenger ferry with duty-free shops, self-service restaurants and subtly-lit casinos. It was a landing craft. And that, in case you don't know it, means one of those things you see all of those troops involved in the D-Day landings wading out of. More sardine can than ship. There was no overhead cover in the event of rain, and as for any really bad weather (as in tropical storms and hurricanes), then all the better for the

Royal Marine skippers and their bouncy crews to practise their skills.

But what did we care? We were laughing. We not only had ourselves a chopper flight but we'd also have a whole afternoon and a night in Belize City before the rest of Rideau Camp caught up with us.

Because we were making our own way, early, up to APC, the army had failed to reserve any accommodation for us until the following day, which was a negative. But on a more positive note, this meant we weren't accountable to anyone either. No one would miss us. And since APC was such a large base, containing soldiers, airmen and even the odd sailor, so long as we didn't piss on the lawns, no one was likely to hassle us.

Call it telepathy, or mutual degradation if you like, but as soon we touched down at APC both Dave and me knew that we were instantly destined to go where the lights are bright (and cue . . . Petula). We dropped our kit off with a mate who worked in the battalion orderly room and headed for the main gate. Once there, we cornered one of the camp guards and asked what the deal was to get ourselves into town.

Apparently we had options. We could either cross the road to where (as he put it) that line of 'niggers' were waiting for the bus, or we could go and see those 'black bastards' over there, who were taxi drivers hanging around APC for soldier pick-ups, though we must be sure not to give them any more than ten bucks for town.

'They're all of 'em filthy, robbing black cunts,' the guard was kind enough to inform us.

Now call me quick, but I got the impression that this soldier didn't go a lot on Belize and was even a twink of a racist to boot. However, in the army at that time (and I'm not even sure that it's all that different today) he was hardly a rarity, and nor was our reaction to his prejudice, i.e. none. Maybe we should have had a quiet word in his ear and said 'Hey man, don't be like that, 'cos we're all equal you know,' and then followed it up with a quick chorus of 'Ebony and Ivory'. But we didn't. We just took it as the norm and ignored it.

So, what about downtown itself, then? All right for a laugh, was it? Recommend any particular parts of it, could he?

'It's a fucking stinky shit-hole,' the guard replied, 'full of fucking dope-smokers, prozzies and lazy bastard jungle bunnies.'

He made it sound like he was an expert on the place, so I just thought I'd enquire (and of course I knew what his answer would be) how many times he'd actually been down to Belize City.

'Twice,' he told me.

And how long had he been in Belize?

'Five months.'

See, I was right. And the sole reason why his brain of little expectation believed that the whole of Belize City was overrun by dopeheads and whores was that the only places he'd ever visited were the clubs at which the cabs had dropped him and his muckers off when they were out on the piss.

Even though I understood many things about soldiers in general and their habits, I never could make out blokes like Private Enoch here. They got posted abroad, thousands of miles away from the shitty British weather and their depressing surroundings and deprived upbringings, and then never left camp. They just weren't interested in anything local. And if you asked them why, they'd just say why the fuck would they be? Who wants to go out drinking in a place that's full of 'ignorant blacks' when you can get pissed up at the NAAFI on British lager at duty-free prices? It was a shame, though, I always thought, because that isn't exactly travelling the world and meeting interesting people, now is it?

'So the whole place is steaming with prozzies and dope-smokers, you say?'

'Yep. Fucking everywhere they are.'

'And we get the taxi from over there, right?'

'Yep. Over there.'

The taxi we ended up taking (whose driver, incidentally, did not rip us off) dropped us bang in the centre of town, right by a narrow swing bridge that crossed one of the city's canals. Now normally, when you think of canals, you tend to think Venice or Amsterdam, brightly painted barges, romantic café-bars by the water ... but not in Belize you don't. This canal was basically dead. It was almost motionless, dark black in colour, and God help anyone who fell in and swallowed a mouthful.

After the tranquillity of Punta Gorda, downtown Belize City was noisy and crowded. It had narrow streets with few pavements and was bustling with people who didn't even stop to pass the time of day. Up until 1970 this had been the capital of Belize, but, in true Third World tradition, after independence the government had built a new capital in Belmopan, a Belizian Milton Keynes situated some fifty miles inland. In fact, though, the movement of the capital wasn't quite as mad as might at first appear, because Belize City, which is right on the coast, had been swept into the sea by hurricanes a number of times over the years.

Being soldiers, there were really only two things Dave and me wanted to do in Belize City: buy booze and drink girls. Museums and other centres of culture would have to wait.

After purchasing two grams of cocaine on a street corner (well, we were innocent then and had never had it before), plus a few dollars' worth of the cheapest but finest Mary-do-you-wanna-dance in the whole wide world, we spent the rest of the day (and how appropriate) in a nightclub, where it was more than possible to meet ladies of ill repute from 8am onwards.

The club, when we found it (and it wasn't difficult) had a resident band playing, who sounded to me like the greatest musicians on the planet – although the joint we'd smoked on the way there may just have clouded my judgement somewhat – and out the back was a kind of motel where the bar girls did what bar girls, we hoped, do best.

By the time one of them sauntered over to Dave and me and our ten-dollar bottle of white rum that would only have cost us six dollars in PG, we were more than ready to party on up.

Back at the Mira Mar all of the bar girls on offer were black Belizians, but here the majority of the ten or so that were on duty (it was a quiet afternoon) were 'white chicks'. Most of them originated from neighbouring Mexico, but others, like the one we got to strip naked, were escaping from their various miserable lots in El Salvador, Guatemala and Nicaragua. Quite why, on this occasion, we decided both to fuck the same girl I can't now imagine. We weren't particularly perverted, so all I can think is that it was a gang-bang-type boys' thing. And it wasn't like it was illegal or anything (although paying for it probably was).

When we suggested to the girl that all three of us go out back together, it was obvious that she'd already been there, done that and had the smear test, because she didn't bat an eyelash. However, we had to understand that there was to be no group discount and it would still cost the same as doing her separately.

As I snorted another line of what I now know was the most expensive baking powder in Belize, I looked across at Dave and watched as he took hold of the girl's hair and tried to push his dick down her throat as far as it would go. By this time I was sitting naked on the end of the bed, once again living a crucial moment in my life when I was finding it hard to get hard.

It wasn't because I had to do it in front of Dave, either, because, if I'm honest, we'd fucked lots of girls together before (all right, three . . . no, thinking about it, make that five). And why not? We were healthy young paratroopers serving our country, so we deserved such pleasures. Didn't we?

It was at this point that I remembered Kalgoorlie, and, like I said, it was with a sense of loss. Just for a second or two, as I looked around the room at Dave humping away and at the grass and coke on the bedside table, I felt a little sad. Like I'd lost my way a bit.

Well, that would be the grass, though, wouldn't it?

After I had not sinned, penetratively speaking at least, and Dave and the girl had settled the row about him wanting to have another go because I hadn't and we'd paid for two goes (apparently there was no way she was again going to go through the experience of having Dave go through her – and who could blame her?), we pocketed the 25% refund (cheap bastards, I know it), waved *adios señorita* and went for a stroll along the early evening seafront to smoke some more Scooby-Dooby Doo, where are you.

We followed the coast for maybe a half-mile or so, passing from dilapidated buildings and rotten wooden jetties littered with piles of honking rubbish, with vultures circling above (no bullshit), to the nicer part of town with its wide views of the sea and its row of hotels providing rooms for the mainly pink-skinned tourists.

We stopped at a park bench that looked out across the ocean and lit up one of the joints that we'd knocked together back there with Miss El Salvador. In between tokes I looked around, the way you do, taking in the nice palm trees and the passing black faces, when, would you believe it, there it was, two storeys high and made completely out of wood: a Kingdom Hall of Jehovah's Witnesses.

Maybe, if I hadn't been quite so stoned, the flashback to my youth that automatically followed my second sighting of a Third World Kingdom Hall (there was one back in PG as well) would have brought with it a twinge of guilt. After all, I had been sinning, and this time on double double time. Oh, but fuck that! I was enjoying myself, which was more than I ever did during my fifteen years of tag-along service to Jehovah God.

'Pass the splith.'

When our joint was all gone, we picked ourselves up and set off again on our travels. We had walked for about two blocks when we happened upon the Fort George Hotel, which we had heard all about down in Punta Gorda.

'Oh, so that's where it is.'

Inside, the Fort George (apart from its sea view and its staff who could all speak fluent English) could have been any posh hotel in London. It had air conditioning, overpriced drinks, poolside waiter service, and a menu with prices that soon put us back into our lowly squaddie pay packets. Mind you, it wasn't expensive to the point that we couldn't afford a couple of drinks, so once we'd asked directions to the bar we soon found ourselves sitting on two tall stools, cold beer in hand. A nice place it was as well, the bar, and it looked all the better to us because we hadn't had access to such Western-style luxury in months.

'Wow! Is that carpet beneath our feet?'

After we'd spent five or so more than pleasant minutes there, an American guy who was sitting at the bar beside us started up a conversation. Dressed in sport casuals and probably in his mid-thirties, judging by the key that was placed on the bar next to him he was a resident of the hotel. Not Peace Corps, then. His opening line I wished I could have put money on (but even if I could, such would have been the odds that once I'd paid the tax I'd only have ended up losing).

'You guys are English, right?'

'Right.'

Our fellow lounge lizard's name was Larry and he was 'out of Miami' and in Belize to buy tropical fish for American aquariums. A nice enough chap he was as well, and since he was a go-get-'em American businessman and we were poor underpaid soldier types, he insisted on paying for all the drinks. Terrific chap he was. In fact, so generous was Larry that when he excused himself to go off to the john (by which he meant the bog, of course) we couldn't help but wonder whether Larry might not be a Sodomite. Oh well, if he tried it on with us we'd just punch him in the teeth and then bite the heads off all his goldfish.

When he returned, Larry partially put our minds at rest about his sexuality by proudly producing some pictures of his wife back home in the States. (Don't mean nothin'. What about that Rock Hudson bloke? How many photos with chicks could he have shown you?) She was a looker as well, and we had to admit it:

'You're a lucky man, Larry.'

Larry then asked us if we were married (he was at it again) and I said that yes, I was.

'Oh, great. Can I see a photo?'

Although I had my wallet on me, since it had never contained a photograph of my wife Carol I didn't have one to show him. Larry, I could tell, couldn't work this out and thought it more than not normal that a man wouldn't carry a photograph of his wife around with him, especially when they were separated by so many miles. Maybe he had a point.

In the end we stayed at the bar chatting with Larry until it was time to set off for the camp. We got along with him like a petrol dump ablaze, but, although we both got pissed out of our brains, at no point did Dave and me so much as mention marijuana – which just goes to show how all the 'ears have walls' stuff we'd been taught in Northern Ireland must have sunk in. Mind you, just before we left the Fort George, we both went to the 'john' and knocked up a couple of numbers, which we put to good use as soon as we hit the streets.

The next morning it was army life again and time for our parachute jump. And hung over or what. But like they say, if you can't go on the piss till five in the morning and still get up at seven to go do a jump, then it's time to buy out. We held a little barrack-room conference about ground training before the jump and everyone agreed that if they didn't give us some, then we weren't supposed to jump, because we hadn't done parachute training in ages. Not that we really needed any, but rules were rules – when it suited us.

To our pleasant surprise (well, we wouldn't *really* have wanted not to do the jump, would we?) at APC they had everything you needed to practise leaping out of a plane with. There were mats to roll about on, ramps to jump off, even parachute harnesses hanging from the rafters. So the jump was on.

It wasn't all bad news, though, because it was to be done without equipment (which meant there would be nothing to pack and no weight to lug around) and with only eight men in each stick (which meant not many men in the air at one time, so less of them to collide with). But guess what else – and this was the big one – no hours and hours of low-level flying over the ocean before we jumped.

In parachuting terms, none of us had done such a jump since basic training, so we tried to look upon the one in Belize as a 'fun jump'. *Tried* to look upon it . . .

For me the highlight of the jump, when we finally got around to it in the afternoon, was a photograph that was taken on the plane. No, really. Fabulous I look in it – all warlike and debonair. By chance, sitting next to me was I dare say the army's only soldier of Chinese origin.

'You see that one there? That's me, that is, when I was attached to a unit I'm not allowed to mention, jumping into Laos in 1978.'

'But wasn't the war over by then?'

'Exactly.'

The jump itself was just like any other. Oh well, we've all gotta die some time – out the door – helpless feeling of falling – chute open – thank fuck for that! – now, where's the trees? The drop zone upon landing ('. . . *and* knees together, *and* bend a little . . .') was great: a soft ploughed field that was a pleasure to roll about in. And what was also nice was that the whole of the local suburb-cum-township had turned out to watch the mad white men (and let's be honest, this really confirmed it) throw themselves out of aeroplanes by numbers.

Nicer still, in the spirit of laid-back free enterprise that was Belize, for fifty cents a local kid would carry your chute off the DZ and back to the truck for you. Of course, me, I get the one who's so small that he can't manage to carry it all the way, so while he ends up with only the reserve, I'm suddenly sweating like a European in full combat gear ('*and* . . . you can take the helmet off, Ken') who's lugging a heavy parachute across a ploughed field in thirty-five degrees of humid heat.

Luckily, though, before I suffered too much weight loss someone else set up another little parachute collection business and I was able to employ my second young Belizian of the day. Gave 'em both a whole dollar I did as well.

What a great guy.

I know.

Ammo nights

What with Rideau being an army camp and all, there were, as you can imagine, a lot of things that needed to be guarded – from us lot in our sleepy beds, to the washing hanging out on the line, right up to all that ammunition we kept in a compound outside the camp. (Well, we weren't going to sleep next to it.)

Thanks to the way things deliberately are in the army, doing a guard duty at Rideau Camp was exactly like doing one back in Aldershot but with the central heating turned up full: two hours on, four hours off, and in between as much tropical moaning and, if you were lucky, sleep as you could manage. Since I was a lance corporal I should, theoretically, have been second in command of the guard whenever I was on it, but because Rideau Camp did overflow with one-stripe wonders I only once did a guard as 2i/c. And even then I complained about it. For you see, if there was one perfect place to have an illicit smoke while in your soldier suit, it was while on ammo compound guard duty.

The ammo compound was situated a good quarter of a mile from the main camp and could only be reached by a dark walk (well, at night anyway) along a single-lane dirt track that led to its only gate. About half the size of a football pitch, it was enclosed by a mean-looking wire fence topped with whirls of barbed wire and surrounded on three of its sides by jungle. The big bonus was that when you were on guard inside it you locked yourself in, which meant that no one could creep up on you if you were doing something you shouldn't have been. There were always two men on compound guard together, so it helped to get on it with a mate. Naturally, whenever we could wangle it (and between us we could wangle most things, given the time) Dave and me would 'do guard' together.

The official deal, when inside the compound, was that one soldier was supposed to remain in the organic bus-shelter type structure that was there in case of wet weather while the other one patrolled the inside perimeter. The real deal was that both guards would sit under the shelter on the two plastic chairs provided, with their webbing off, their weapons on the floor and their feet up. The compound was in contact with the outside world by means of a field telephone, which had a wire that led all the way back to the guardroom and the guard commander's desk. When your two hours of stag were up, before your replacements could leave the guardroom the guard commander had to phone the compound to advise you that they were on their way. The reason for this warning call was that both the ammo compound guards were armed – and we wouldn't want any mistaken identity mishaps, now, would we?

No we would not.

Thinking about it (and I do have to think), doing guard duty in the compound was the only time while I was in the army that I was ever stoned in charge of a weapon, and a loaded one at that – which, although the thought never crossed my mind one iota at the time, was not really a very bright thing to do. What if we were attacked? Where would my aggression come from? And I mean that most sincerely, folks.

In reality there was about as much chance of there being a Guatemalan soldier on the other side of the fence as there was a polar bear. All the same, with a smoke in you, walking around with your machine gun, moon over the jungle, fuck knows what sort of creatures chirping and croaking a backing track . . . the mind could create. I often had this thought that if I was in a Hollywood war movie right now, I'd be the guy who gets crept up on and has his throat silently slit. And what if there was a sniper out in the jungle? A guard walking around the inside of a locked compound that was surrounded by perfect creep-up cover (someone just like me, say) would be little more than a fairground target: quack-quack, ping!

Mind you, on a more positive note, when it comes to doing guard duty, being in a mental state of paranoia is not necessarily such a bad thing. In fact, I'd go so far as to say that it's a good thing, because at least you're watching your back. As the old Vietnamese proverb says: there's nothing wrong with having a nervous guard dog.

Being soldiers, and therefore part-time philosophers, with time on our hands while sitting in the ammo compound we couldn't help but lean back in our chairs and ponder how we'd hit the place if we were the bad guys. 'Easily' was always the conclusion, because we knew that if we were in their place and it was them sitting here instead of us, then they'd be dead very soon.

'What do you reckon? Sniper's round?'

'Yep. Right between the eyes.'

'Fucking dead meat we'd be, mate, and we wouldn't know a thing about it.'

'There are worse ways to go, though, eh? By the way, there's a little lit-up red dot on your face.'

'Really? Funny that, 'cos there's one bobbing up and down on yours as well.'

By chance (I'd even go so far as to say by lucky chance) I happened to be on ammo compound guard with Dave on the night we had the pleasure of experiencing Belizian rain for the first time. And when I say rain, I mean rain like we could not believe it. We'd been told about the rain in Belize – warned, if you like – but we did come from England, so we tended to believe that there wasn't a lot you could teach us about rain, mate. We'd seen it all, stood in it all, got soaked by it all. But not like it rained in Belize we hadn't. That first night we actually heard the rain coming before it arrived, although when this rumble that had started in the distant jungle grew louder and louder as it beat its way towards us, we didn't realise what it was immediately.

'What the fuck's that noise?'

'Dunno.'

'Do you think we should report it to the guardroom?'

'Dunno.'

And when it did finally reach us it was like someone had just turned a waterfall on. As our little grass shelter was open on three sides, you would have expected us to get soaked, but in fact the rain was so heavy that it fell dead die vertically, like a wall of see-through steel. Very impressive it was.

One night we got caught in the rain while walking back from PG because we'd missed the last transport from town (with good reason, I might add), which was not very pleasant at all. We struggled even to stand up in it, let alone run for cover, and in about two seconds every inch of us, right through to our underwear, socks and paper money, was pissed wet through.

Now, the good reason we had for deliberately missing the last transport back was that that very night we had bought ourselves a half-pound of grass – the way you do – and rather than risk carrying such a package in an army vehicle, we had cunningly elected to walk back to camp instead. As the rain fell and the lightning kept flashing up seconds of daylight, the dirt road back to Rideau quickly turned into an orange thick shake of mud, so the only thing for it was to try and find shelter under some trees (though please *don't* try this at home).

With the rain continuing to bucket down, a set of headlights appeared from the direction of PG, and lo and behold, if it wasn't an army Land Rover. Now what was that doing out at this time of night?

Like everything you bought in Punta Gorda, our grass was wrapped in a large brown paper bag. Since we now didn't fancy walking back from town after all and it was only half a pound of grass, and soaking wet to boot, Dave threw the bag into the jungle and we waved the approaching Land Rover down.

Inside with the duty driver were two drunken sergeants who had been having their own night out on the town (mind you, we hadn't bumped into them and we'd been just about everywhere, so where had they been and what had they been up to?). Naturally, the other soldiers thought it just hilarious how wet we were. And so, come to think of it, did we, but for a different reason. Yes, you've guessed it. We woz stoned again – though not very, by our standards. Which leads me on to the truth, the whole truth and nothing but the truth, and I say this because I wouldn't want to be held responsible for any urban-type myth of the dope world.

For PG, the half-pound of grass we'd bought that night wasn't exactly top drawer. In fact, it was the mildest grass we ever smoked in Belize (though we probably wouldn't have thought it that mild if we'd been rolling it up in Clapham). A couple of days after we'd lobbed it into the jungle, because we were going to be on guard that night and had no other smoke left, Dave went off in search of it. When he found it, it looked pretty much like anything else in the world would have looked if it had been sitting at the bottom of a swimming pool for forty-eight hours. The bag had all but disintegrated and the grass was 'like fucking wet spinach'.

To dry it out, Dave spread the grass over a corrugated metal roofing sheet that he'd found down by the rifle range and left it to bake in the midday sun for a few hours. When he went back later to pick it up, the grass was dust dry, and that night in the compound we were able to smoke some of it. To our surprise, it was now dynamite, head-ripping gear. What the scientific reason for this vast improvement was I do not know, but getting wet and then being baked dry again had definitely turned up its potency dial.

Somehow (rushing, I guess, or as close to it as I ever got in Belize) before setting off for the compound that night I had picked up the wrong set of webbing from the guardroom floor. I didn't notice this until I was well on my way to a happy state of relaxation in my plastic chair and started searching in my ammo pouches for goodies to feed my munchies. As soon as I dipped my hand in I knew something was wrong. I may not have known much about anything, but one thing I did know for sure, because I'd checked and double-checked, was exactly where I'd put my Bounty bars. And they weren't there.

As if by telepathy, at that moment the field telephone rang and it was another member of the guard asking if one of us two had picked up the wrong webbing. Well, I obviously had, hadn't I? So I told him yes. At this, the soldier whose webbing I'd picked up by mistake immediately said he'd come over and bring mine to the compound so that we could swap them back. When I told Dave we had a visitor coming, he immediately processed this information to arrive at the same thing I was wondering. Why bother? After all, webbing tends to be webbing, and it was a tidy walk to the compound and back just to get hold of something you certainly didn't need in the guardroom.

'Wonder what's in it that he wants so badly?'

It would take him ten minutes to reach us, so we had a look. There were two things of interest. Firstly, the naughty, naughty boy had some marijuana (yes, that's right: grass) tucked into his ration-pack drinks bag. ('You mean it's *not* herbal tea?')

Well, we weren't going to grass him up. It was an idea, though, because it would have earnt us some Brownie points and marked our cards as fervent anti-dopers at the same time, which had to be good camouflage by anyone's standards. A shade hypocritical, mind you. Or we could pull him about it and let him know we belonged to the same club and his secret was safe with us. But then again, why? It wasn't like we needed the friendship, and if, at a later date, he was to take a fall, he might just throw our names into the pot to make it easier on himself. So we did the wise thing. We put it back whence it had come and made like we'd never seen it.

The second thing he had that was of interest (and this we definitely had not seen, if anyone asked) was a letter from his wife. Now, we wouldn't have read it, honest, except that it was already out of its envelope, and when we opened it up to see what it was (note the 'we', by the way) we couldn't help but catch the lipstick smudges. And what smudges they were. The first was a pair of heavily lipsticked lips kissed into the paper, the next two were obviously lipsticked nipples, and the last was back to lips again – but those of the lower region of the lady's anatomy.

Well! P–lease.

Having seen the pictures, of course, we couldn't resist taking a quick peep at the words. And if ever there was a case to be made for the authenticity of all those personal letters they print in top-shelf magazines, then this was it. Very rude and straight to the point it was.

The soldier, when he turned up at the compound to pick up his drugs and filth (and really, I don't know what the army is coming to), played it totally cool. Mind you, he *was* one of the most boring and uninteresting men I've ever met, so who could tell – maybe he was always like that? Not that I'm judging him for being boring and uninteresting. In fact, in the army I liked men like that, because they were usually the ones that were harmless.

But who'd have guessed that he was a smoker?

How many years on?

How many years on?

Well, one year it was ten years on
  and it was like they remembered me.
I saw moving pictures of my battlefields
  on my colour TV.

And I saw Stevie and I saw Tom,
  smiling faces, cam cream on,
and then I saw Stevie and I saw Tom
  lying dead at Goose Green – cam cream still on.
Stuff like that.

As I write this now, my six-month stint at Rideau Camp is
sixteen years ago. Looking back on it, as it is with any period of
time that's recalled (in my case, even the first two days of last
week), there are bits of it that I can recollect in great detail,
others where I can kind of pick out the odd moment, say a
particular event on a particular day, and then there are the
whole days, from dawn to dawn, about which I don't remember a single second.

And there's nothing wrong with that. Normal is what that is.

But there's one day when I was in Belize . . . No, we'd better
make that (one, two, May 28th is three, June 14th) . . . there
are four days when I was in Belize that I really should be able to
recall but I can't. I remember nothing at all about what I did,

who I was with, how many drinks I had (and unless I was on guard duty on the 28th of May 1983, I just must have had a whole hoopey-load of drink) or what I said. And I just must have said: 'One year on, hey! The first anniversary of the battle for Goose Green.' Even if I only whispered it to myself, I must have said that.

I can tell you about other 28th of Mays, other Goose Green Days, since Belize: the places I've been to on that date (bars and pubs, mainly), how drunk I got, how angry or sad or happy I was, and, over the years, every losing combination of all that. But I can't tell you about that first 28th of May in Belize, and because it was the first one, today – naturally enough, I suppose – I reason that I should be able to recall at least something about it. After all, only one year on, it certainly wasn't like I'd forgotten the Falklands.

Up at Air Port Camp, the RAF (and God bless 'em, because they were the real deterrent) owned whatever you call a row of Harrier Jump Jets. A bit of a squadron I think it is.

Like everything British and military that was stationed in Belize, every now and then these aircraft went on exercises. As far as I could make out, the Harriers' task in the event of war breaking out was to zip to the border and start dropping bombs and shooting fast exploding-type things at anything that fell into the category of Guatemalan and advancing, with triple Green Shield Stamps for the tanks.

So one bright sunny morning I'm sitting at Rideau having just returned from the morning run to the airstrip and all I am in the world is open to sell stamps, when out of nowhere – and I really do mean absolutely nowhere – two Harrier Jump Jets fly low-level right over my post room.

Zoooom!

Today I smile and laugh when I say I did shit myself, but within point zero of a second I was back at Fitzroy the day the Argentine jets blew the Welsh away. I hit the bastard ceiling with fright, and then I legged it outside. When I got there (and it didn't take long) I found I was not alone. Almost the whole of the camp was 'al fresco' and coming down off a panic attack as well.

As I looked over at the nearest soldiers, I could see that there was this sort of mass embarrassment going on. All anyone could think of to do was try and make a joke of it and openly admit, but with a silly smile, 'Shit myself I did. Fucking RAF!'

'Wankers!'

'Shitheads!'

'Arseholes!'

Some nights up at Rideau it would rain like none of us had thought possible, and along with this would come strobe-light lightning and thunder that sounded like the earth was being torn in two. The first night that we were all tucked up in our little beddie-bye-byes and along came a tropical thunderstorm, I thought the camp was under shell fire. I did, honestly. OK, I can laugh about it today, but boy, was I scared. Although, when a voice from the darkness beat its way through to me and asked 'Are we being fucking shelled or what?', once again I realised I wasn't the only one.

Both in Belize and over the years since, I've had the odd violent dream about the war, and, as you would expect, me getting shot or blown up is a common one. Then suddenly I wake up dripping in sweat, just like in the films.

I've also dreamt of the war happening all over again, with me, the Argies and a whole load of other people with guns. Only it's always taking place somewhere else: on the council estate I was born on in Swindon, in the fields of my granddad's farm in Cornwall, over the playground of my first infant school . . .

When I was at Rideau I once dreamt that Argentine helicopters were landing on the streets of Punta Gorda (up by the cemetery, fittingly enough). As luck would not have it, when this dream invasion started I was in town all on my own, carrying a rifle and wearing a helmet (did I even have a helmet?). As the choppers landed and the first troops jumped out, I had to decide on the spot whether to stand my ground and fight or make a tactical retreat el pretty damn pronto. And as the first bullet whistled towards me I woke up.

Stuff like that.

Kenneth Yes!

It would be nice for me to be able to blame all that dope-smoking in Belize on the fact that I'd taken part in a war only twelve months before. Messed me up it did, guv. Made me turn to dope. But it didn't really, because I got into smoking dope in uniform some four months before I ever heard of the Falkland Islands.

In November 1981 I found myself sitting on a snow-white beach in Kenya where the scene around me looked pretty much like a Bounty advert, except that in my commercial paradise all the beach girls, who were mostly holidaying Italians and Germans, were topless. Even now I can distinctly remember sitting on the hot sands of Dinani beach and saying to myself: 'Do you know something, mate? It was worth going through all of that Northern Ireland bollocks just to have ended up sitting here now.' In fact, so good did everything appear that it made the whole thing about joining the army in the first place seem like the work of a genius. There again, I *was* an Englishman out in the midday sun.

We had travelled to Kenya to take part in a six-week soldier training thing, because although the British army had pulled out of Kenya in the 'sixties, at any given time there was always one battalion of British infantry soldiers stationed in the country on 'exercise'. Our time in Kenya was split between three separate locations that catered for three different types of possible African warfare: jungle, semi-jungle/semi-desert and all-out desert.

Our company's first stop was the jungle training venue, and once off the plane at Nairobi's international airport it was all aboard a four-ton army truck for a very pleasant five hours along what go for roads in Kenya.

Our camp, when we got there, turned out to be of the tented variety. It consisted of maybe thirty or forty small two-man tents, three larger tents that acted as Company HQ and stores, and two other tents playing the parts of cookhouse and NAAFI.

On our first night I took a stroll round the inner perimeter of the camp and found myself drawn, like a curious moth, towards a small fire that was flickering in one of the camp's corners. Gathered around it, sharing a bottle of beer, were five or six local workmen who had been employed by the army to help in the field kitchen. When I walked up to them they all smiled and nodded a happy 'jambo' and I was invited to join them. I sat down on the upside-down empty cooking-oil drum they'd offered me as a seat and joined in the conversation as best I could. Almost straight away I became aware of a smell that seemed more than a little familiar to me. If I was correct, it was the smell of burning grass. Doing a quick scan of all the faces, I soon found the one that was sucking on a joint.

The beer they were sharing was being passed round the campfire in the same way that we in the West would pass round a joint at a party. When the bottle got to me, much like in an old film where the white explorer whispers to the female lead that it's a big-time insult in these here parts to refuse the bowl of sacred monkey brains, I made a point of not wiping the top of the bottle before I took a swig.

After I had passed the beer on to the next man (who, I noticed, wiped the rim with his T-shirt before putting it to his lips – the cheeky cunt) I was passed the joint. I was in two minds whether to accept it or not, but then I thought, well, there's no way any other soldiers can see me, and even if they do, I can just say I thought it was a normal cigarette. Which, as excuses go, was a pretty good one, because the joint was made from a hollowed-out cigarette that had had grass pushed into it. So I had a toke or two and we talked about this and that, and very interested they all were to hear about the paradise of a Western town – i.e. Aldershot – that I lived in.

When the joint reached me the next time round, I asked the guy sitting next to me if he could get me some of this 'ganja' stuff. Since we were all the best of pals by now, he said of course he could, although he'd have to pop into town tomorrow afternoon to pick it up. My problem with this was that the next morning I was due to go away and play soldiers in the jungle for three days.

When I got back he'd still be here and so I'd still be able to get my grass, but what about the time between now and then? So I asked if he had any on him that I could have, buy, borrow or whatever to tide me over for a few days. He said 'sure' and disappeared into his tent, reappearing a few minutes later with what looked and felt like a piece of folded-up newspaper. I said thank you very much, very, very, very much, and stuffed it into my trouser-leg map pocket. Before bidding farewell I once again confirmed our appointment for three days' time (same field, same campfire) and then headed back, happy as a sandboy, to the tent.

Back at my tent I opened up the newspaper to see what I'd got, and I reckoned that I now had about half an ounce in my possession. Kenya, was all right.

The next morning I packed away my kit and paraded for my three-day African nature ramble. Now, according to the plan as it had been explained to me, there would only be three of us on our little jungle excursion, i.e. me, the OC and a colour sergeant. So I was more than a little surprised to discover that we were to be joined for the three days by a young lieutenant from the 16/5th Lancers, which is a cavalry regiment. As far as I could make out, he had joined the army because 'Daddy' had been in the army, just like his daddy before him, and they all drove armoured cars and played polo, and when 'one' was not sleeping in the officers' mess one retired to one's hice (as he pronounced it) in the country. Now apparently – and I should point out here that this may not be entirely accurate, even though us paras all believed it as gospel – the money a lieutenant in the cavalry got from the army each month wasn't enough to cover his mess bills, so it stood to reason that they all had private incomes. Which meant, in three words, that to us paratroopers cavalry officers appeared, acted and talked like an alien species.

Around mid-morning we stopped for a smoke break and I grabbed a shovel and disappeared into the undergrowth to have a quiet crap. When I found a suitable spot I dug a suitable hole, squatted down and let squeezing commence. While I was there, not knowing what to do with my hands, so to speak, I thought: 'Hey, groovy, Ken – why not bang up a neat little one-skinner?' And that's what I did.

I probably smoked no more than half of it before dropping it into the hole and adding it to the rest of my recyclable waste. When I got back to the group, everyone else was still sitting around looking like no one was in any particular hurry to get anywhere. At one point I was leaning up against a fallen tree, trying to unwrap an old and sticky Spangle without getting any goo on my fingers or sweetie-wrapper paper in my mouth, when it hit me – bang! – like someone had just flicked the light switch. My first thought (and it was amazing that I was still capable of one) was fuck, am I stoned. My second was one of regret for having talked myself into allowing myself to get like it in the first place.

While I was trying to come to terms with the way the jungle around me was now starting to appear (Hey, fuck, man . . . I'm in *the jungle*), Lieutenant Charge-of-the-Light-Brigade was squeaking away about something to the group in general. When he'd had his say, he turned to me, of all people, and asked me what I thought about all that. Although I had been nodding away while he talked, and letting out the occasional little murmur of agreement in well-judged places, I hadn't taken aboard one single word of it.

Luckily, we were all in the army and I was a private and he

was an officer, so all I had to do was fall back on the old 'I don't know, sir', uttered in my most deeply simple born-on-a-council-estate-and-failed-my-eleven-plus kind of way. And boy, did I want out of there before anyone wanted any more answers out of me. Fortunately, the OC decided he'd had enough of sitting around and gave the order for us to move on out.

A couple of miles of wading through the jungle later, we reached the spot where we were to lie up for the night, and because there were only four of us in the patrol, the OC and the cavalry lieutenant basha'd up together while I got to share a ground sheet with the colour sergeant.

Once we'd all settled in and got a brew on, well, then there came some very exciting news. The young cavalry lieutenant, while on a small walkabout, had discovered what he believed to be elephant tracks ('Well, whoopee shit,' thought I) and wouldn't it just be a dandy thing to go follow them? Me, personally, I didn't think so, and as elephant fever gripped the rest of the camp, I volunteered to stay behind and keep an eye on the kit. After all, better safe than sorry. We wouldn't want it to get nicked in our absence.

'But who's around to steal it?' asked the lieutenant with cunning officer-type logic. 'We *are* in a jungle you know, private.'

'I know, sir. But the monkeys, sir. Terrible thieves they are, sir.'

And actually, as far as baboons are concerned, that's a more than fair assessment.

So off into the undergrowth the three of them trotted, while I settled down to a bit of peace and quiet. With a nice mug of tea in my paws, a fag in my mouth, a tape in my Walkman and my headphones on, I was just fine, thank you very much for asking.

This is the life for me, I thought, sipping my tea and boogying along with the music. All I needed now was another smoke. Not that I needed one, because I was still a teeny-weeny bit stoned from the one I'd had earlier, but everyone else was out of the way, and I might not get another chance over the next couple of days.

There was a slight problem with my wish for a spliff, though, and it didn't have a thing to do with the conveniently forgotten self-promise I'd made earlier in the day not to smoke any more of Kenya's finest, which had disappeared as soon as everyone else had. No, my problem was that I had no papers to roll it with. At home, whenever you run out of Rizlas there's always one to be found somewhere: tucked under the settee cushions, screwed up in the bin, hiding under a seat in the car or behind some paperback on a bookshelf. But out in the jungle..? So that was that. No more dooby for me today.

But then I had a brainwave of the very inventive culinary kind. 'I'll eat some,' I thought, 'that's what I'll do.' So I dug out my mess tins and rations and settled on a tin of mixed veg and another one of minced beef. Once I'd got these under way over a hexam stove, I threw in what I had left of my grass – and Bob's your uncle.

I was part-way through heating up my special meal when back came the elephant trackers.

'Any luck, sir?' I called out to the cavalry officer.

'No. No joy. *Most* disappointing.'

'Yes, sir,' I agreed, 'most disappointing.'

I could tell from the way he looked at me that he was thinking 'Hold on a moment, chaps. Is this soldier being insubordinate?' Before he could have another thought, though, I wrong-footed him by asking, in an interested and enthusiastic manner, if we could continue the search in the morning. There was nothing I'd like more than to see some real live elephants, because I'd only ever seen the ones in Regent's Park. Day trip from the slums it was, sir. Bought us ice cream they did. And fish and chips afterwards.

Meanwhile, the colour sergeant walked over to where I was sitting and dropped his webbing on the floor next to me, muttering under his breath, 'Fucking elephants! Stupid cunt'll 'ave us out looking for unicorns next.'

'Did you not enjoy that then, Colour?'

'Lukowiak . . .'

'Yes, Colour?'

'Shut the fuck up!'

'Yes, Colour.'

There was a short pause, then he asked what I was cooking.

'Mixed veg and mince, Colour.'

'Oh good.' The colour sergeant then started to rummage through the pouches of his webbing, and as soon as he began doing this I knew what was coming next. Sure enough, he held out two tins of food and said: 'Chuck these in with it, will you.'

As you can probably imagine, it immediately struck me that to do that would not be an act of the greatest wisdom. Not that I had a lot of options. I did think about telling him to go take a running fuck and cook his own food, but if I'd done that I would only have woken up either in hospital or at a court martial, and I didn't fancy either of them. I could, of course, just come straight out and tell him what was in my stew, but when I thought short and soft about this, I didn't think so. I could, alternatively, not tell him what was in it (which sounded a bit more like it), or I could (and this was getting better) acciden-tally knock the mess tin over, thereby rendering its intoxicating contents unfit for human consumption.

What would he do to me if I did that, though? He wouldn't be a happy bunny if I fucked up his food, that was for sure, and he'd also be certain to let me, and everyone else he met over the next six weeks, know just what a clumsy wanker I was.

So really there was nothing else for it but to open his tins, throw his food in on top of mine, stir it all up and then hope. And I did have a slight hope . . .

If I remembered correctly (and I must have, because when-ever one of my army muckers asked if anyone had seen 'Memory', it would be me they were looking for), when I first starting smoking marijuana back in Australia in 1975 I had tried it maybe five or six times before it had any effect on me. And, as I'd since come to learn, this delayed reaction was by no means unique to me.

Nevertheless, as I mixed his food in I kept reminding myself: I

113

must not stir the contents of my mess tin too vigorously; I must try my very bestest to keep what's his and what's mine at separate ends of the pool.

'What are you buggering about at now, Lukowiak? Stir the fucking stuff up properly. Come on, I'm hungry.'

Oh well, it was his brain, even if it was my fault. So I stirred the fucking stuff up properly.

It was then that I had a brilliant idea of the type I'm so brilliant at having – i.e. the type that comes just too late to save the day. Why hadn't I just tipped my own food out on to the jungle floor before getting around to adding his? So simple. Much like my good self, really. Twat.

Far too quickly, the heating-up was done and it was time to spoon the colour sergeant's share into his waiting mess tin.

Two spoonfuls later, he turned to me and asked, 'Did you drop the fucking thing or something?'

'No, Colour. Why?'

'It's full of twigs.'

He had a point. It *was* full of twigs, and no doubt a few seeds too, if you cared to look.

'They must've fallen down off the trees,' I lied. 'Would you like me to make you something else, Colour? I've got a nice chicken curry and rice you can have.'

'No point. You'd only go and fuck that up as well.'

(Bet I fucking wouldn't.)

So there we were, both spooning away, and with every mouthful I was looking out of the corner of my eye to see if the colour sergeant was still with me here on planet Earth. I began to wonder how long it would take to hit him. I, myself and me had only eaten dope before on three, maybe four, occasions, but from what I knew about it, it was much slower to take effect this way than when you smoked it. Judging by the times I'd eaten dope back in Bristol, I estimated that it would be about forty-five minutes or so, call it an hour at the most, before he discovered what was going on.

But what could I do? Nothing much, except wait and carry on hoping that the colour sergeant would prove to be immune to the effects of heated-up herbal cannabis. So, when we'd both finished eating and he lay back to have a nap, I decided to have a little lie down myself.

As I stared up through the trees, life didn't really look that different from being camped in a forest in Wales at the height of a heatwave. Come to think of it, though, it definitely sounded different. When a bird (or was it a monkey?) let out a loud call, this was quickly followed by a call from something else, which in turn was answered by another call, and so on until noise had broken out from all corners of the canopy.

At one point, what I thought was definitely a monkey this time let out a shrill 'eee-eee-eee-eee' sound. Next to me the colour sergeant sat bolt upright. Turning only his head, he looked slowly to the right, and then to the left, and then up into the foliage of the trees above. A bird squawked, and the colour sergeant instantly squawked back.

Uh-oh . . . shit.

Another bird then let out another squawk, and once again the colour sergeant came back with a perfect imitation of the sound it had just made. From then on, for about five minutes, every time something in the jungle had its say, the colour sergeant immediately echoed it.

By this time I was aware that the secret ingredient in our tinned meat and two veg had started to creep up on me as well. In fact, it had already arrived in a driverless Chieftain tank. However, I couldn't enjoy it for panicking about what the colour sergeant might do next.

I soon found out.

The OC wandered over, with young 'Lieutenant Flashman' in tow, to where we were sitting. They reached us and stopped, and the colour sergeant and I both looked up.

The OC then said something like 'Colour Sergeant, you were in the jungles of Malaya during the Borneo crisis, weren't you? Since we have a little time on our hands, and find ourselves in the jungle, I thought you might like to give us the benefit of your experience and tell us something about jungle RV procedures?'

The colour sergeant thought about the OC's request for a few very long and very silent moments before replying with a very blunt 'No!'.

Even though the OC had only *asked* the colour sergeant politely if he would *mind* giving us a little talk, his words were, in effect, an order. Behind the OC, I noticed that the cavalry lieutenant was having great trouble coming to terms with what he had just heard. A senior NCO saying no to a major? I could see his mind frantically scanning the pages of his Sandhurst manuals in search of what to do in the event of such a crisis.

In truth, of course, there wasn't a lot anyone could do but get back to what they had been doing before.

'Oh!' said the OC in surprise. 'All right then. Maybe tomorrow?' And with that he about-turned back to his basha with the lieutenant once more in tow.

Later that same day, when the effects of the grass were finally, thankfully, beginning to wear off, the peace of the jungle was interrupted by the sound of steel cutting into wood. I took a look over to where the OC and the lieutenant were ging-gang-goolying it and could see that the lieutenant had his machete out and was chopping away like a very happy eager beaver at various pieces of fallen tree. Oh well, all the best to him.

About an hour later the chopping stopped and he walked over to where I was sitting, with his camera in his hand.

'I say. You wouldn't mind taking a photo of me in my bivouac would you?' he asked.

Well, I fucking would actually. But hey, I was a private and he was a lieutenant, so I had no other choice but to smile and answer 'Certainly, sir.'

Like the good soldier that I was, up I got, took his camera from him and followed him over to his part of the woods. When I got there I soon discovered what all the noise had been about. He had made himself two wooden wigwam-type frames, between which he had hung a hammock. All in all I was quite surprised, not to mention impressed, because I couldn't have built anything like that. So I said so.

'It's very good, sir. Where'd you learn to make one of them then, sir?'

'In Belize. I was there for six months earlier this year.'

'Oh! We're all going to Belize next year, sir. Is it a good posting, is it, sir?'

'Bloody good tour. Sort of thing a chap like you would revel in.'

Chap? Did he really call me a chap? Well, yes he did. He was always saying it. My chaps, your chaps, our chaps . . . even, in the case of an enemy, 'their chaps'.

Mind you, fair's fair, he might only have been able to converse in fluent 1940s black-and-white film dialogue, but he was to be proved right about me and Belize. For when I got there, revel in it I certainly did.

Night had already fallen when we arrived back at base camp after our three days and three nights of wandering through the overgrown wilderness, and my first thought was to find my friend the camp workman, who by now would hopefully have a nice bag of grass waiting for me. Once I'd cleaned my weapon and kit and packed it all away for the night, I changed into my tracksuit and headed for his tent. On the way I passed a small group of soldiers who were playing three-card brag under candlelight in the camp cookhouse tent, but apart from them it seemed that no one else was up. Fine by me.

When I reached the local workers' tent, although their campfire was still smouldering, like nearly everybody else they had already turned in for the night. I gently pulled back the tent's canvas flap door and poked my head into its pitch-black interior. I couldn't see a thing, but I could hear the sound of several people sleeping.

When I whispered to see if anyone was awake, someone stirred and fumbled for something in the darkness, and then a torch was switched on. Holding the torch, sitting up in his sleeping bag on a camp bed, was my new best mate.

'How are you, my friend?' he enquired. 'I have been waiting for you.'

I assured him that I was fine and asked if he'd managed to score me any ganja.

'Oh yes, my friend. But I am sorry, because I could only manage to get you one half-pound.'

On hearing this, my brain called a time out. Excuse me, but did he just say 'one half-pound', as in nine ounces (or is it seven)?

'Er, did you say *half* a pound?'

'Yes, my good friend. I am sorry, but it was all I was able to purchase.'

All he was able to purchase.

He then reached under his camp bed and pulled out a zip-up sports bag, which he proceeded to place on his lap and zip down. Out of the bag he pulled a brown paper parcel – in fact, make that a very large brown paper parcel. Once I was over the shock of the size of it, my next concern was how much that much was going to cost me. And more to the point, would I even have enough on me to cover it? There was only one way to find out and that was to ask him.

'How much would you like for this?'

'Well, my good friend, I was wondering if you would be prepared to exchange the tracksuit you are now wearing for this?'

'Excuse me? I'm sorry. The what?'

'The tracksuit you are now wearing. I was wondering if you would be prepared to exchange it for this?'

He was wondering.

'Ooh, well, I don't know . . . Oh, go on then.'

Zip went my tracksuit top (available in two colours, £12.99, Top Shop, east corner of the shopping precinct, Aldershot) and then I told one of the nicest men it has ever been my pleasure to meet that I'd be back in two minutes with my bottoms. Sorry, his bottoms.

It wasn't until the following morning that I got to have a good look-see at what I had purchased. And shit, there was a lot of it. In fact, come to think about it now, back then it was the most dope I had ever seen in one place at one time, never mind own. And own it I certainly did – which presented the problem of what to do with the stuff. I still had over a month to do in Kenya, and as I was living out of a suitcase and a bergan, everywhere I went the grass was going to have to go with me.

I found what I believed to be the perfect hiding place in the lining of my sleeping bag. But even so, although I was bound to smoke a fair amount of the grass between then and my return to the UK, I was sure to still have loads of it left, so I was either going to have to dump that or somehow smuggle it back home with me.

Luckily, the problem solved itself, sort of.

By the time I got to leave Kenya there wasn't enough of my ganja left to get a gnat stoned. Even an English one.

Lazy men, crazy dogs

Throughout the world it has become standard practice, whenever the British army sets up base on foreign soil, for it to provide jobs for a few people from the surrounding area as part of the deal it strikes with the country concerned. Belize being no exception to this rule, each of the army camps there employed a whole bunch of folks who went under the collective heading of 'local workers'.

At Rideau, if you didn't count the women who ran the laundry down by the stream or the girls who worked in the NAAFI, there were four such workers employed on camp. By local (meaning Punta Gorda) standards, if ever there was a job that lifted its occupant up a notch or two on the social scale, not to mention dropping them into the regular income fast lane, then it was cleaning up after the British army at Rideau Camp. If you were i/c the toilet blocks up there, then positively rolling in it you were.

It's true to say that none of the local workers at Rideau exactly slaved for their money, either. (Yeah . . . and look who's talking) In a permanent camp such as Rideau, the chances were that any job as a local worker would also be a job for life, because the army very rarely sacks anyone (its motto on the employment front tends to be 'punish rather than remove').

I believe too – strangely enough, perhaps – that even if a local worker found himself being lorded over by the very worst type of triple-striped military racist, his job would be fairly safe. Because that racist would more than likely be working class himself, and, upbringing still being what it's always been, he probably wouldn't like to be seen as responsible for someone else losing their job, even if they did look a bit different from himself. (Well yes, OK, I suppose there could be one or two exceptions.)

The time arrived, as time so often does, for my post room to be painted, although I was given no prior warning of this great event. In fact the first I knew of it was when a man turned up at my stable door one morning, paintpot and brush in hand. The man in question was a local worker named Colin (nearly all black Belizians have names taken from the Old Testament) who was the camp's resident odd-job man and also the 'head' local worker.

Now, I don't want to give away too much of the plot here, but let's just say that in later years I was to get to know a thing or two about painting (of the walls and emulsion variety) and by then, if you were to ask me how long it would take to slap two good coats on my old post room's walls, I'd have priced it at six hours and still been ripping you off for two.

So, come the morning of his third day and the good news that Colin here was just about to make a start on the second coat, even I began to notice that this job was taking a tad longer than it ought to have done.

In Colin's defence, I should point out that he was only allowed to paint while I was there, which did mean that he was stopping and starting all day, because I was nearly always not there. He could, of course, just have been left on his own in the post room to get on with it – but the regulations would never have allowed that, even though he wouldn't have touched a thing, I know, never mind stolen a thing. However, to the men (and that's me included) the mail was sacred, so they would not have wanted anyone near it who wasn't authorised to be.

By chance, during the afternoon of the first day of 'Colin Paints the Post Room' we were blessed, halfway through it, by a visit from the battalion RSM, who had basically gone AWOL from the bullshit that was Air Port Camp and was hiding out in Rideau. (Incidentally, 98% of all that bullshit up at APC was *caused* by the RSM.) On Colin's third day in my post room once again we were paid a visit by the RSM, who couldn't help but notice the continuing presence of Colin and his pots of paint.

'How long's 'e bin 'ere, then?' the RSM asked me behind Colin's back.

'Three days, sir.'

'Three days! What's 'e doing – putting it on with a fork?'

(Everybody laugh.)

Because he was an RSM, and therefore quite genuinely believed within his battalion-bound mind that just about everything and everyone belonged to him, he couldn't just let Colin get on with it. Had to go and say something, didn't he. Which was:

'And how much fucking longer's it going to take you to finish in 'ere then, mate? Picasso didn't take this long to paint the fucking Sistine Chapel.'

(Nobody laugh – please.)

Now, what normally happens when an RSM has one of his humorous little digs is that the recipient is expected to come to attention and start chanting the mantra of 'Yes, sir' in reply to everything that's said. What Colin does, though, is that he very deliberately puts down his paintbrush, slowly turns to look at the RSM, smiles calmly, and then proclaims in the broadest possible white man's idea of a Jamaican accent: 'You don't rush the brush, man. You live fast, you gonna die fast.'

And then that was it, really. What could you say in reply to that? The RSM walked off defeated, I got on with the post somewhat happier, and Colin carried on painting like he was using a fork.

Anyway, there I was, seventeen and a bit years later, sitting in this bar in Wales enjoying a pint or two with a mate of mine called Denzil (nearly all white Welshmen have names taken from the Old Testament).

Now Denzil, see, he was in the Paras as well, right? Only he wasn't in 2 Para with me, he was in 3 Para, see? So, when I was in Belize in 1983, Denzil was in the UK. But a year later, in 1984, my mate Denzil, he goes out there with 3 Para.

So Denzil and me, we're chatting away about Belize and what it was like, when Denzil starts telling this story about some local worker who's painting one of the offices at Holdfast Camp, and it's taking him so long that eventually he's pulled by the RSM.

And as Denzil tells this story, it's all there – 'don't rush the brush', 'live fast, die fast' – word for word. Naturally, as soon as he's finished I put him on the straight and narrow by telling him that he is, in fact, full of shit and accusing of him of quoting from an event that happened to me in Belize in 1983. But he won't have it, and to this day he still claims that I'm making it all up and that it all really happened a year later and in another part of Belize.

So hey, maybe I'm psychic!

In one of the back streets of Punta Gorda there was a house that belonged to some rich people. Dave and me had never had the pleasure of meeting these people so we had no idea what it was they did for a living, but we could tell they were rich because their house had a high tennis-court fence round it and was guarded by two mean-looking free-range dogs.

And the dogs really were nasty, savage bastards right down to their metal-spiked leather collars. I couldn't tell you what breed they were, but they looked like the type of beast you might end up with if a Rottweiler raped a Dobermann.

Whenever the house was on our route, a good fifty yards before we reached it these dogs would start to go crazy. And as soon as we hit the gate they'd be there waiting for us, ready to bark us all the way along the fence. Being paras, and therefore brave – not scared of nothing, us – we would stand on the other side of the fence and stare back at the two dogs, which (with a bit of luck) would drive them all the more crazy.

But if you thought that was as crazy as crazy dogs got, you should have seen 'em go when we poked 'em in the face through the wire with sticks.

Our game of 'Winding up the Guard Dog' would normally be brought to an abrupt end when the maid rushed out of the house, cursing the dogs in Spanish.

One sunny Sunday afternoon Dave and me were once again strolling the backstreets of Punta Gorda (and no prizes for guessing what we were passing between us as we wandered along) when we turned a corner that brought us on to the street where our friends the two dogs lived. And no sooner had we hit the cross-breeze of the junction than, sure enough, the two nasally racist mutts started barking at us like mad.

Now where was something to poke 'em up a bit with?

We were just about to start burrowing in the undergrowth for whatever was sufficiently long and sharp when, horror of horrors, the scene ahead suddenly turned into something out of a cartoon film (one that wasn't very funny). Looking down the road I was just in time to catch the sight of both dogs slithering sideways in an attempt to change direction as they broke out on to the road at the speed of light. Straight away two key words flashed through my mind: 'gate' and 'open'.

Now whether your actual dogs have actual birthdays I'm not too sure, but if they do, then as far as these two canine guerrillas were concerned, not just their birthdays but Christmas, Easter and every other major celebration had all arrived at the same time . . . and guess who was on the festive menu.

Now me, to be honest, in the two seconds I had to view the dogs skidding to a halt before they started to charge my way, I shat myself I did. Because the dogs were bound to see this as payback time, and boy, had Dave and me run up a debt.

So we did what any combat-hardened paratroopers would have done in similar circumstances: I ran like fuck in one direction and Dave ran even more like fuck in the other.

A quick glance over my shoulder was enough to convince me that this was a race I wasn't going to win, so I leapt over a small garden fence and climbed up on to the second-floor balcony of the house it belonged to.

Now the thing was, these hounds must have been smarter than we thought, because they seemed to have got it all worked out. One of them (my one) had obviously said to the other: 'I'll take the tall good-looking one and you can go for the ugly little fucker, OK?'

Where Dave had got to and whether he'd escaped from his dog I neither knew nor cared. I had my own skin to save.

In the end the fight with my dog came down to a standoff, with me hanging from the balcony out of reach and the beast below leaping up and down on the spot in a frantic but vain attempt to sink his teeth into me.

The stalemate was only broken with the appearance of the Spanish maid (where the fuck had she been all this time anyway?), who simply called the dogs and they skulked off back towards her with their tails between their legs.

And where was Dave? Up a bloody-great tree, that's where. And neither one of us was coming down from our perch until we'd got signed statements from three impartial witnesses all swearing that the guard dogs were now safely back under lock and key.

As the dogs trotted back to her, the maid had let out a torrent of Spanish abuse in our direction. Since she wasn't asking for a rum and Coke or a bottle of beer, we didn't understand any of it, of course. Funnily enough, though, we could still tell what she was saying almost word for word.

It went something like: 'Next time you two soldier pricks wind up our dogs, I'll just let the fuckers have you. Now piss off and don't ever come back.'

'So what did you do then?' asked Denzil.

'Well the first dog reaches me, right? And he leaps up, all teeth bared and snarling, and immediately I grab him one-handed by the throat and start smashing the fucker's head into the nearest tree. You should have heard that little bastard yelp! Didn't fuck with me again, I can tell you.'

'Ken . . .'

'Yes Denzil?'

'You are *such* a lying English shit.'

'Actually, Denzil, I'm more Polish than anything.'

Holiday time!

Midway through my six months in Belize (and get this for a taste of working-class squaddie life) Carol flew over from England so that we could holiday together in Cancún, Mexico. Believe it or not, having your wife come out to join you for R&R was not an uncommon occurrence while on a tour of Belize, although the fact that wives could get a flight on a pay-for-meals-only deal with the RAF did have a lot to do with it. In fact, it had everything to do with it.

Having kissed Rideau goodbye in the morning and flown up to Belize City along with my mail (and that's dedication for you), I met beautifully white-skinned Carol off her flight from Brize Norton, and from the airport we caught a taxi into town.

Because I was on holiday an' all, I'd brought with me a couple of ounces of grass. I figured that as we'd be in Mexico for ten days, this should be *mucho* plenty to last me.

On arrival at our hotel in Belize City (which, I might tell you, cost us a fucking fortune) the first thing I did once we'd settled into our room . . . well, you can probably guess, eh? Virile airborne trooper, hasn't seen the wife for three months, gets her alone in a hotel bedroom, she's just come out of the shower wearing nothing but a hand towel . . . well, like I say, you can guess. Rolled myself a nice joint, didn't I?

That night we somehow found ourselves walking the poorly lit backstreets of Belize City (all right, so I got us lost) and on the corners of most of them stood little groups of young black guys, who, as we passed, just couldn't resist calling out

126

comments of the suggestive sexual kind to Carol. Halfway down one particular street I realised we *really* shouldn't have been where we were, and as we passed another gang of youths smoking dope on a corner, yet again Carol was greeted with an earful of sexual innuendo. (Although in fact, come to think about it, 'Come suck my big black cock, honey!' is a tad more than your actual innuendo, isn't it?) Naturally enough, me, inside, I'm fuming by now and all I want to do is go over and push the illegitimate person's teeth down the back of his throat. But even then I wasn't quite that badly in need of psychiatric help, so we just kept on walking.

Now this place was definitely not Belize as I knew it. In the three months that I'd been going to Punta Gorda I'd never once heard a Belizian say anything even moderately offensive, and yet here among the 'city folk' we were getting it every twenty yards. (Bit like being in Paris, really.) So after two nights and three days of the delights of Belize City, like its open sewerage system, its electricity supply based on the principles of roulette and its instant new friends on every corner, we decided it was high time to head on north to Mexico.

By the time we were due to leave I'd near-on smoked half my holiday stash of dope already. I didn't think anything of it, but Carol did, and I began to feel a certain tension in the air whenever I rolled myself a joint – especially the ones before I got out of bed in the morning.

From Belize there were only two ways you could get to the Mexican border: you could either take the bus (or, if you like, coach, as we Brits tend to call any bus that goes more than a couple of miles beyond the local shops) or alternatively you could spend a few days walking all the way.

The Belizian bus we caught looked just like it had been left over from the filming of a St Trinian's movie. I'll grant you it didn't have suspender-clad schoolgirls hanging out of every window, but by the time we reached the border it seemed to contain just about all the rest of God's creatures. The bus stopped maybe five or six times along the way, and each time the number of animals aboard caught up a bit more with the number of people. At one point, being English and predictable, one of us (all right, me) couldn't help but come out with the obvious remark, and the very next stop, wouldn't you know it, on gets a chap with two chickens in a wire cage . . . and a stainless steel kitchen sink.

For some reason, probably not a million miles from smoking too much dope, it hadn't dawned on me, until our bus slowed down as it approached the Mexican border, that we were going to have to pass through customs. I did have a little panic at this point, but then I thought: Why would they even bother to look? After all, what sort of dickhead smuggles marijuana *into* Mexico?

I needn't have worried anyway, as it turned out, because our luggage never got to leave the bus. At the border all we did was pull up in a car park, get off the bus, walk through one door, get our passports stamped, walk out another door, get back on the bus and then drive off into the sunset. I could have had a whole suitcase full of the stuff.

Once the bus had deposited us at the bus station we booked into the nearest large hotel, which turned out to be more than pretty fine for us. It had a fantastic big two-level swimming pool, great food (though none of the staff in the restaurants spoke any English – well, they just don't try, do they?), and in our room, which was large and air-conditioned, was a cute little fridge that I was subsequently to learn was called a mini-bar, although at that time it was a new one on me. When I opened it I found that my mini-bar contained a variety of goodies: beer, chocolate, miniature bottles of spirits, chocolate, both red and white wine, chocolate, soft drinks (mixers) and lots of things snacky. In fact, its contents made me realise just how many little luxuries I'd been missing out on while I'd been in Belize.

In case you haven't yet had the privilege of open access to a mini-bar, there are two things you should be made fully aware of (although unfortunately, in Mexico back in 1983 I hadn't been). Firstly, the goodies therein are overpriced to the tune of at least three times what you'd pay for them in your local supermarket, and secondly, you should never be in possession of the key to a mini-bar when stoned out of your mind on A-grade sinsemilla.

So as soon as we hit the hotel room and had gone through the 'Oh this is nice . . .' routine, to Carol's annoyance I knocked up one of my famous little one-skinners, lit it up and then turned the key that opened the door to Munchiesville. Two hours and a week's pay later, I was still cross-legged on the floor in front of the mini-bar and had done just about the whole of the Who's Who of booze the American way. Well, I *was* on holiday.

We stayed in Chetumal for two relaxing days, during which we left the hotel only once (that was adventurous of us), to return to the bus station and book our onward journey to the coastal resort of Cancún.

Surprisingly, the Mexican 'coach' we eventually took really was a coach, and I must say it was better than anything you could have climbed aboard in England at the time. Mind you, who really needs air conditioning and Spanish videos in England?

On the journey to Cancún we stopped at the Mexican equivalent of a service station, where we were able to leave the coach for ten minutes or so to stretch our legs. I wandered into a café-type place and, with the aid of sign language and the girl behind the counter's pop-song knowledge of English, ordered two Cokes to go. And do you know what the girl did? She flipped opened the two bottles and poured their contents into two plastic bags like the ones you used to take goldfish home in when you won them at the funfair. She then popped in two straws and tied the bags at the top with a couple of wire twists. At first I couldn't work out what this was all about (maybe foreigners weren't trusted with glass?), but later it was explained to me, by an American who knew about such things, that in Mexico the bottle was worth more than the soft drink it contained. Foreign travel, eh? What an eye-opener.

Described in all the holiday brochures, not to mention the R&R puff for British Forces Belize, as 'the new Acapulco', Cancún had miles of golden sand fringed with a row of high-rise hotels. When we finally reached its gates, Cancún looked like a horrible cross between Benidorm (but for Texans) and Miami (only with everyone able to speak English). And as it was all geared up for American tourists of the package-tour variety ('Oh *really?*'), by Mexican standards it was expensive to boot.

One morning, having heard just one too many conversations that jumped from dollars to herpes to guns to drugs and then back to dollars again, we caught a ferry over to a small island that lay thirty minutes off the coast of Cancún.

The Isla Mujeres, as it was called, turned out to be much more like it. Although the place was still fairly touristy (and why not? – this was the famous Yucatán Peninsula), unlike Cancún it did at least appear to have some local people who actually lived in it, and, bar one high-rise hotel that sat on its own clump of rock out in the bay, there wasn't a single building over two storeys high. As in the whole of Mexico, most of the tourists on the island were American. Here, though, as opposed to the suitcased variety they tended to be the back-packing type – folks like us, who were making their holiday up as they went along.

At the jetty, no sooner had we popped our bags on the ground than we were approached by a man asking if we wanted a hotel. Well, we could hardly deny it. I asked how much a night it would be and what the rooms were like, but maybe he didn't understand English, because all he did was pick up one of our bags and head off up the road with it. So what could we do but follow?

Luckily, when we got to his hotel we found it really was just perfect. It wasn't too expensive, the room and bathroom were clean and tidy, if basic, and the balcony looked right out over the sea, which was was no more than fifty yards away.

Once we'd unpacked (and I'd had a joint), Carol and I took our first stroll through the backstreets of the island, where we soon discovered that the thing to do here, if you were on holiday, was to hire a moped. Oh yes. Now, to be honest, I'd never been in charge of a two-wheeled motorised vehicle before. I'd been on the back of a motorbike a few times, but I'd never taken the helm. So this was all a bit of an adventure for me.

Easy it was, though. A twist of the wrist to go, a squeeze on the brake to stop, and Batman! So from then on, if you were looking for Ken and he wasn't sunning himself on the beach (or skinning up in the hotel room), then he was out and about exploring the Isla Mujeres on his moped.

I soon realised that I'd heard of the place some eight or so years earlier – when I was living in the Western Australian desert, believe it or not. At that time *Jaws* was on at the cinema and so the subject of sharks had never been bigger. One afternoon I came upon a copy of the *National Geographic* that contained a feature on the 'sleeping sharks' of Mexico, and guess what? It turned out that these sharks got their heads down on the Isla Mujeres (or, to be precise, just off it in the wet bit). For a not unreasonable fee you could, if you so wished, rent some scuba gear and go down and give one of them a big hug and, double bonus, have your photo taken while doing it.

I must confess that this photo opportunity, and especially the prospect of showing the pictures around the NAAFI when I got back to Rideau, appealed to me no end. However, the thought of being that close to anything with sharp teeth like what sharks have more than erased such a foolish fantasy. Well, maybe not the fantasy as such . . .

'Yeah, well, they're all man-eaters, of course, but you know me. Danger's my middle name, mate.'

'I thought it was Philip?'

The part of the island off which the sharks slept had a small wooden jetty and hire shops for snorkelling and aqualung equipment, which, when I arrived, were just being set up for the day's business. While the rows of flippers were being hung out, Mexicans dressed in white Mao suits and sandals were sweeping and cleaning any surface they could find. I bought a Coke and sat on a quiet rock near the jetty, looking out over the ocean and back towards the high-rise skyline of Cancún. In the distance I could see a small dot of a boat, which, as time passed, grew larger and larger until it eventually docked at the jetty next to me.

The vessel was a small ferry not dissimilar in size to the one that had transported us from the mainland, except that it was newer, faster and definitely had more Americans on board. Full of them it was. Now, if you'd shown me a group photograph of the people leaving the ferry and asked me who they were, I'd have guessed that they were either a warm-climate golfing crowd or escapees from the casualwear pages of a late 'seventies mail order catalogue. They were, in fact, day trippers from Cancún who had come to experience some real Mexico.

So I'm sitting on this rock in Mexico, minding my own business, clutching a Coke (deposit paid) and tokin' a joint, when over wanders this larger-than-two-lives middle-aged woman. And already I've taken a dislike to her, because I've had to throw the joint I'm enjoying into the sea.

The woman was wearing a loose T-shirt over a pair of shorts so tight that I couldn't help but wonder if she had a best friend, and on her head was a cardboard sun visor like the ones poker-players wear, with 'Coca-Cola' printed on it. When she reached me she stopped and, without so much as a 'good morning', asked: 'Anywhere around here I can get a Coke?'

Now, in view of the fact that I was actually holding a Coke at the time, if you'd asked me (and she did) I'd have said that the answer to this one was more than fucking obvious. By way of reining myself in so as not to blurt out some offensive piece of razor-sharp wit, I paused for a moment to choose my words. Before I could make a selection, though, she had come at me again.

'Do you speak English? Coke–a–Co–la,' she said, pronouncing it slow enough for even a dimwit like me to understand. I tell you, it was lucky she'd caught me on a good day (and stoned).

'Yes, I do speak English,' I informed her. 'I *am* English.'

'Oh *really*?'

And off she went with all the usual chat: she adored the

English accent, didn't I think Benny Hill was a genius, wasn't the Queen just wonderful, and what *about* those Monty Python guys – were those guys funny, or what? Eventually she got around to asking what had brought me to Mexico. Was I on 'vacation'?

I explained that I was 'kind of' on 'holiday', but only from Belize, where I was serving as a member of Her Majesty's Armed Forces.

'Oh *really*? Is that like the military?'

'That is the military.'

'Oh *really*? And what is it you do in the military?'

'I'm in the air force.'

'Oh *really*? And what do you do in the air force?'

'Well, I used to be a fighter pilot – F14 Messerschmitt Jump Jets, British Aerospace Migs – but now I'm on astronaut training.'

'My God! I didn't know you guys even *had* astronauts.'

'We don't. That's why I'm in training.'

Before I could get around to taking the joke a bit further before giving her a good laugh by admitting that it was all just my English sense of humour, the woman turned and bellowed out at the top of her voice, 'Hey, Muriel. This guy's an astronaut!'

'No, no. I'm not really,' I said hurriedly 'It was just a joke. You know, like those Monty Python guys?'

'It was? Oh, you had me there. That English sense of humour . . .'

And about fucking time.

If the island did have a drawback (apart from the tourists, that is), then it was that there was only one bank. One day, having run out of local currency, the way everyone used to before there were cashpoints, Carol and me headed towards it to swap some pounds and pence for pesos.

After queuing for the best part of a Mexican hour, when we finally got to the counter the swarthy moustachioed Latin pimp stereotype who was running it was pleased (and that was the thing – the little shit did seem exceptionally pleased) to inform us that they didn't change 'Engleesh' money. They changed American dollars, of course, and Canadian ones, and even French francs, but as for sterling . . . 'Eet's no good.'

That was rich, I thought. A man who gets paid in Mexican pesos trying to tell me that my pounds were worthless.

Luckily, Carol had a credit card. Unluckily, according to Pancho Villa here we couldn't have any pesos off that either. So our only other option was to take a day trip all the way back to starship Cancún to find ourselves a proper bank – one that had glass in its windows and was run by people who had the ability to use telephones. (I knew we should have gone to Benidorm.)

After catching an almost empty ferry back across the water, we waited by the roadside for a taxi to take us into Cancún centre. Waiting there beside us were a dark-haired couple, maybe just a little older than us, who had travelled across with us on the ferry. Taking them for Mexican because we'd heard them speaking to each other in Spanish, we'd smiled the odd acknowledgement whenever the boat lurched but hadn't attempted to talk to them.

When a cab eventually arrived, guessing that the other couple must be headed for the same place we were, I turned and asked in loud, slow English if they'd like to split the lift into Cancún, backing this up with a steering-wheel mime followed by a quick point-point in the appropriate direction.

'Sure. Thank you,' they replied (in quite fast English). But then they added that they felt there was something we should know about them before they accepted our invitation, in case it made us want to change our minds. Which was interesting. Maybe they had herpes?

It turned out that the thing they thought we might object to was that they were not Mexican (well, hey, neither were we!) but Argentinian, although they both now lived in New York and so had realised that we were English, not American. And I don't know why, really, but on hearing where they were from, straight away, inside, I was overjoyed. I'd never before met an

Argentine who wasn't dressed in uniform. Come to think of it, I'd never met an Argentine without a gun in my hand.

I said, Carol said, we both of us said: 'That's fine.' And I added that I was deeply sorry that our two nations had gone to war (and deeply was the word). I then went on to explain that there was something I felt they should know about us – or, to be precise, me – which might make *them* want to change their minds. But when I told them all about my part in their General Galtieri's downfall, it didn't seem to matter. In fact, I do believe they were just as happy about meeting us as we were them.

On the taxi ride into town the couple admitted that, although they had felt a sense of national pride when the Malvinas were regained by Argentina, they'd been against the junta and regretted all the violence and oppression that came with it. And I said I could understand that.

I, in turn, told them that although I'd never even heard of the Falkland Islands until the invasion, let alone known where they were, I now knew all about them – because some of my friends had died there. And they said they could understand that.

After we'd done our business at the bank (with a little help from our Argentinian friends), the four of us had a few drinks together in a bar and later took the same ferry back to the island. Over the next few days we were to see quite a lot of the couple and eat out with them several times. But although we all talked more or less non-stop, the Falklands War was never again mentioned.

A major benefit of going around with people who spoke the local language emerged when we went out shopping with our new Spanish-speaking friends. As a 'man of the world', and one who had done a bit of travelling in his time, I liked to think that I knew all about bartering and that no shopkeeper would ever pull the wool over *my* eyes. Well, dream on, Ken.

One afternoon, when I was out and about on my own, I bought myself a T-shirt. The guy selling it, from a blanket on the ground on a street corner, had originally wanted, let's say, ten pesos for it (I can't remember the exact amount). But I wasn't one of your American tourists, who just opened their pocketbooks and handed over whatever was asked. Oh no, he'd picked a tough cookie in me. After ten minutes of heated negotiations I'd knocked him right down to seven pesos. And proud of myself I was, too.

Next day, needless to say, my Argie mate goes and buys the exact same T-shirt from the exact same guy in the exact same spot – only he gets it not for seven, not for six, not five, not even four, ladies and gentlemen . . . He pays just two pesos: a *fifth* of the original amount I'd been asked for the thing.

From then on, any time we wanted to spend money, we got our new-found friends to go do it for us.

As the lazy days passed on the island, we danced at discos on the beach, met yet more wonderful people, ate fabulous food, and whenever we sat on the sand to watch the sun go down, even Carol had a hit on a joint. But alas, she had her office back in London waiting, and I had my post room back in Belize.

So, with a sad farewell to our new friends and a promise to write (though of course we never did), and another promise to ourselves to return one day (and we never did that either), we returned to Belize via the same bus route that had brought us from it. When we arrived in Belize City in the late afternoon, on the say-so of a taxi driver we booked into a more than nice little Colonial-style hotel situated on the seafront, just a little way up from the Fort George. After dinner I went out on my own to stretch my legs and, although I neglected to mention it to Carol, to see if I could score some more dope. (But you had some dope? Yes, but I wanted some *different* dope.)

I wasn't far from the street where Dave and me had scored before when we were up in town parachuting, so I went to the same place, and sure enough, in less than a minute I'd managed to score five ready-rolled joints. As there's never any time better than 'right now' to have some grass that's already rolled (unless you're under water, I suppose), I walked back to the seafront and struck one up. A few puffs later my throat was feeling a bit dry and the rest of me didn't like it, so I decided to pop into the Fort George for a quick drink. Standing at the bar, I was just about to order when who should come in but Larry, the tropical fish buyer from Miami who I'd met there before when I came to the Fort George with Dave. Oh well. He was harmless. Larry was again in Belize buying fish for the tanks back home, and 'Oh boy!', was it a surprise bumping into me again. I explained that I couldn't stay long because my wife was waiting for me back at our hotel, but I did hang around long enough for him to buy me a couple of drinks. Small world, though, eh?

The following morning I saw Carol off on her RAF plane back to England, snuck a quick, nervous joint in the airport car park, and then caught the afternoon flight down to Punta Gorda.

In my absence an engineer corporal had been standing in for me, and I can't deny that he'd done a fine job, handing everything back all shipshape and Bristol fashion. Tragically, also in my absence Dave had been drilled into by some exotic insect that had then set up house under his arm, which had resulted in him being sent home for treatment. This, I cannot begin to tell you, was a major blow, as Dave had been my one true 'mucker' in grass and every other thing I'd got up to in Punta Gorda.

Naturally enough, any soldiers whose R&R hadn't arrived yet but were hoping to go to Mexico wanted to know all about my travelling experiences. So I told them. And dead interested they were, I can tell you.

'How come these sharks don't rip your face off, then?'

'Well, they're asleep, aren't they?'

'But I thought you said sharks don't ever sleep and never stop.'

'Well, they're not so much asleep as stoned out their heads. Something to do with a freshwater outlet that fucks up the oxygen content of this particular bit of sea.'

'Went down then, did you?'

'Couldn't stop myself.'

'Got a photo, have you?'

'Naah. Wasn't allowed, was I?'

'Why not?'

'In case the flash woke the sharks up.'
'Lying shit!'

Shortly after my return from Mexico I was invited to a party up at Tom's. Tom was an American Peace Corps worker living all alonesome in a house in PG, a big gentle giant of a Texan who, like myself, was a bit of a dopehead. Hence the friendship. The party started at a barbecue over a fire in the back yard, but as darkness drew in it moved to the top front porch of the house. By the time I'd just about had enough and was ready to go check out the Mira Mar, who should arrive but two good-looking white girls I'd never seen before, who, it seemed, were both Peace Corps workers visiting PG for the weekend from their base in Belize City. So I decided to stay. (Wise move.)

The drinks flowed and it ended up with just me and one of the girls, a Linda, alone in the kitchen. And talk about forward . . . I went to reach for another beer out of the fridge and when I turned back round she grabbed me and gave me a big pashy on the mouth, tongues and all. Then she wanted to know if I smoked marijuana, because if I did she had a couple of ready-rolled joints in her jeans. We couldn't just light up in the kitchen, though, because she could lose her job for it as much as I could, so we went outside and stood by the remains of the fire. Halfway through the first joint she fell to her knees, unzipped my trousers . . . and you can guess the rest. And they say there isn't a god?

The next day I happened to be house-sitting in PG for some other Peace Corps friends when Linda turned up on the doorstep, having heard on the grapevine that I was staying the night. I let her in, we had a smoke and a Coke, and then it was all much the same as the night before, except that now we had a bed.

Strangely enough, or at least, today it seems that way, I never once thought about Carol either before, during or after my sex and drugs bouts with Linda. Mind you, to be fair, it wasn't as if I was hurting anyone. Was it?

Is that a wrap?

Like most of the major turning points in this tale (and this one's the oil tanker of all of my manoeuvres), I no longer have any clear recollection of the precise moment when I eventually decided that it would be a first-class act of brilliance to smuggle home some Mary-do-you-wanna-dance. Hey baby, wanna take a chance?

As you know, the idea had been constantly crossing my mind since day one, so I guess one day the lollipop lady didn't show up and the thought got to hang around on the pavement far too long.

There was a trigger, though – something that finally made me say to myself: 'Aah, fuck it!' And that I do remember. All of a sudden I stopped receiving my regular supply of mail from home, or, more accurately, letters from Carol. It got to the point where, because I hadn't heard from her for so long, I started booking phone calls home. But each time the phone rang in the flat at Aldershot, no one heard the tree falling.

So that's my first excuse out the way.

Once I'd finally decided to go ahead with it, I also decided to follow the example of my predecessor the engineer corporal (he of the King Edward's cigars) and wrap my contraband in a suitable amount of military clothing before posting it on home. We were now on the last leg of the tour and soldiers were beginning to post home all of the excess stuff they'd acquired over the past five months, so the parcel trade was already well and truly up. And what do more parcels make? They make more cover.

Having drawn up plan mail-home-a-whole-heapload, I trotted off to see Demas and place a cash-up-front order for four pounds of Belize's finest, which I figured would be enough of an amount to make the exercise worthwhile financially, while at the same time not making the parcel too big.

The night after I'd put in my order I caught the duty vehicle back into town and returned to the little shack that Demas called castle. It should have come as no surprise to me just how large a home-made brown paper sack containing four pounds of grass actually is, but it did. It was huge, and the more I kept thinking about it, and how it would look all wrapped up and stamped, the huger it got.

Fortunately (because I know dopehead me, and I so easily could have forgotten), I'd remembered to bring a sports holdall along with me, and with a little bit of physical persuasion I just about managed to cram into it the contents of my future parcel home. My overworked brain had already figured out that it wouldn't be a move of wisdom to catch the late-night duty vehicle back to camp, just in case someone got all 'what's in the holdall?' with me, so I decided to walk back – although that in itself wasn't going to be an exercise entirely free of risk.

At the time of night that it was, there shouldn't have been any vehicles either coming out of or driving back to Rideau camp, and so it might just be possible for me to walk the two miles back to camp without meeting one. But you never did know. What if a couple of bored sergeants had decided on a little unplanned trip into town? Well, if I saw any headlights then I'd just have to lob the holdall into the bush. The problem there, though, was that if it was a military vehicle there were ninety-nine chances out of a hundred that it would stop and offer me a lift, which would mean I'd have to come back the next day to pick up the grass – if, of course, I could find it.

What I'd have to do instead, I decided, was throw myself into the bush with it and hide until any approaching headlights had passed. Sure enough, halfway up the road to home I spotted a set of lights coming from the direction of Rideau. Luckily, while I was in Northern Ireland I'd patrolled miles of country lanes at night diving in and out of hedgerows every time a car passed, so I was well trained. Mind you, there's a bit of difference between ducking under a bush at night in Ireland and hiding behind its counterpart in Central America. In Ireland the main hazard was stepping on a sleeping cow, whereas in Belize any bush might be home to any number of creeping, crawling nasties. (I tell you, the places I ended up in for the sake of marijuana.)

A couple more vehicles passed, which again caused me and my grass to hit the bush, but none of them belonged to the army so in fact all that bobbing and weaving was for nothing. Still, better safe than sorry, eh?

Having almost escorted my newly-acquired dope all the way home, the next hurdle was passing the guard on gate duty. It was highly unlikely that he would stop me and ask to look in my bag, but nevertheless he did have the right to search anyone and/or thing that came into the camp, which meant that the possibility was always there. So let's worry.

When I reached the gate, it came to pass that the man on stag was a friend of mine and I came to pass under the barrier with no more than a nod and a 'You're back early'. I headed for the sanctuary of my post room, where I locked myself in and took the grass out of the holdall for a proper looksee.

Under electric light it looked even bigger than it had in Demas's shack, and once again I began to worry about just how big my parcel was going to be. The best thing for it (and this I realised straight away, which was more than bright of me) was to find some way of compacting the grass. Looking around, it was plain to see that the heaviest thing in the post room was me, so I popped my grass on to the floor and spent the next five minutes making like Zebedee in *The Magic Roundabout*. Only maybe I wasn't all that bright after all – boing! – because I wasn't heavy enough, and even after doing my impression of a happy kangaroo for ages I didn't succeed in reducing the grass down to much smaller than it had been in the first place.

Oh well, when faced with a problem that has no immediate

solution, sleep on it. So I did. And the next morning, after I'd done my duty with the outgoing mail and closed my door for lunch, I returned to the problem of having too much marijuana in my post room. And who'd ever have believed that could be a problem?

Now, as I like to point out to myself on regular occasions, I'm not completely stupid, so the obvious answer (i.e. dividing my ill-gotten bounty into two separate parcels) had crossed my mind more than once. My problem with this one, though, was that I really wanted to get it all over with in one hit, and if I did split the dope between two parcels, then it stood to reason that I automatically doubled the chances of it getting intercepted somewhere along the line. And I didn't want that to happen now, did I? It was while I was continuing to mull over my 'little problem' that its solution finally came to me via my hearing apparatus – for there was an awful lot of noise going on outside.

Opening my post room door I could see that the noise was coming from a four-ton truck that had somehow managed to wedge itself into the gap between the guardroom and Company Headquarters. Without a second thought, I put my grass into an empty postal sack and sauntered outside. I then got behind the truck, which was doing a series of small three-point turns in an attempt to get out of the corner it had boxed itself into, and popped my sack under one of its rear wheels. When the truck came back again it ran over my dope (great song title that) and hey presto! It was flatter. I repeated this operation three or four times, and each time the grass got smaller and smaller. But just as I'd decided that it had had enough of being run over by a four-ton truck, I got interrupted.

'What the fuck are you doing, Lukowiak?'

It was the camp sergeant major. And really, what is it with these people and their habit of sticking their noses into other people's business? I mean, had I ever once walked up to him and ask what the fuck he was doing? Sir.

'It's rubbish, sir. From the post room. I'm trying to flatten it a bit. Make a bit more space.'

'I thought you burnt your rubbish?'

'I do sir, but not every day. So it piles up. And you know me, sir. Tidy's my middle name.'

'Really? I though it was Cunt.'

And with that, off he strolled to give the driver of the four-tonner some grief.

The truck idea really did work and the volume of the grass was now considerably less. So, with that little problem solved at last, I locked the post room again and headed off to my hut in search of items suitable for parcelling it up in. I had an abundance of spare clothing and so the selection for my parcel wasn't difficult. After wrapping my load in a jumper and a pair of combat trousers, I sat down to write a piece of creative fiction: the customs declaration.

The following morning I purchased some stamps from myself, making quadruple sure that I used more than enough to cover the postage, and then escorted my parcel to the airstrip along with the rest of the mail. Normally, once I'd seen the mail safely aboard the plane I didn't hang around for take-off, but this time, feeling a sense of occasion, I stayed on. And as the plane lifted off and disappeared over the trees towards Belize City, I waved my parcel *au revoir* and then wished myself luck.

That very afternoon (and wouldn't you just fucking know it?) I was having a quick flip through all the incoming mail before sorting it into its various pigeonholes when, lo and behold, I finally spotted one from my wife. For the first time since I'd been at Rideau, everyone else's mail had to wait while I opened and read my own. And it was bad news, bad news. My baby dun gone and left me. It seemed that Carol had moved out of the flat in Aldershot and was now sharing a flat/house/igloo (she didn't say) with a girlfriend in Crouch End, which, according to the new address she'd given me, was somewhere in North London.

Carol's excuse, or reason if you like (and I did like), was that she worked in London and commuting from Hampshire all the time was wearing her down. She was training it to the City and back every day, and for what? I was away playing soldiers, so she was only returning to an empty flat in Aldershot – where, she might add, she had no friends or social life. If I just liked to think about it (and I didn't like), I knew that her reasons for moving to London were good, sound, logical ones, and yet at the same time I felt there was something not quite right about the way they were being put across to me. Pushing in my own twisted thoughts between the lines, I began to feel that I wasn't being told the whole story.

On top of all of this, the bad news meant that there was now nobody living in the flat to which I'd just posted off four pounds of marijuana. And just fucking super, that was.

By the time Carol's bombshell had hit home it was too late in the day to phone her at work, but the very next morning I booked a call through to her office and finally I got to speak to her. Although my main concern should have been the fact that she'd left home (and possibly me as well), it wasn't. What my mind was now doing overtime on was what was going to happen to my parcel if someone didn't go and pick it up. I'd always appreciated that Carol would more than likely be at work when it arrived and therefore the postman would pop one of those little cards through the door telling her to collect it from the local sorting office. But what if no one did? How long would they keep it there?

(I could just see it, and it would be more than typical, this would. The grass gets home clean as a whistle, but no one picks it up. Next scene in the movie: my parcel has done an Elvis and I'm holding it once again in the post room in Belize.)

Over the phone Carol told me she was returning to Aldershot 'most' weekends to pick up the mail and so she would collect my parcel for me then – but why all this concern over 'a parcel of clothes'? (If only she knew. Not that I was going to tell her.) She also assured me that on my return to England she would come back to the flat in Aldershot. So that was all right then. But why no mail lately? Well, she'd been busy. Which again was . . . all right then.

But I couldn't really work out what was going on. In fact, by the time I put the phone down I was feeling more than a little

144

uneasy, although I realised that all I could do was wait. Wait and see.

And then I fell ill. Mind you, I say 'fell', but 'plummeted head first off the highest building in town' is more like it. In five days I lost almost a stone in weight, and then along with that, overnight, literally, I developed a not-very-attractive-really all-over skin rash and at the same time became the front runner for the title 'Mr Depression Belize 1983'.

Eventually I took myself off to see the camp doctor, and when I sat down in front of him and began to explain my condition, for some reason I burst into tears – which was not really an airborne-type thing to do in front of an officer. The doctor, whose name was Hughes and who was one of the true heroes of Goose Green for the lives he and his men had saved that day, took one look at me and said, 'I think you need to go to the hospital in APC for a few days, Ken.'

This was *really* worrying, because not only had he used my Christian name but he'd used it in a sentence and in a way that was both kind and understanding. Oh shit, I thought, maybe I really was very ill?

I was put on to the next helicopter out of Rideau and on arrival at APC, doctor's note in hand, I reported to the camp's hospital. After the statutory one-hour wait I was led into the office of the head quack, a sensible-looking full colonel with white hair and glasses.

He read the note from Dr Hughes, asked me to strip and then closely examined my skin rash. Then came his first question:

'Do you know any local girls?'

Now fortunately, I had been in the army long enough to understand that when the good doctor here came out with this, what he was really asking was: 'Have you shagged any of the whores in Punta Gorda?'

'Me, sir? No, sir. Certainly not!' I replied, all offended. 'And besides, sir, I'm married.'

With this the colonel took off his glasses, looked me straight in the eyes and said (only without moving his lips or making any noise): 'Yeah, like *that* makes a difference to anything!'

He then sent me off to have my blood, urine, saliva and any other fluids they could squeeze out of me tested, and once that was all out of the way I was shown on to a ward and led to the bed that had been designated as mine. I got undressed, put on a very fetching little pyjama top and settled down for a nice rest in hospital. And it was different, because I'd only ever spent one night in hospital before, and that was only when I was nine and had cut my head open. (Well, *I* hadn't. It was more that someone else had cut it open for me. Anyway, I got concussion and so had to spend a night under observation.)

It took all of the worst part of ten minutes of sitting there in my new bed for me to realise that the swings in hospitals are great ('cos it means you don't have to do anything), whereas over on the roundabouts . . . God, is it boring.

There again, most playgrounds have more than just swings and roundabouts, so with a bit of luck, over at the slides there might just be some nurses – as in slim, white, sexy, funny, caring chicks. Wheel 'em on in.

So far all I had seen by way of nurses was a male lance corporal of the RAF Medical Corps, who I don't think fully appreciated the significance of that piece of paper they'd made him sign right after the Official Secrets Act. But never mind. According to the soldier dying in the bed next to mine, later on – on came the night nurses.

'You mean, like female ones?' I asked.

'Oh yes.'

Hey! Rock 'n' roll.

But I should have known, really. I mean, when did any man ever walk into a bar and meet just the type of woman he'd been fantasising about? Exactly. So why should hospital be any different?

The best way I can describe the nurse who did finally come on duty that night is to ask you to think of the Tom and Jerry cartoons. Now bear with me on this one, but you know that black maid who occasionally appears and screams 'Thomas!' at the top of her voice before booting the cat up the arse and out the back door? Well, if they ever make a Tom and Jerry film using live actors, then this nurse has got the part (unless, of course, Maya Angelou is also up for the role).

On the first occasion when I pressed the buzzer by my bed because I wanted to ask something of her, when she appeared she gave me a big, jolly smile and enquired, 'What is it, child?'

Child? Did she call me 'child'? Now hold on a minute please. I am not a child, I'm a lean, mean killing machine. A sick one, I'll grant you, who, as it happens, is just a bit too lean at the moment – but I ain't no child. Mind you, she *was* big and I really was sick. So what did I say? 'Could I have a glass of water please, miss?'

'Of course you can, child.'

She said it again! If she calls me that once more I'm going to say something. I am *not* a child. Boy, is she lucky I'm ill. And here's the joke: without realising it at the time, I was very ill indeed.

It became time for lights out. I lay on my back, and after a few minutes, through the darkness I could hear her. That nurse. She must have been in her office at the end of the ward, because her voice was faint and so I couldn't catch every word, but I was getting enough to know that it was me she was talking about. Then another voice joined hers, only this one was male and speaking Polish. The nurse said something back, also in Polish, and the two of them went on talking for hours. Meanwhile, I lay in bed for hours listening to them. My father was Polish, so I knew a little of the language and every now and then could pick out a few words. It was me they were talking about all right. The Polish Secret Service had discovered the parcel and were plotting to use this knowledge to blackmail me into becoming a spy.

Eventually I had heard enough to know that I had to run. The Belizian nurse was a Polish agent and I had to get away, so I slowly slipped out of bed and crept along the ward. I would have to pass the office they were sitting in, but if I could do that, then I'd be free.

When I reached the point of no return, I glanced through the wedged-open door and found the office empty. I knew (and I really did know) that I hadn't been dreaming. The nurse had definitely been in this room with a Polish agent – and yet they weren't here now. The office had no other door, so they must have escaped either up through the ceiling or down through the floor. I looked under the table and even tilted a filing cabinet, but I couldn't find any trap door. And then I heard footsteps. Men in boots, and a lot of them, were marching quickly down the corridor. I couldn't see who they were, but some sort of deep survival instinct took over and I knew straight away that they were AK47-carrying Russian soldiers. If they caught me in the office with the secrets I would be dead. So I ran back to my bed and pretended to be asleep.

Again I lay in the darkness for hours, waiting for the ward doors to be thrown open and beams of torchlight to cut through the darkness. In the end I became so tired of waiting and worrying that I didn't care any more. They could catch me, torture me, kill me . . . all I wanted to do was sleep.

But I couldn't sleep because of the sand. It must have been when I was in the office. That fucking bitch of a fat nurse had slipped into the ward and put sand in my bed. I jumped out of it and, cursing under my breath, began to brush the sand off my sheets. After a few minutes' effort I'd managed to get rid of all of it, so I jumped back into bed. It was no good, though. There was still sand in my bed. I tossed and turned, but no matter how hard I tried to get to sleep, the sand wouldn't let me.

I decided that I wanted to look at some of it, so I got out of bed again, ripped off my sheets and walked off to the washrooms with them. Once I'd got them under the light I soon discovered that it wasn't sand that had been driving me crazy, it was washing powder. This was supposed to be a hospital, and yet the fuckers – and they were all fuckers, the whole fucking lot of them – they couldn't even rinse the sheets properly. The fucking brigadier was going to hear about this. Now, where does that cunt live? The cunt lives here somewhere. Fucking bastards! Look at this sheet. Fucking washing powder!

I left the washroom in a rage, and the only thing that saved the brigadier from being dragged from his sleep was me noticing a row of large built-in cupboards. I opened the door of the first one and – lo and behold – it was home to about five hundred neatly folded sheets. I pulled one from the pile and tore it open. It was covered in washing powder. I pulled out another one, and then another, and another, and then a whole pile of them, and then another whole pile. And every single one of the bastard things was covered in washing powder. I was fuming. Here I was, ill, and these bastards, all the shitheads who ran this place, they wanted me to sleep on this shit!

Life was so unfair, so fucking unfair, that all I could do was fall on my knees and weep, like a child after all. It was no good, I'd just have to give in and bear my burden until morning. So I went back to my bed, and I was still lying there awake when the first tasks of the morning routine began to be carried out on the ward.

Before breakfast arrived I did finally manage to slip into sleep, only to be woken again, sweating, at eleven by a very, shall we say, 'pissed off' matron (who was a major, no less, in Queen Alexandra's Royal Army Nursing Corps). Before I could even get out a polite 'Good morning, ma'am,' she was shoving a clipboard under my nose and handing me a pen. She wanted me to read (and she assumed that I *could* read?) and then sign immediately her hospital equivalent of the Boy Scout pledge: I promise to be out of bed each day before eight, I promise to shave each day by eight, I promise not to walk around the hospital without my slippers on, I promise to . . .

Before I could get through the list, never mind sign the pledge, the matron explained, in the tone of voice you might hear on a 'bend over, you naughty boy' chatline, that she was not prepared to put up with my kind of behaviour on her ward. In future, when the doctor did his morning rounds I would be awake and I would be shaved.

Well, I'm afraid that was it.

I can't remember what I said to her word for word, but I know that by the time I'd got to the bit in the first sentence where I should have slipped in the word 'ma'am', I'd replaced it with 'you stupid dyke bitch' – which, as you can imagine, went down a hoot. As for her 'useless fucking lazy staff', the nurse of last night was now a 'fat bitch', the male nurse I'd seen earlier was a 'poofter wanker', and the people who washed the sheets, they were the hospital's 'overpaid chimpanzees'.

By now, of course, the rest of ward had switched on to fact that there was entertainment of the finest calibre going on over at bedspace seven and everyone was listening in. When I got to the end of my speech, I gave matron a defiant 'what have you got to say to that, then?' stare.

Now to be honest (not that I cared either way at the time), you would have expected her to blow her top, wouldn't you? But do you know what she did? Nothing. Or as good as. She simply said 'Oh really?' (though not at all like an American tourist) and then walked off the ward. Well, good riddance to bad rubbish, that's what I say.

She soon came back, though – only for 'Matron II (And This Time It's Personal)' she didn't come alone. Top of the guest list was the colonel, who was escorted by two male nurses and had taken his glasses off. Being the highest in rank, he got to say the opening lines.

'Now, what's been going on here?'

And at that, off I went again on full rant. Midway through, to prove my case I jumped out of bed and led them all off to the linen cupboard, from which I grabbed a pile of sheets from a shelf and threw them on to the floor.

'Look at this!!' I screamed. 'Fucking washing powder!!'

I think the moment when the light of understanding hit my by now totally enthralled audience was when I got around to warning them of the night nurse's involvement with the Polish Secret Service. Going into great detail, I told them all about her nighttime rendezvous with the Polish agent – and if they didn't believe me, then all they had to do was go and find the trap door.

But do you know what? They told me they already knew about her. Oh yes. They'd had their eye on that nurse for a while now, and they thanked me for all my good work in finally uncovering her. Of course, they'd need me to make a full statement to Military Intelligence . . . 'Of course,' I agreed happily . . . and of course yet again, we wouldn't be able to do that on the ward, would we, because you never knew who might be listening? So if I'd just like to go into this little private room that they'd got out back and wait for a while, they'd go and notify Military Intelligence and also get the camp guard to arrest all the women who wash the sheets.

It was such a relief to know that sanity had finally been restored to the world that I was quite content to let them lead me away to quietly await my interview with Military Intelligence.

By the way, I was now a very important man, they told me. And if Polish Intelligence got wind of the fact that I was about to be interviewed by British Intelligence, then they'd probably try and kill me before I could talk, so it would be best for me to be in as safe a place as possible. A room with bars on the window and a big metal door that no one could force open, say. That would be safe. What's more, because all of this was so important to national security I'd have to be given a truth serum before I was interviewed, just in case I was actually a double agent. And that seemed reasonable too, so I let them inject some into my arm.

And you'll never guess what? I really was very, very ill indeed.

When I finally woke up it was morning again and the RAF male nurse who I hadn't been too kind about the day before was standing by my bed. Although he wouldn't let me have a drink until after the doctor had seen me, he was all right with me and even asked if I could remember anything of the events of yesterday.

'No, not a lot really,' I admitted. So he gave me a quick reminder.

'I fucking never called her that!'

'You fucking did.'

My next visitor was a doctor I hadn't seen before, who had

come to give me the results of my tests. Before he got around to that, though, 'just out of interest' he wanted to know if I was aware that the matron's husband was a colonel in the SAS.

('I fucking never called her that!')

('You fucking did.')

Having enjoyed passing on that little gem, the doctor went on to tell me about my tests.

'Well, it's good news, son. We've come to a conclusion about what's the matter with you.'

'You have, sir? And what is it, sir?'

'You have a Non-specific Tropical Disease,' he informed me confidently.

'And what does that mean, sir?'

'Well, in layman's terms it means . . . er, well . . . it means you've got a disease . . . a tropical one . . . and we don't know what it is.'

Fortunately, he did at least know what to do about it (allegedly), because he put me on a course of antibiotics.

Three or four days of completely sterile inactivity passed, over the course of which all was forgiven and I was returned to the wards. And day by day, in every way, I did get better and better. My rash almost disappeared, I put on a little weight, and even more importantly, all in all I began to see the world as a better place. Smile please.

During this time there was, naturally enough, a lot of debate as to how I'd caught whatever it was I had. At first I put it down to candle-at-both-ends syndrome (though I could never have passed this theory on to the doctors) because, looking back on my time in Punta Gorda, I couldn't remember a day when I hadn't been either stoned or drunk, or, come to think about it, usually both. But could that be true? Every day for nigh on five months? Well yes, it was true. Although I'd never stopped long enough to realise it before, I had smoked dope every day without fail, including while on holiday with Carol in Mexico, ever since that very first night when Rosie led Dave and me to Demas's door.

The real cause of my illness was discovered when I had to

provide answers to a questionnaire that was read out to me one day, and the question that clinched it was the one about whether I'd 'had any contact with mildew'. Well, now you come to mention it . . . One afternoon I had come in from sunbathing all hot and knackered, and, not fancying lying down naked on my coarse blankets, I'd got down a bedspread from on top of my wardrobe, where it had been lying folded and unused for months. It was only when I got back up and went to fold the bedspread up again that I noticed that it was covered in mildew.

'Aha!' exclaimed the doctor. 'That will be it.'

I was almost all well again and about to be discharged when, out of nowhere, I suddenly got one of the biggest frights of my life. Into the ward one afternoon breezed the battalion adjutant and the chief clerk. Now this in itself wouldn't have been too bad, because I knew that under Queen's Regulations (or something like that) any soldier in hospital is supposed to be visited every day (or it might be each week) by someone of higher (or it could be equal) rank, from his own unit (and that bit, I know, is gospel), or else everyone faces a firing squad. But that wasn't the reason for their visit.

The two men got to my bed and both smiled and asked me how I was, which was nice of them. And then before either of them had said another word, the adjutant stopped a passing nurse and asked if there was somewhere the three of us could go to have a little chat of the private variety. With this I nearly died on the spot, and no matter how hard I tried to convince myself otherwise, I just knew that the game was up. The parcel had been discovered.

The nurse pointed towards a door that led through to a small private room reserved for soldiers who had BUPA. (Really.)

It took us no more than thirty seconds to walk from my bed to that room, and yet within that time I managed to run through every nightmare that surely awaited me, including listing all the things I would be losing: job, house, freedom . . .

But what was the point? The bottom line was that everything was now over.

The door was closed behind us, and me, I'm still dying (so it's handy I'm in a hospital). Then, before you could say 'Bake me a cake with a file in it, babe', the adjutant asked me a question. And what a question, because it had nothing to do with dope or parcels or Her Majesty's Customs or anything even remotely illegal. No, all they wanted to know was whether I would be interested in taking up a one-year posting to Sandhurst.

Oh, the relief! Oh, the pure joy! And thanks for asking, but really, what the fuck would I want to go and hang out with a load of officer new-boys for? I mean, Sandhurst! My arm would drop off with all that saluting. So thanks again, but I'm happy where I am. Sir.

And with my rejection of their offer, off the battalion adjutant and the chief clerk trotted.

Once they'd left the ward I did start to wonder if maybe they'd been winding me up. I mean, what was so special about asking me if I wanted a new posting that they had to lead me away to a private room to do it? Maybe they suspected something and were just testing my reaction to being led away like that?

I worried about this for days and my mind wasn't put at rest until I was finally discharged from hospital (yes, all better again now, thank you for asking). Having run into a very happy battalion orderly room clerk in the NAAFI at APC, I discovered that the reason for his joy was that he was being posted to Sandhurst for a year. Like they say, one man's meat . . .

At Rideau Camp I returned to a post room that was in a right mess. However, as far as I was concerned this was perfect, because one of my concerns during my enforced absence had been that the soldier sent from APC to fill in for me would find out just how little I actually did in a day and pass this information on.

Luckily, the uniformed wonder in question was a full CPL, and (dare I say it?) from 'up north', who tended on average to spend eighty per cent of his day moaning about his lot in life, so he was always likely to complain about his stint at Rideau, no matter how little he did there.

Because my absence had been so sudden, what with me nearly dying and all, there had been no proper handover between us (as in me saying things like 'Would you like to count the stamps one more time, corporal?' and 'You just get them to sign here, here, here and here') and as a result, for starters the stamp money was down. In truth, of course, it had probably never ever been up and almost certainly would already have been short when I was flown off to the hospital at APC. But my replacement hadn't noticed when he arrived and so he took the shortfall to be his own fault. Oh well.

Not only that, but it seemed he had had great difficulty in handling the main, if not the only, pressure that went with working as post clerk, which was, on average, during waking hours, having someone ask you every thirty seconds when the mail was due in. The reply to this question was simple enough, though. You simply told them (depending on the time of day) either 'three o'clock' or 'tomorrow afternoon', adding (depending on their rank) either 'sir', 'sergeant', 'corporal' or 'mate'. Or, if the person asking didn't fit into any of those categories, then the answer was: 'The same time as yesterday, and the day before that, and the day before that, you mindless fucking moron.' But for some reason this constant questioning had really got to my replacement and I could tell that he was only too happy to be giving up the position of Post Clerk, Rideau Camp. Which reminds me . . .

'When are you going back to APC then, mate?'

'Dunno. Gotta phone the chief clerk and find out.'

'There's a phone next door.'

'No hurry.'

Yeah, right. So I phoned for him.

And guess what? Although the chief clerk didn't actually say as much, I could tell that they didn't really want him back at all.

This was strange, though, because more hands make less work, and there's nothing those boys up at Battalion HQ liked more than less work. So of course, off went my troubled mind again. What was going on? Was he here to replace me permanently? Was I about to be lifted? Where was my fucking parcel?

My mind was to be put at ease after me and my new comrade in stamps had sat down to our first Coke together in the NAAFI. In fact, and I wouldn't want you to think I was overstating this, not only was my mind to be put at ease, but without even realising it at the time, I was also about to learn an important 'life lesson' of the type that's worth its weight in cocaine.

About two seconds after I'd paid for the Cokes (well, it was only fair, after all the stamps he'd bought), the corporal started telling me all about his wife back in England, or, more accurately, what his wife was up to back in England. Apparently she'd been shagging everything in uniform that moved (and there's an awful lot of moving uniforms in Aldershot) and had now left him for some 'crap-hat' from the REME.

To be honest, like most men I really didn't want to hear any of this and would have appreciated a rapid change of subject, but he was obviously very disturbed by it all and just couldn't let it go. One minute he was telling me how his wife was the biggest spunk-swallower in Aldershot, and the next he was weeping on about how deeply he loved her and how much he wanted her back.

The poor man was in such a bad state that he didn't care who he talked to about his wife's nocturnal habits, as I was to find out when I phoned the chief clerk again, using the cover of not understanding something (which was a good one, because in the army there are quite literally tens of thousands of people wandering around every day not understanding one thing or another). During our conversation I cleverly brought up the subject of Corporal Married-to-a-Right-Dog and enquired if the chief clerk was aware that he was having some marital difficulties (not that it was difficult to guess the answer to this one).

It turned out that the reason they had sent him to Rideau in the first place, and then made him stay there, was that he'd lost the plot so badly that he'd been going around embarrassing not only himself but also quite a few people with pips up at APC. On discovering this, on the one hand I was thinking, 'So you dump the poor fucker on me, you bastards,' and on the other I couldn't help but feel a huge sense of relief, because it meant that my parcel paranoia had been no more than that – paranoia.

That and guilt. They make the world go round, you know.

And it got even better, because the chief clerk then gave me a piece of good news. Some soldier's mother had died back in England (which wasn't the good news) and he was going home for the funeral, so my replacement could now be sent up to Holdfast Camp to replace him.

'Oh, that's sad, chief. There's a chopper tomorrow morning. Shall I tell him to be on it?'

So the corporal went on his way and Rideau and my post room returned to how it had all been back in the good old days, before I had been taken ill and fate had lumbered me with a walking, talking agony column.

The morning the corporal left I once again phoned Carol at work and just like that – snap! – my burden, Lord, was lifted. (I know, I should write gospel songs.) The parcel had arrived safely in Aldershot and Carol hadn't even had to go far to collect it. The postman, on finding no one in, had simply left it with the people next door. It had made it!

Now you would have thought (and I certainly did for a while) that the unnerving experience of sending home one parcel containing illicit dope would have been more than enough for me, but this proved not to be the case. Even though I knew not only the risk I was taking but also just how much anxiety had been involved in mailing the first parcel, before long I found myself deciding to send another one.

I've sometimes wondered, looking back, how I found the courage to go through it all again, and do you know, the only thing I can put it down to is that my Falklands experiences had made me brave. I mean, why worry about a little thing like that? It's not like there's someone shooting at me.

And that's my second excuse out of the way.

Like I said, I hadn't planned to send another parcel. Like so many other things in life, it just happened.

Because of my stay in hospital I hadn't seen Demas for over a week (which, apart from my holiday in Mexico, was a record period of time since I'd been in Belize) and I'd never had the opportunity to tell him where I was going beforehand, so I figured, rightly, that he must have been worrying about what had happened to me. (After all, he was the one who had sold me the dope.)

On my very first night back at Rideau I signed myself out in the guardroom and caught the duty vehicle to PG. After a few quick 'welcome back, guy' drinks in the Mira Mar, I set off alone and walked the few streets to Demas's door. Once I'd knocked and identified myself, the door quickly opened to reveal a man who was more than happy to see me. Demas had indeed been worrying. I was invited in, and less than thirty seconds later my other record-breaking run (of over one week's abstinence from dope) was at last over.

I had always assumed, since every time I'd seen him he'd had a pipe of grass in his hand, that Demas would also be fond of the odd tipple, as in booze. By way of saying sorry for having to go away without telling him, I had therefore brought him a bottle of rum from the NAAFI. It was none of that local Caribbean rubbish, either. Proper white rum it was, all the way from England. But Demas didn't want it. He was grateful for the thought, but, as he put it, he didn't 'do' alcohol. Drawing from his pipe and then handing it across to me, he passed on a few words of wisdom on the subject: 'Alcohol is an ignorant drug. If you take a lot of it, you become ignorant.'

That night I stayed there with Demas, sitting sharing his pipe and his stories, longer than I'd ever done before. And as he told me again all about the time he'd spent in Scotland, where he'd been employed as a forestry worker during the war (no, not *the* war – the Second World one), I couldn't help but think how strange that must have been. But enough thought.

Before I finally had to leave, or I was going to miss the duty vehicle back, Demas trotted off to his bedroom, had a little rummage around, and then returned a few seconds later carrying a large brown paper bag. So, no mystery about what's in that, then. But apparently, this was the gear, this was. When the bag was opened I guessed, drawing on my vast experience in these matters, that it held about a pound of nothing but heads.

'This is all right, isn't it?' I asked.

'Yeah, man.'

'Not seaweed, is it?'

'Oh, how I wish it was. I love boiled seaweed and conch.'

And just like that, before my mind could even begin to replay any of the nightmares of sending the first parcel home, I was up and organising the second. Or, if I wasn't yet organising it, I was already mentally counting up the cash.

So, it was nighttime in PG once more and there I was, out strolling in the moonlight, bombed out of my brain, with a pound of dope under my arm in a brown paper bag. And do you know what? I'll be fucked if I'm going to walk back to camp tonight, I thought, I'll go back in the duty Land Rover.

As stupid as you like, I trotted off back to the Mira Mar and put in an order with Chico for one plastic carrier bag, which, I can tell you, was some mean luxury item in Punta Gorda. Because I was his great, great friend (How was I now, by the way? Oh yes, and could he have some cigarettes tomorrow?) the bag came free, and once I'd put the grass into it I could have been carrying anything. No one would know what was in it – or so I chose to believe.

When the duty vehicle arrived I was the only soldier waiting for it, and when I climbed in the back, the driver didn't even notice my carrier bag.

And then it was post room, some more clothes from my summer combat collection, wrapping paper, tape, stamps, customs declaration, kiss bye-bye and off to the airstrip.

Easy as that?

Easy as that.

The wait for my second parcel's arrival in England turned out to be nowhere near the torment the wait for the first had been, either. More by chance than anything, on the Saturday after I had sent the second parcel I phoned the flat in Aldershot, at what would have been late morning UK time, and Carol was at home, picking up her mail and a few more clothes.

Since I was due back in a couple of weeks, I naturally wanted to know when it was, exactly, that Carol would be moving back to Aldershot. She didn't know, it seemed, because although she didn't tell me she wouldn't be coming back, she didn't confirm that she would either. What she did say, though, was that another parcel had arrived for me that morning. Brilliant!

'Yeah, it's just a few more clothes . . .'

'I opened it, Ken.'

'Oh.'

Then she said it: 'When you get back I won't be here. I want nothing to do with this.'

And with that, she hung up on me.

Like I fucking cared. Who, me? You wouldn't get me going on like that poor dumb-fuck corporal who'd stood in for me in the post room.

And just to prove it, during my very last week at Rideau Camp in Belize I did another two more parcels home: one to the flat in Aldershot and one to the barracks.

Handy it was, having two addresses.

Home's where the heart is

Just like it always had for Andy Pandy, it became time to go home. As you may have gathered by now, apart from the bit when I was in hospital I'd quite enjoyed my time in Belize, and if they had wanted to extend my stay, I wouldn't have minded. But why would I? I'd hardly worked myself into the ground, I'd seen a little more of the world, including Mexico, I'd met more than a few interesting people, and some Americans, plus – double bonus – nobody had wanted me to kill any of them. I'd also got to smoke a small truck-load of grass, which (if you could find it in the first place, of course) would have cost about the same as buying a large bungalow back home. On the down side, yes, it's true that we'd all been away from our loved ones and family for six months, but the way things seemed to be going between me and Carol – what did I care?

My last day at Rideau landed on a Sunday, which gave me a good opportunity to say goodbye to the friends I'd made in PG and to enjoy one last walk of its streets. Oh, the dope I'd smoked walking around this place. I took a camera with me and took pictures of buildings and street corners that I felt had been significant in some way, and today I still have those photos (they annoy me, though, because something gritty must have invaded my camera and every one of them has a wide scratch running horizontally across it.)

Whereas I had arrived at Rideau by helicopter, I got to leave it by landing craft, a means of transport that was only ever used for heavy stores or large troop movements. The craft, which was to take us up to Belize City for our flight home, left from the wooden jetty in Punta Gorda, so my last view of PG was looking back at it from out at sea. If we'd left by helicopter, I wouldn't even have got a last sighting of PG, and it seemed fitting to be able to wave the place goodbye, because if I would miss anywhere in Belize it was Punta Gorda, not Rideau Camp.

I had genuinely liked PG. The only people I ever exchanged cross words with there were other soldiers and I never met a single local I didn't like. It was an easy-going place, where life was so much slower than it was back home – harder, of course, but more relaxed. Gazing back at PG for the final time, I realised how sad I was to be leaving it behind and hoped that one day I might return to its shores. (Though not on a landing craft, please.)

The journey from Punta Gorda to Belize City followed the coast north and lasted I don't know how many hours. But I don't even want to remember those hours on the landing craft, never mind write about them. It was dark most of the way, the sea was rough and the journey long, it rained for ages without let-up, and, just to top it all off really nicely, the Royal Marines who were doing the driving thought it was a great laugh, especially the bit where we paras all started throwing up overboard.

When we did finally arrive at the port in Belize City the sun was just coming up, and boy, were we a happy bunch of troopers to be walking on dry land again. The movement timetable didn't have us flying out until the following afternoon and so transit accommodation had been arranged for us at Air Port Camp. As soon as I knew that we weren't being 'stood down' until noon the next day, I changed my clothes, cashed a cheque I wasn't too sure about in the pay office and then caught a taxi into Belize City. I got the driver to drop me by the swing bridge in the centre of town as this was close to a particular street I wanted to visit (mind your own business – all right), and I hadn't been walking along the pavement for more than a minute when who should I bump into but Linda. She was carrying some folders and was on her way from one Peace

Corps office to another, so she couldn't stop, but boy, was it nice to see me, and what was I doing tonight? Well, I *had* intended to stay in and re-read the RAF booklet on safety procedures for long-haul flights, but . . . if she had nothing on, why didn't we meet up at the Fort George (say around seven?) and then we could have nothing on together.

Well, what a stroke of luck that was, eh? And what more fitting way to spend my last night in Central America than in the centre of an American? I hadn't planned to stay in town for the night, but with 100 per cent guaranteed hardcore on the menu, suddenly there didn't seem to be any good reason why I shouldn't. Or was there? As the old Polish proverb that my father once told me goes: 'When your prick is up, your mind is down.'

Actually, when I came to think about it, I'd signed myself out in the guardroom when I'd left APC, hadn't I? So, come whatever time their cut-off for return to camp was, if I still wasn't signed back in they'd report it to my battalion's duty officer. And that meant . . . well, probably not a lot more than a bollocking. But then you never did know, did you? If the officer on duty was a wanker (and you can phone Ladbrokes yourself for the odds on that one), I could end up on a charge, or, even worse, on rear guard over leave. Knowing the way 'punishment swaps' worked in the army, it was more than likely that they'd want me to enter into a deal (of the sort you can't really turn down) whereby they'd agree not to charge me if I volunteered to do rear guard over leave. And I couldn't have that, could I? When I got back to England I had parcels to unwrap and places to go, so the last thing I wanted was to be hanging around in Aldershot.

Another problem was that if I was going to stay out all night then I'd have to pay for a room at the Fort George (well, I couldn't expect the poor girl to pay – she was a charity worker), so I'd have to go back to camp first anyway to cash another cheque. But what else could I do?

(Well, you could always call it off, Ken – after all, it's only sex. And it's going to cost you a lot of money, what with a taxi to camp and back again, the cost of the hotel, plus drinks of course, not to mention another taxi back to camp tomorrow . . . Oh yes, and you *are* still married, remember.)

Once I'd cashed another cheque at the pay office, I left APC again, this time conveniently forgetting all about the signing out in the guardroom bit, and caught a taxi to the Fort George Hotel. There I checked into a single room – which I knew would be cheaper, although I'd still get the exact same room as if I'd paid for a double – and waited for sex on a plate, partially financed by the American taxpayer, to arrive.

I like a girl who's punctual, and bang on time Linda arrived at the hotel lobby for our seven o'clock rendezvous. We had a drink in the bar and then I offered her a second, which she declined, although she did wonder if I happened to have any grass on me. *Did* I have any grass on me? So we retired to the comfort of my room and, basically, the party was on.

At one point, not long after we'd put out the first joint, Linda pushed me backwards on to the bed, unzipped my flies and was just about to get all oral when she stopped, looked up, stared me straight in the eye and said: 'I've been looking forward to this all afternoon.' *And* down (two, three), up (two, three) . . .

I only mention this because since that night I've remembered those particular ten seconds of my life, especially the words, many times. (Like when, Ken?)

From there on in, my last night in Belize was just like a Swedish Erotica film circa 1975, with me playing big-boy John Holmes (she even had on one of those silk neckscarves). In fact, anyone would have to admit that, as last nights go, it was a pretty fine one. But then, why wouldn't it have been? It wasn't like I had a concession to go and spoil things. Not for one minute did it cross my mind that I might be doing anything I shouldn't. Like they say, what the old wife back home don't know about don't hurt her, does it?

Arriving back in England (and where's the welcome like we got when we flew in from the Falklands, then?) was to prove to be one of life's more expensive experiences. It was also to prove what a full-on wanker I could be (all right, can be) at times.

After passing through immigration at Brize Norton, we had an even chance of having to go through customs just like anybody else arriving in the UK – which was why I hadn't got twenty kilos of grass in my rucksack. This was just as well, as it turned out, because HM Customs did turn up for our flight, even if it was only in the form of two pushed-together tables with a bored man in uniform standing behind them. And as we all shuffled past the tables in single file, the bored man in uniform was stopping no one. Until I got level with him. All very friendly, he wanted to know if I was all right, was I, and if I'd enjoyed my time away. Well yes, I had, thank you very much for asking. Mind you, it was good to be back and, by the way, could I go now?

Well, just out of interest, since he *had* stopped me and it was his job to ask, how many duty-free items had I got with me: fags, booze, perfume, that sort of thing? I told him that I was only carrying the two hundred cigarettes we were allowed and a bottle of spirits, and then, starting to undo the straps on my bergan, I asked if he'd like to have a look at them. 'Oh no, that's all right,' he said, and sent me on my way.

Now, while in Belize, with the aid of the never-never from the NAAFI Dave and I had both bought ourselves a Rolex watch, and just as I was lifting my bergan on to my back again, the customs man noticed mine.

'Nice watch,' he remarked.

'Yeah, do you like it? It's a Rolex.'

'I thought it was. Expensive, they are, aren't they? Tell me – if you don't mind me asking, that is – how much did you pay for that, then?'

'Seven hundred quid,' I said proudly.

'Seven hundred, eh? That sounds cheap for a Rolex.'

'Yeah, it is. It'd cost you over a thousand here.'

'Really? So you didn't buy it here, then?'

'No, I bought it in the NAAFI in Belize.'

And as soon as I had said it I realised what I'd done.

'Well, I'll tell you what,' said the customs officer with a smile, 'you give me fifty quid and I'll let you bring it into the country.'

Fifty quid? He must be fucking joking!

He wasn't, needless to say, and no matter how much I argued, he wasn't having any of it. So what could I do but hand over the money? Except that I only had about twenty pounds in cash. And no, I couldn't send it on to him later (even if I did double promise). However, the army had come prepared for such eventualities. The customs officer informed me that our pay office had set a up temporary location, not dissimilar to his own, in the arrivals lounge, so I could go and cash a cheque there and then come back and give him the money. And do you know what? When I went meekly off to get the Nazi bully-boy his blood money, he even had the cheek to make me leave the watch with him, like I was going to do a runner or something.

But never mind him, what about me? All I need have done was tell him I'd bought the watch in England, or better still not wear the thing in the first place. What an idiot!

After I had reluctantly paid up and got my watch back, the next happy welcome-home event was the handing-in of my camouflage jungle suits. Or not, as the case may be.

Now, no one had told anyone that immediately on our arrival home they'd want their kit back, so Arrivals, when I finally got there, was full of cursing soldiers unpacking their bergans. Not only had it never crossed my mind that they'd be quite so keen to get the jungle kit back (were they going broke or something?), but I'd used mine to parcel up the dope, so I didn't even have anything to hand in. Never mind, though, because surely they'd let me hand mine in later, when we got back to Aldershot? Would they fuck! And I was now the proud owner of two brand-new suits of clothing, jungle, camouflage – or at least, I would be as soon as they found army form 1033, which would prove that I'd once signed for them. (By the way, if ever someone's telling you they were once in the army and you're not too sure that they're telling the truth, ask them what a 1033 is. If they don't know, then they must have been in around the time of the garden of Eden.)

So, England. Fucking great to be back, eh? It had only been ten minutes ago that I was on my knees kissing the runway (it's a Polish thing – or it might be Catholic, though I'm not) and yet already it had cost me a hundred quid, and outside it was drizzling slow grey rain. Land of Hope and Glory.

I was just about to board the coach to Aldershot when it didn't get any better. I got stopped by a sergeant major from one of the rifle companies, who told me to stay were I was while he found my name on his nominal roll. I was just about to say aloud: 'Hello, is anybody in? All those people you line up every morning, you've not seen me in among them, have you? I'm not in your company!' (or something like that), when he found my name on his list.

'Lance Corporal Lukowiak, isn't it?'

Could I deny it? Probably not.

'Yes, sir.'

'Ten pounds please.'

'You fucking *what*?'

'You fucking what, *sir*, I think is what you mean. And, if you must know, it's your voluntary contribution to the corporals' mess whip-round for Corporal X'.

'Corporal *who*?'

'I'm sorry?'

'Corporal who? *Sir*.'

'Better. Corporal X. He had a very bad vehicle crash in Belize and is now in hospital and may be crippled for life. I take cheques, by the way.'

And really, not that I begrudged it, but please, get me away from these people before they take any more fucking money off me.

Once we arrived at the barracks in Aldershot, after a few hours of last day at school-type stuff (though without the blancmange, musical chairs and postman's knock), the battalion was stood down for two weeks' leave.

It was early evening and already dark by the time I walked the short, windy distance from the barracks to where I lived, and the flat, when I got there, was empty and cold. So my homecoming wasn't at all like it is in the films, where the returning soldier gets greeted on the doorstep by his joyful wife, and I guess, just for a while, I felt a little sad for myself. Poor me, eh?

Oh well, I still had my parcels.

Once I'd found them, in the cupboard under the stairs, it wasn't too long before life didn't look so bad after all. I turned the telly on, switched the fire on, put the kettle on, got my slippers on . . . got it all on. All I had to do now was sell some of me grass. Oh yes, and see the wife.

The next afternoon I caught a train up to London to go visit the house where Carol was now living. At Waterloo I had to change from train to tube, which meant walking through the station to get to the underground bit. Now call it culture shock if you like (or maybe too much ganja in the toilet on the train up), but on the way to the tube I just had stop and have a sit down. Even if you added up all the people I'd seen altogether during the six months I'd been in Belize, I don't think it would have come to the number of people milling around in a single minute at Waterloo. A very strange feeling it was, as well. There was definitely a bit of the 'what are we all doing running around like hamsters in a wheel?' about it – not to mention the 'I wonder how many of these woman had sex last night?'.

Having finally managed to convince myself that I could handle being in the metropolis again (Oh look, there's a Burger King!), I caught the tube north to find Crouch End. When I reached Carol's house she was in and waiting for me, and when you haven't seen someone you love, or at least think you love, for a while . . . well, you know, you tend to be happy to see them even if things aren't that great between you. And it was really nice to see her again.

Once she'd shown me her room and given me a little guided tour of some of the rest of the house, we went off to the nearest pub and had a drink. As far as the parcels were concerned, and, more importantly, what was in them, Carol told me point blank that she didn't even want to discuss it. And as for our future together, at this moment in time she wasn't sure, but she felt that it might just all be over.

Being a real man (it's what real men do), I immediately wanted to know who he was, this man I assumed she must be having an affair with. I mean, why else would she want to leave me?

But do you know what? I was right for a change, and it turned out that the bloke in question was the man who owned the house she now had a room in. That was always Carol's trouble – she just couldn't lie.

For some reason, I was badly hurt inside when I discovered that what I'd suspected all along was really true. I wasn't going to let Carol see that, though, so all decent and reasonable-like I said my goodbyes and headed off back to Aldershot.

Once I got back to the lonely quiet of the flat I tried to make myself look on the bright side of life, because after all, here I was kind of single again, and the way I'd been behaving lately, maybe that was how I wanted it? But I wasn't happy. How could she do that to me? What had I done that was really so bad? I mean, it's not like I'd ever once so much as laid a finger on her or come home all drunk and nasty.

Oh well, I still had my marijuana to fall back on.

Strangely enough, today I'm not too sure how much I had waiting for me when I got back from Belize. I can't even remember exactly how much of it I ended up selling, although I'd guess it was about six or seven pounds. What I do remember, and shall never forget, is that it wasn't quite the breeze I'd always imagined it would be. You'd think it would be every dopehead's dream to have a pound or two of their favourite herb tucked away upstairs in Narnia, but it wasn't that simple. In fact, I hadn't got a clue about the grubby cash business of moving dope by the pound. Who should I offer it to, and for how much?

I knew it would be easy enough to sell small amounts to friends, and that I did, but when it came to any more than half an ounce, they just didn't have the pockets. Moneywise it's true to say about dope that the slower you sell it (as in the smaller the quantities) then the more you make. However, although I'd never sold dope myself before, I had bought it enough times back in Bristol to know that people who sold it regularly in small amounts had their phones ringing and people knock-knocking on their door day and night. In an army flat there was no way in the world that I could have that happening.

So, almost a week into my leave and with Carol away living in London, there I was in Aldershot really needing to sell some of the stuff that was stinking out the spare room – because, thanks to that last night in Belize and the extra money I'd had to pay out at Brize Norton, I was more than broke.

My lucky break came out of the blue when I received a phone call from an old friend who lived in Manchester. At the end of our conversation, knowing he was a toker himself, I asked him for his address so that I could send him a little present, and later that day I filled an audio-cassette case with grass and posted it off to him.

The very next evening my friend rang again to thank me very much for the parcel and to enquire whether, by any chance, I might be able to get hold of some more of that particular grass. Apparently it was the best he'd had in years – maybe even ever.

When I asked him what he meant by 'some more', as in a precise weight, he just said 'Any you can get.'

'What if I could get two pounds?' I asked.

'That would be great. Can you get that much?'

Although it was really a slight break from the etiquette of these things, my friend also asked me if the grass was mine.

'It might be,' I replied, playing my cards close to my chest like I'd seen them do at the pictures. He said he'd take that as a 'yes' and then asked if I'd be around for the next hour.

'For you,' I said, 'I'll be around for two.'

He took all of ten minutes to phone me back, and when he did it was all good news. If I could come up to Manchester tomorrow, he'd pick me up at the station, take me to see a couple of third parties, and Robert's your uncle. But there was, of course, one more thing to discuss: like how much, mate? I didn't really know the going rate, so I let him tell me. Five hundred a pound, he said, which included him being covered for his efforts. I told him we had a deal and that I'd see him tomorrow as arranged. Just before he hung up, though, he asked if there was any chance of me making it four. I should coco.

I was then faced with a problem which, surprisingly, I hadn't even thought of before, and that was how to weigh the grass. The best equipment I could come up with was a small set of plastic kitchen scales, on which I could just about weigh a pound before it fell off. I weighed out four single pounds and then cunningly checked them by taking them down to the post office and weighing them on the parcel scale there as well. It came to a little over the four pounds, which, allowing for the paper it was wrapped in, sounded just about right to me.

The next day, being near enough penniless, I set off early because I needed to get the train fare together to get myself up to Manchester. At that time, if you banked with the National Westminster Bank (which almost everybody in the Parachute Regiment did, because it was their forms they'd pushed in front of you back in basic training) an army ID card acted as a twenty-pound cheque guarantee card. However, when you cashed a cheque at the bank, the date of your transaction was punched into the little calendar at the back of your cheque book, thereby ensuring that you could only cash one cheque on any one day.

If you needed more money than this, the way around it was simply to have more than one cheque book, which could be achieved by never using up all the cheques in one book before you started on a new one. I now had three unfinished books in my possession, so I cashed one cheque at the bank in Aldershot and bought my train ticket to London, and when I got there I cashed another two at the first couple of NatWest branches I came across. With that done, I made my way to Kings Cross, where I phoned my friend (whom I'll call Martin to protect the guilty) with my estimated time of arrival before hopping aboard the next train to Manchester.

On the way up there I locked myself into the toilet and knocked a joint together. Now this is something I've done many times, and I know I'm by no means the only one because I've come across the debris of joint-making many times in train toilets, i.e. tobacco on the floor and the butt of an unsmoked cigarette floating in the bowl. The thing is, though, that dope (and especially grass) honks to high heaven, so especially if you happen to have a few more pounds of the stuff hidden in a bag back under your seat, smoking some in the bog is not a very clever thing to do. Of course, doing something not very clever was hardly a first for me.

Martin was on the platform waiting for me when the train pulled in, and as he walked me to his car he told me what he had arranged.

Our first port of call was to be the home of an old girlfriend of his, who wanted to get hold of half a pound and was prepared to pay three hundred pounds for the privilege. After that we were going to drive over to see another friend of his, who would take whatever I had left and give me five hundred a pound for it, paying the same, pro rata, for any odd amount that might be over.

When we got to Martin's ex-girlfriend's house the first thing to catch my eye was a camouflage jacket hanging up in the hall, which had badges and corporal stripes sewn on the sleeves. It turned out that the girl's boyfriend was a corporal in the Territorial Army, and of course, me, being the mouth that I was at the time, couldn't help but inform her that I was in the regular army and had fought in the Falklands. Airborne I was (she was very good-looking).

Once the girl had made us all a coffee and all three of us had had a sample smoke, I went on to tell her all about Belize and how I'd smuggled the grass home from there. Looking back on it now, I realise what a fool I was to talk about this so openly, but I guess I did it because at that time I never really believed for one minute that there was any harm in it.

Much as I (genuinely) would have liked to, we couldn't sit around all night drinking coffee and chatting away, 'cos we still had business to do, so Martin and me made our apologies and the nice young lady counted out the three hundred smacke-roos, which I stuffed into my pockets.

We got back into the car and set off for location number two, which was apparently no more than ten minutes away. When we got to the house, we were met at the door by two men and led into a small sitting room. On the carpet by the sofa was an old set of black wrought-iron kitchen scales (exactly like the ones my mum used to weigh flour on when I was a kid).

Seeing the scales set me off worrying in case the weighing I'd done back in Aldershot hadn't been accurate enough. I didn't want these guys to get the idea that I was trying to turn them over. Not that they were a couple of hardened criminals or anything (in fact, they were students from Manchester University), but I still didn't want them to think I was ripping them off.

They were able to weigh what I had in one go, and – thank you, Lord – it came to just over three and a half pounds, or one thousand, seven hundred and fifty pounds if you were talking about the sterling variety.

I'd never counted up as much as £1,750 in cash that belonged to me before, but I'd checked much larger amounts of other people's money when helping out with the nightly count at the casino I used to work in. So if there ever was a moment in the whole of my time as an evil drug-runner when I was on top of things and did actually look like I knew what I was doing, then it was when I was counting out the cash. With the £300 I'd picked up from the TA corporal's girlfriend, I now had over £2,000, which was a lot of money back then. Oh yes, in those days two of you could go out for the night, see a film, have a meal, get pissed and still have change from forty quid.

My original plan had been to stay the night at Martin's and catch a train back to London in the morning. But, as the business had gone much quicker than I'd thought it would, there were now enough minutes left for Martin to drop me back at the station in good time to catch the last train down to London that same day.

We said our goodbyes in the station car park. I thanked him, then he thanked me, and then we both thanked our lucky stars. If any more of the grass came my way, I was to be sure to let him be the first to know. Well, now that he came to mention it, if his friends did want any more, I happened to have another five or so pounds back in Aldershot. So I told him to give us a ring when he'd got something sorted. Sorted.

Just as I was about to board the train to London, like a good Boy Scout I opened my wallet to check my ticket. And as soon as I did, I noticed straight away that my army ID card was missing. Shit! What should I do now? Get on the train anyway? No, I couldn't do that. Losing your ID card was big shit in the army, and if I'd lost it anywhere then it had to be here in Manchester. Or was it? I started to go through the mental checklist that we all resort to whenever we lose something.

When did you last see it?

On the train up. I showed my ticket to the inspector and the card was in my wallet then.

Or was it? I wasn't too sure. One thing about dope that no one can deny is that it is not a memory-enhancing drug. The harder I thought about it, the more I wasn't sure when I'd last seen my army ID card.

I'd definitely had it when I was doing my round of cheque-cashing in the morning, so I must have lost it at some point between going to the last branch of NatWest up to a short while after getting out of the low bucket seats of Martin's car. Martin's car! That had to be favourite for where it was. I quickly ran back outside, hoping to catch Martin before he drove away.

When I got outside, it was like a scene from a French *film noir* as I came to an abrupt halt at the sight of Martin's car pulling away from the curb and disappearing out of earshot into the city traffic.

I walked to the nearest phone booth and called his house. I knew he wouldn't be back yet, I'd just seen him leave, but his wife would probably be in, and she could pass on a message for him to search the car as soon as he got home.

It then crossed my mind that maybe I'd left my card on the train after all, or maybe I'd dropped it in the station some-where. Either way, it would probably be a wise move to go and report the loss to British Rail, even if it was just to show the army that I'd made an effort. So off I went in search of the lost property office, and – would you believe it? – joy of joy's, a BR employee had found my ID card by the platform barrier and handed it in.

Although, for some reason, they didn't want to take it, I left behind a twenty-pound tip for the person who had handed it in and told them all to go and have a drink. (That was a lot of money back then. Oh yes, one person could go to the pictures, have a meal, get pissed and still have change.)

So, good news at last, except that by now I'd missed my train back to London and was going to have to spend the night in Manchester after all. But when I phoned Martin's house again, he still wasn't back from dropping me off and it was now anybody's guess what time he would be.

All I could think of to do was to go into town and find myself a hotel. After all, it wasn't like I couldn't afford it. I found a vacant taxi at the station and asked the driver to take me to whatever he thought was a good hotel – meaning a big one, preferably with a disco. The one he dropped me in front of was fine from the outside, and inside it was certainly better than what I was used to by way of transit accommodation. It cost, though, and when I said I'd be paying in cash the nose behind the reception made me pay up front. Oh, and by the way, they only had an 'inner room' (whatever that was).

The room was OK, but, unlike in the American-type hotels I'd stayed in on my travels, the single room I'd paid for was just that and had only one single bed. Also, when I opened the curtains to look out at Manchester by night, I discovered why the man downstairs had described my room as 'inner'. Behind the curtains was a wall, which decorwise matched the rest of the room, but there was no window. After a while I decided I didn't like this lack of windows at all (what am I, in Beirut or something?) and so, after taking a shower and cunningly hiding my money under the mattress (far too obvious for anyone to look there), I used my status as a resident to gain free admission to the disco in the hotel's nightclub. How's it go? 'Night fever, night fever . . . you know how to do it.' Big, loud place it was as well, or certainly by Aldershot's standards, and once I'd smoothed my way to the bar and ordered the standard Southern Comfort and Coke (yes, I *do* want Coke in it), it wasn't too long before I was chatting up a more than good-looking young lady.

So, what a bit of luck that I'd lost my ID card, then. After a few dances (well, they played Lionel Richie and 'All Night Long', didn't they), not to mention a few more drinks, the girl wanted to know if I fancied going on to another place she knew that stayed open even later than the nightclub. You know me – if there's one thing I love it's 'even later', especially of the alcoholic variety – so off we trotted, and on the way, halfway up an alley, I got more than fifty per cent of what it was I was working towards. And I'd never been there before, but wasn't Manchester a nice place?

I also took the opportunity to ask the girl if she happened to smoke, as in dope, because if she did, I'd got one rolled. Once I'd lighted it up and passed it over, I warned her that it was the business, I did. But she seemed to know what she was doing, so who was I to roll her back?

Eventually (and I hope this place has got a sink) we got to where she was taking us, which turned out to be no more than a lock-in in a small pub. To enter, we had to knock on a side door and get viewed through a little hatch, but as soon as my escort was recognised the door was opened and in we were beckoned. Inside, it really was no more than a normal pub, and if you ask me (judging by all of the paraphernalia hanging on its walls, not to mention the music coming from the jukebox), a pub with an Irish theme. Tell you what, though . . . for a lock-in the place was very busy and much louder than you'd think they'd have wanted it to be.

We ordered our drinks from a barman who seemed to know the girl I was with, and, after a bit of a push through the crowd, found a couple of seats to squeeze into. For some reason, while we were in the disco the girl and I hadn't got around to asking each other what we did for a living, and what brought this fact to my attention now was that I was looking out over the top of my drink, taking in the room, when I noticed an Irish flag on the wall. In an instant I realised, and call it survival instinct if you like, that it probably wouldn't be a good idea for me to mention my occupation out loud in this place.

Luckily, before we could get around to any chit-chat the girl I was with suddenly decided that she was really stoned and started to make like Mogadon Woman. This I could handle, because I don't know why (well I do, actually), but I didn't much like it there and would have been quite happy to split. In fact I was just about to suggest leaving when we were joined at our small table by a man holding a collection tin, who, going by his accent, was a real 'Belfast Billy' – except that there was no way in the world that this man's name was Billy. To my horror (and I really do mean horror – after all this was England, for fuck's sake), he was collecting for the families of Republican H-block victims. And what was worse, the girl I was with knew him and introduced me by announcing: 'Seamus, this guy's got some really great gear on him.' Well thanks very fucking much for that, you daft Doris. Seamus then wanted to know if there was any chance of him having a smoke, and so, seeing it as a way of at least getting away from his collection tin, I said I'd go off to the bog and bring him back a little.

Pushing my way through the crowd towards the toilet, I couldn't help but feel that this was not a good place for me to be. If anyone here were to find out that I was a member of the dreaded Parachute Regiment, things could turn out more than nasty. And it wasn't only bad from that point of view. If the army ever found out that I'd been stoned out of my playpen and drinking in a pub that at the minimum was filled to the beams with Republican sympathisers, then that wasn't likely to go down too well either.

By then I was starting to feel more than a little claustrophobic and wanted nothing more from the world than to be allowed to get the fuck out of the place, like now. But it wasn't that easy, because the Gents was at the other end of the room from the side door that led outside. And do you know what (and hopefully this was the last time ever) – I really wished I'd never gone and smoked that last joint what I did. My salvation came when I got to the men's toilets and, just like in the movies again, found an outside window that I was able to climb through and disappear into the shadows.

Which only goes to show that sex isn't, always, everything.

Despite my late night and too many drinks, the next morning I awoke in my hotel cell all bright and breezy (as you do, I suppose, when you've got two grand stuffed under the mattress). After I'd checked out of the hotel and found out what time the trains left for London, I thought I'd spend an hour or so walking around Manchester and doing some shopping, because when I came to think about it, there were quite a few things I wouldn't mind acquiring now that I had a bit of cash.

So I shopped till I dropped.

The first thing I bought myself was a pure wool light grey suit. It cost me well over a hundred pounds but was more than worth it, especially once I'd picked out the shoes, shirt and maroon tie to go with it. Next on my list of consumer wants was a brand-new Walkman – one of those ones you could adjust the tone on. And of course, if I treated myself to the Walkman then I'd need a few new tapes as well (and isn't it funny how we can always remember where we were when we bought a particular record?), so I got Paul Simon's 'Still Crazy After All These Years', because I liked him (and that was me), and Joni Mitchell's 'Blue', because Carol liked her. I also purchased a red Antler suitcase (God knows why) and a bottle of my favourite aftershave at the time, Eau Sauvage.

As a further treat I upgraded my ticket to first class for the train journey back to London. Once I'd had a quick joint in the toilets I put Joni Mitchell into my Walkman, and, with the aroma of Eau Sauvage in the air and my Rolex watch and nice new shirt-cuffs on display, settled back to enjoy the first of several whisky and lemonades. Before long my mind started to drift towards thinking about Carol, and all of a sudden (and it was sudden) I realised that I wasn't happy without her and wanted her back.

I knew that she had been unfaithful to me, but, if I was honest, I was hardly in a position to throw stones in that department.

By the time I got to London I'd worked myself up into becoming well and truly emotional and had very sensibly decided to go round to Carol's house, hospitalise the boyfriend and then drag her back to 'the Shot'. (You know how it goes: 'You didn't marry a namby-pamby civvy, woman – you married a trooper!')

When I arrived there, having made a short pub stop on route, the female flatmate was in but Carol and Romeo hadn't come home from work yet. The flatmate let me in, though, and was even kind enough to make me a coffee. On a trip to the bathroom I sneaked into Carol's room, found the small album that contained our wedding photographs, thought to myself 'How could she?' and then tore each and every one of them up. Left them in a spread-out pile on the bed I did. That would show her!

While I had been upstairs acting out my frustration, the flatmate had been busy downstairs phoning Carol's boyfriend to let him know that there was a six-foot-two paratrooper at the house who wanted to kill him. The boyfriend's response to this was to make two phone calls – unfortunately, in the wrong order.

His second call was to Carol at her work to let her know that her mad husband was round at the house and threatening vengeance. The first call, though, had been to the police, who soon turned up on the doorstep – expecting I don't know what, because when the doorbell rang and I looked through the curtains, the scene outside had turned into a TV-style siege: three police cars with flashing lights and four, five, six . . . seven policemen. My first thought was that I was carrying drugs (a good first thought to have when the police are knock-knocking on the door) and that I'd have to dump them, quick. I also had a lot of cash on me, but I figured that if they asked me about that I could explain it away as money I'd saved while overseas serving my country.

I ran to the bathroom, locked the door and began searching

for places to hide my 'personal'. I could, of course, flush it down the toilet, like they do in *Miami Vice*, but that would mean I'd never see it again, which would be far too sad a parting. I found a near-perfect spot behind the front panel of the bath, which, once the grass was safely hidden, I fitted neatly back into the slot I'd forced it from. I then had one quick run-through of my pockets to make absolutely sure that I'd got it all, and turned to leave the bathroom.

Just as I was about to unlock the door, someone tapped on it from the other side. I was going to call out and ask who it was, as if I couldn't guess ('Hello, 'ello, 'ello!'), when a male voice, all nice and calm and calling me 'Ken, mate', asked me to do him a favour and open the door to let him in. *Let him in*? Couldn't I come out instead? When I did open the door, standing outside the bathroom was the biggest policeman I'd seen since the Brixton riots. Huge he was, and the sort of the bloke that, if you were going to hit him (and you'd have to be mad to even consider it), you'd have trouble knowing where to so that it would hurt. He wasn't looking for any violence, though, because he was my mate. He'd had the situation explained to him and all he wanted to do was put me in his car and take me to the railway station.

'It is Waterloo for Aldershot, isn't it, Ken?'

I allowed the officer to lead me outside, past the midget ('cos he *was* small) who I'd come to London specifically to kill and a crying Carol being comforted by her girlfriend. As they put me in the back of one of their police cars, my final view of Carol weeping there on the pavement left me feeling not too good about myself.

On the drive to Waterloo, though, it became clear that the policemen were more than a little on my side in the argument. If you asked them, the only thing I'd done wrong was turning up and announcing that I was going to beat the wanker up. I should have just gone ahead and done it. After all, he deserved it, what with me being a Falklands war hero and him being a scumbag who had run off with my wife while I was away in Belize. And it's got to be said, but what a nice couple of guys these coppers were, and understanding as well. With what I'd done already – which apparently, although it amounted to no more than threatening violence, was mucho plenty – they could have pulled me in and basically caused me lots of big trouble with the army if they'd wanted to.

Surprisingly, or maybe that's what some cynics might think, this wasn't the first time the police had been more than decent to me in situations where they could have been right shits.

On my first night back from the Falklands War I had stayed with my sister in Bristol, where, before joining the army, I'd worked as a croupier in a casino. ('Well it wouldn't be in an abattoir, would it, mate?' . . . although they are quite similar, in a way.) That night, pissed out of my mind to the point where I could hardly walk, at three o'clock in the morning I decided to climb into the car and set off through Bristol city centre to visit the old slaughterhouse. Five minutes from the casino I looked in my rear-view mirror and saw behind me a flashing blue light, and straight away I realised that if they breathalysed me, then I was done for.

But do you know what? I didn't give a flying fuck.

When I got pulled over and wound down the window, the first officer who came over asked me to step out of the car. And why I was worried about the breathalyser I don't know, because there was no way they needed one of those to tell that I was drunk. They asked me for my licence, but I didn't have it with me at the time so I showed them my army ID card instead. That did the trick nicely. They wanted to know what regiment I was in, and when I said the Paras they asked if I'd returned home from the Falklands that day, because they'd seen paras arriving back at Brize Norton on the television news.

And that was it. As soon as they knew I was a homecoming hero, they simply asked if I had enough money on me for a cab, which I did, and then advised me strongly to get one home. I could pick the car up in the morning.

Which, in anybody's language, was a right result.

*

Back at work, I remembered the corporal from Belize and how he had embarrassed everyone by going on and on about his wife leaving him. I was *not* going to be like him, I vowed.

Let's do it all over again

Here's some madness for you. Carol was still away living in London, the money I'd earned from the grass was well on the way to being all gone, and even worse – get this – I had no smoke left for me to escape with. Within a week of selling the last ounce of it to a friend on a promise, I was on a train bound for a bookie's in Finsbury Park, which believe it or not was the nearest place to Aldershot where I knew I could score some smoke. I still had some of the money left, but as a wise man once said (I believe it was Free Wheelin' Franklin of the Fabulous Furry Freak Brothers): 'It is easier to get through times of no money with dope, than it is to get through times of no dope with money!'

When I arrived at the betting shop it took me the best part of six seconds to spot a black guy who I felt was not disappearing outside every two minutes with various people just 'cos he had a need for fresh air. Mind you, I hardly needed to be Banacek to work that one out. All sorts of suspicious-looking types were sliding up to him and whispering in his ear, then he'd whisper back and then off they would go outside together.

And to this day it never ceases to amaze me just how suspicious people can look when they're doing their damnedest to appear the exact opposite. The flash of the eyes and raised eyebrows signalling across the room, the silent nod of agree-ment to the person they're about to pass something to, then the quick hand-under-the-table movement, which everyone catches because it's nearly always followed by a fumble and

183

panic as they both try to pick up whatever it is they've dropped. Really – it would be less obvious if one of them jumped up on the table and shouted: 'Got the gear for me Harry?' while the other one put some scales on the bar to prepare for the weigh-in.

So I placed a couple of bets, and to show what a nice honest, open guy I was I started up a bit of loudish good-natured gambler's banter with some of the shop's other victims. Which is not a hard thing to do in a bookie's, because there are nearly always a couple of people who are winning, and winners just love to talk about how clever they are. Losers, on the other hand, they tend to keep mum (unless, of course, they're cursing the world that's treating them so unfairly). Eventually, I shuffled up to the guy I needed to speak to and asked him right out if he knew where I could score some grass. Without a blink, he turns to me and he says: 'Are you a policeman?'

'No, I'm not a cop. Do I look like a cop?'

'Yeah, you do.'

Six-foot-two above sea level, steel blue eyes, short hair, dressed neck to toes in casual menswear from Burton's . . . he had a point. But then again, would a plain-clothes policeman come in here and try to buy dope, looking like me? Far too obvious. Aha, but is it? Because sometimes the obvious becomes the un . . . (I'm sorry, but I had enough of that doublethink in Northern Ireland, and I'm not getting into it all again in a bookie's in Finsbury Park.)

So to get it all over with, and to prove that I was not a policeman but the squaddie I kept trying to telling him I was, I showed him my army ID card and then topped that up with my even more impressive army rail card, which carried a colour photograph of my handsome self with the name of my unit stamped right across it: 2 Para, pal.

'A para? Were you in the Falklands then, mate?'

'Well actually, I don't like talking about it.'

Twenty minutes later, after I'd run him from the sands of San Carlos Bay to the tarmacked streets of Port Stanley, and our RAF VC10 home again afterwards had finally landed safely at

Brize Norton airport, I asked once again if he knew where I could score some grass.

And no, he didn't know.

A point of etiquette here for you. Now at this juncture I could have said, 'Look mate, no offence meant, but I did not get off the banana boat yesterday. I've seen you popping outside with your buddies, and I am half Polish, you know, like that Banacek bloke.' But to have said that would have been impolite. So instead, I put it another way.

'How much you got on you? I need an ounce.'

That one did the trick. He looks at me and thinks for a bit, and then he says, 'It'll cost sixty pounds.'

'I've got sixty pounds. You got an ounce on you?'

'No, I'll have to go and get it. And I need the money now.'

He needs the money now, bless him. Get fucking real. Banana boat and all that. No way is you getting the money up front.

'OK. Then I can't get it for you. Bye-bye, soldier boy.'

And he had me. But just to rub some salt into the wound as I too quickly folded and agreed to his terms, when I handed over the cash he dug another five pounds out of me for a taxi. So me, Mr Nobody's Fool, all I could do was pass it over with a wish and prayer. Not that I really needed the stuff or anything. Like they say, your marijuana isn't addictive, is it?

He said he would be about twenty minutes, which in anyone's language means more like thirty, but after he'd been gone forty-five and I was starting to think 'He's still not back,' it all suddenly became much, much worse. Because in that time I'd lost over two hundred quid on the horses . . . and how much is that doggie in the five trap? By now I'm fully involved. To try and claw some of it back I threw a large amount on an odds-on favourite, and it got hammered. By now my brain has completely gone – ho, ho – and I'm betting on every race, having almost forgotten about the guy who's gone off with my money to get some grass.

Fuck the grass.

In short, I lost a load, as in about six hundred quid. And I'm pissed. Because he's not back after an hour and a half, so he's obviously not coming back (the robbing dark-skinned shit), and to top it all off, I've just gone and lost an annoyingly large amount of money in the wait.

I was down to my last hundred pounds when in through the door, all puffed out and smiles, came the guy I'd given the money to for the gear – Ganja Man, slower than the fastest snail. It took me about half a second to work out what his game had been. He'd been hoping that by now I'd have fucked off and he could keep the money, or if I hadn't fucked off, he'd just hand the money back and say he couldn't get any, and he'd lost nothing. I fucking knew.

Well, I was wrong.

He had an ounce of grass for me, and looking at it, it appeared as though he hadn't ripped me off either. It looked a good ounce.

'Sorry I was so long,' he apologised.

Now six hundred quid down, so was I. Pissed I was.

I left the bookie's having completed the task I'd set out from Aldershot that morning to do (you're the man, Ken), but – and there was nearly always a but with me – in the meantime having also managed to create a big fuck-up.

Changing trains on the way back to Aldershot, I stopped off in a small bookmaker's near Charing Cross Station in London, where, a little surprisingly, I won some of my lost money back. Not all of it, but enough to lift my spirits a bit.

On the train back to the home of the British army I went to the toilet and had a smoke of the grass I'd bought, and I had to confess that by English standards, and certainly considering it had been bought on spec from a man of Afro-Carribean extraction in a bookie's in North London, it was good gear. So I was sorry for everything I'd thought about Ganja Man, though he could have done my impulsive self a big favour and been a bit quicker.

But whatever, good gear or not, I had to confess that all this was madness. I was madness. I'd had pounds of the stuff a couple of weeks ago, and now I was spending the money I made selling it buying other grass at hugely inflated prices, and . . . and losing four hundred quid while doing so. I was fucking mad, me. Puff, puff.

And sitting down on the toilet in the train, choo-choo, puff, puff, having a long look at life, there was only one thing for it. (Well actually there were about forty things for it, but there was only one that took my fancy.) I had two weeks of Christmas leave coming up in December (and don't get smart, because you can end up having fucking Christmas leave in June in the army) and I could go back. I could fly my own way to Belize and roll me over, lay me down and do it all over again. Just one parcel of ten pounds, say. Who'd know?

And once the thought had arrived, it didn't take long for me to agree with my own bad idea.

By the time I stepped off the train in Aldershot it was break out the suntan lotion because I'm going back to Belize. No U-turns and just like that. Which was stunning really. A major, major decision thought up and agreed in thirty seconds while stoned on a toilet in a train. But then again, the way I saw it back then, Carol was gone (and who could blame her?) and the army, when I thought about it, career and all that, I didn't give a fuck about any more for some reason, and so why the fuck not, eh? Like what did I have to lose? Well, nothing. And what did I have to gain? Well, everything. Well, money at least, like in cash. And dope, of course, like in grass. And what do we all love? We all love cash and we all love grass.

Speaking of which, I didn't actually have enough cash to fly me back to Belize, or, come to think of it, to score ten pounds of the non-addictive herb when I got there. But then, as I often used to hear them say in the Kingdom Hall of Jehovah's Witnesses, where there's a human will, Satan will always help you find a way.

To protect the guilty, I'll just say that I managed to borrow some money from someone who knew I was good for it. With interest, of course. The date for my departure was set with the purchase of a plane ticket from a bucket shop in London, and then all I had to do was wait for Christmas leave. And it might as well rain until December.

And then life took a human twist.

I was out in a wine bar in London one Friday night, with a civvie mate of mine and his girlfriend, when, the way you do, I struck up a conversation with a woman who was standing next to us in the very crowded bar. Brahms & Liszt in Covent Garden it was. Her friends were going but she didn't want to leave yet, and so she joined us. We all got pissed – which was good, because that had been the whole idea of going into the bar in the first place – and at the end of the night, when we invited her back to my friend's flat in Royal Oak, she was more than up for it. Ho, ho.

We caught a cab back to my friend's, where we all drank some more wine and had a smoke or two, and then my mate, he goes off to bed with his girlfriend, leaving me alone with Mo. For that was her name.

Well, nothing beyond a kiss and cuddle actually happened that night, because, as I said to her at the time, I wasn't like that. (Lying shit. I was pissed to limpness.) But we slept on the floor together, and the next morning, when I explained that I had to catch a train back to my lonely flat in Aldershot, Mo offered to drive me. Which was kind, really, considering it was a hundred miles or so as a round journey. (Don't you love girls?)

And then, somehow, before you can say 'I'm on the rebound' we're an item and I'm enjoying it. The night we met I had been looking for no more than a one-night stand, but for some reason I really did like Mo. I enjoyed talking to her, and when I told her my poor-me story of how, after I'd been away in Belize for six months, my wife had left me for another man, she sympathised and told me I'd been badly wronged. After all (and poor me again, eh?), only the year before I had been serving my country in the Falklands War. Of which I said, 'Well actually, I don't like talking about it.' And twenty minutes later, after I'd run her from the sands of San Carlos Bay etc, Mo really understood just how badly I'd been wronged.

You know what, though. Even then I wasn't completely all bad and so a large part of me felt guilty that I sat there nodding away at Mo's opinion of my wife's treatment of me, because – and I think quite naturally enough for a young male mind – I hadn't passed on to her the whole story. (I'd left out the bit about all the womanising I'd done while I was in Belize, for instance.) But there again, why the heck would I, Batman? Who ever got sex by being honest, except as a very last resort?

The night before I was to fly off to Belize, I took Mo, who was by now a regular fixture of my leisure time, to a casino in Soho. Mo had never been to a casino before, and as I had worked in one prior to joining the army, who better to introduce her to the joys of comfort gambling than my good self? We were playing blackjack and it was all very much up a little one moment, down a little the next, when Mo went off to the ladies' room. Well, talk about Lady Luck. In the time that she was away I didn't lose one hand, and as with all nice wins when they happen, it happened in a flash. By the time she returned I was up five hundred pounds. Now funnily enough, before we had entered the casino I had, actually, actually said to her that I was going to win five hundred pounds, and that when I had, I was going to leave. So we left.

When we got back to Mo's flat we had sex in the dark on the hallway stairs, which is a lasting memory, and let's be honest, a pleasant one.

Now me knowing me, and sometimes I do stop and think, before I set off from Mo's flat the next morning I gave her fifty pounds in cash and asked her to mail it to me at the flat in Aldershot. You never know, I thought, I might get back from Belize and be broke.

The journey from Mo's flat to Heathrow, and the flight that followed across the ocean to the land of the brave and the free I don't recall a second of. Not even the in-flight movie or the name of the airline that was kind enough to fly me. Which all these years on is probably the dope for you.

Miami, when I got there, I only remember because as soon as

I had made it through customs and into the airport concourse I was greeted and welcomed to America by a short-haired hippy who insisted on shaking my hand and presenting me with a flower. Being English I found this somewhat embarrassing and really wished he hadn't picked on me, although I was polite about it. He then asked if I'd like to make a donation to his cause, which, although he didn't mention it at the time (and that may just be because he didn't know himself) was the purchasing of Rolls-Royce motor cars for the Bagwan What's-his-name.

Unless the RAF were doing the flying, one couldn't fly direct to Belize from England, and I had to wait for three whole nights in Miami before my connecting flight to Belize City left. So, what to do? Thanks to my little win in the casino I had some cash to spare, so why not check my good-looking English self into a hotel and wait out. But where? I didn't know, so, once outside the airport I asked a taxi driver. When I found one he said that the best thing for me to do was go to a place called Fort Lauderdale, which was some xxx miles from the airport. It wouldn't cost that much, 'cos he'd drive me for a fixed fare, and it was all beaches and girls, like Blackpool but with sun, millionaires, yachts, porn, guns and herpes. Oh, and strip joints and topless bars, apparently. But did I really want to go there? A place like that? After all, I was in a sense at work – on a serious drug run, hey!

When we reached Fort Lauderdale we drove up the main coastal strip and I was dropped off outside of a Howard Johnson hotel, which the cab driver assured me would be comfortable and also within my price bracket. What the room cost a night I can't now remember, though I do recall that it was surprisingly cheap when compared with the same sort of hotel back in England, and that the receptionist seemed a little concerned that I didn't have a credit card and wanted to pay in cash.

My room, when I found my way up to it (for it was high, and had I sent anyone a postcard I would surely have put a cross on 'my window'), had two main features that me the Limey couldn't help but get excited about. Firstly, it was huge and could easily have slept six, and secondly the TV had more channels than there are entrants in the Eurovision Song Contest. One of these channels was MTV, which was all new back in 1983 and hadn't reached England yet, although we had heard about it at our quaint post offices in our little villages full of thatched cottages.

My fascination with Music TeleVision lasted a good hour or so before I came to my senses (well, just how much 'Big Country' can you listen to and watch at the same time?) and decided that I should go out and about and maybe meet some American girls. After all, I was in America, so it stood to reason that I had more than the average chance of bumping into one or two of them. So I popped on my new grey suit and my smart new maroon tie and headed off into the Fort Lauderdale night. (By the way, when in America and looking for girls, always wear a tie – what with the accent and all they just might think you royalty.)

I walked along the strip 'cruising', as they say, from bar to bar. By now it was getting dark and I was in Florida, USA and the occasional policemen I passed had guns and this was where they filmed *Miami Vice*, so I was trying to get into the mood of how seedy and dangerous it all was. But it wasn't really, and neither were the bars. For this was Touristville and all the bars I passed through tended to be parts of hotels, which for blocks and blocks along the seafront were all you could see.

One of these hotels was a Sheraton, and, unlike the Howard Johnson I was kipping in, I'd heard of that chain because I'd stayed at the Sheraton Hotel in Perth, W.A. once. So, with a ready-made anecdote should I strike up a conversation, I walked on in. Inside it turned out to be pretty much like all the other hotel bars on the strip: big and wide and open and lit like the meat counter at Tesco's, as in bright with no flies. I smoothed my English self to the bar and found an empty stool and, coolly sipping on my first Southern Comfort and Coke (which, incidentally, was a perfect pleasure to order in America, as not once did some smartarse behind the bar sneer 'Oh, you're not going to put Coke in it, are you?'), I began to scan the room.

It wasn't long before I was catching eyes across the carpet from two good-looking ladies in their late twenties, early thirties or so who were sharing a booth across the other side of the room. One of them, a fluffy blonde type, was dressed in a kind of Southern Belle outfit, all white and layered and lacy, and looked like a cross between Scarlett O'Hara and Bo Peep less the bonnet and sheep. Her friend was also dressed to kill, but only in an American TV normal kind of way, so I couldn't describe her clothes today. Because of their dress I just assumed that the 'gals' were from the South, as in Deep, and although I couldn't hear what they were saying, as they talked I imagined they were coming out with things like: 'Well, I do declare. Is that not a handsome young man over there, Miss Ellie-Lou?'

After fifteen minutes of long-distance flirting (well, I am a good-looking boy) and them making it patently obvious that they were talking and giggling about me (and I hate that, by the way – I mean, I do have a mind as well, you know) I finally plucked up the courage to wander over to their booth.

'Well hello.'

And guess what. They weren't even American, never mind from sweet home Alabama. Guess what they were? Well you won't. Well you might, but probably not spot on.

They were Canadians, you see, but, and it's quite a big but, they were French Canadians from Quebec. Which was handy, as it was the only part of French-speaking Canada that I think I'd heard of.

'Oh, Quebec? How interesting. Are you from Montreal?'

'Oui.'

(Thank fuck for that. It is in Quebec then.)

Although they didn't look like it, and they really didn't, my two new female friends were sisters, who, though originally both from Montreal, now lived in separate parts of Canada and had met up only that afternoon in Fort Lauderdale for a 'vacation' together.

Now me, even back then, I liked to think of myself as a

reasonably well-travelled type, which is why it came as a surprise to me to learn that one of the sisters didn't speak English. Lived in Canada and didn't speak English? Was that possible? I didn't really know.

The thing was that the one who couldn't speak English – who, incidentally, was the one wearing Laura Ashley's 'Gone With the Wind' collection – turned out to be more than a little bit weird in that she read palms (and she just had to do mine) and was also apparently some sort of psychic. What made her all the more weird was that whenever she said something to me she would stare me straight in the eye, and I mean stare, and rattle off a stream of words in rapid French that her sister would just as rapidly translate. And the French they speak in Canada, it ain't like the French I didn't learn much of in 2B when I was twelve. Instead of being spiritually moved by the bollocks she was coming out with (and you can take my word for it, it was all total and utter bollocks) I stared right back into her eyes and thought, 'Do you know, this is just like that scene in *Close Encounters of the Third Kind* where the French scientist is gibbering away to the American scientists in rapid French.' What were the names of the actors again? But I kept smiling, and to be honest I turned it up a notch or two with the proper English gentleman routine. Weird or not, Little Miss Muffet was still good-looking, and so was her sister.

As our evening together progressed and the drinks flowed, the girls put up the idea that we leave the hotel and go in search of some of the famous Florida nightlife, as in 'nite' clubs. Oh well, go on then.

And the next thing I know the three of us are sitting in the back seat of a taxi, which for some reason is taking us to a nite club in Miami, and me, well, I'm a little bit confused. Because I'm sat in the middle of the two girls (sisters, mind you) and both of them are stroking and squeezing the inside of my thighs. Hey, hey! Though to be honest I was a tad nervous, in an innocent, likeable sort of way. Gulp!

So then the two French-Canadian sisters and me are sitting in this quiet side bar that's part of this drop-dead fuck-off huge

Miami disco, having just returned from fifteen minutes of fully clothed sex on the dance floor. And I'm very happy, I can tell you. We're laughing along, drinking our alcohol and getting on just fine, when over wanders this Australian guy (of all races), who excuses himself for interrupting, but he was wondering if it would be OK for him to join us, since we're an odd number and he's out on his own.

Now my reaction to this, and quite naturally enough if you ask me, is 'Well actually, no, it would not be fucking all right for you to join us, Skippy, because I'm on to one of those set-ups with the French word for three in it here. So fuck off.' But of course, with the ladies there I can't say it and he gets to sit down.

It turned out that he was in Miami sort of illegally, as he didn't possess a magic green card but was nevertheless designing a yacht for someone who had the cash to afford him. And do you know what? The ignorant, uneducated, colonial wanker only goes and speaks fluent French, doesn't he? *Merde.*

The four of us talk for a while and then the Australian asks, as he bloody well should have by now, if anyone wants a drink. Then him and *moi* (see how serious I was? I was even learning the language), we go over to the bar to get his round of drinks in, 'cos he can't carry them all by himself. At the bar, sitting on her own and passing the time of night chatting to the barman, is a more than attractive young lady who's dressed in fine clothes and has obviously spent a minimum of three hours in front of the make-up mirror. Standing a couple of feet away from her, we order the drinks, and while we're waiting for them to arrive the Australian and my cool English self swap a bit of small talk.

The attractive young woman turns to me and says, 'Excuse me, but your accent. It's English, right?'

The girl wasn't wrong, so I said so. 'Yes, that's right.' And I already knew what was coming next, because I'd heard it a hundred times before.

'Oh, I just love the English accent.'

She then turned to my new colonial acquaintance and stated with confidence, 'Your accent. It's not English, is it, honey?'

'No,' he replied, 'It's Australian.'

'Oh *really*? God, you speak such great English. Where did you learn?'

Now, had this been six months before, at this point I would have been thinking 'Fuck–right–off–and–die.' But no, thanks to my close proximity to so many Americans in Belize and Mexico, I now knew as sure as day follows night that the young lady's enquiry was a genuine one. Been to college, holds down an office job, even watches the TV, and yet for her the whole wide world stops where the sand meets the sea on Miami Beach.

'Actually, luv, we speak English in Australia.'

'Oh *really*?'

And then, back at the table and a few drinks later, disaster strikes when Kangaroo Joe and one of the Canadian sisters go for a slow smooch on the dance floor. And when they get back it's all holding hands under the table and suddenly they're a couple. Oh well. *Qué será* and all that.

But all was not lost for me, so don't feel too sad, please. For I still had one sister left (and the one who spoke English) and later that very same night, back at my Howard Johnson, with MTV providing the backing track, I allowed her to have her wicked French-Canadian way with me.

So, it was nice to know I was going to be faithful to Mo, then?

(You're the man, Ken.)

Back to Belize for
some more marijuana

Aboard the flight from Miami my mind occupied itself by playing the 'what if?' game. And there were a few of them. Like what if it was standard operational procedure for British military intelligence in Belize to check the manifests of all incoming flights? So what if? Surely I'd only pop up on their screen as a serving member of Her Majesty's armed loonies and no way could they know that I wasn't serving in Belize? But what if they did know? What would I say? I ran through my options and settled on the line that whilst I had been serving in Belize I'd had an affair with an American Peace Corps worker (which was a good one, because it was kind of half-true), on my return to England my wife had left me for another man (which was an even better one, because it was very true) and in my distressed state I had headed back to Belize to be in the arms of my American sweetheart. And if they did check this with Linda and she replied, 'Well guys, we were fucking, but I'd hardly call it love,' I could always turn around, give her the big hurt eyes and bleed aloud, 'Did you not know that I loved you?'

With that settled, my only other nerve problem aboard the flight was the presence of the other soldiers aboard. The last thing I wanted was for one of them to wander over and start up a conversation. So what if? Well, then I was 'Squaddie Boy' returning to Belize after two weeks' R&R in Fort Lauderdale. Not only did I carry a pukka ID card to back this up, I had served in Belize and I had just spent four days in Fort Lauderdale. I could also tell them that I was part of the Jungle

Training Team, which would hint that I was SAS and enough said. But what if it turned out that *they* were Jungle Training Team? Be just be my luck, that would.

I decided that my best bet was to close my eyes and keep them that way until we arrived.

How long the flight from Miami was I don't now remember, though I do know that I didn't get one of those in-flight meals that us working-class types like so much, so it can't have been that long. And thankfully no one disturbed me during it.

When we landed at Belize International Airport, as the plane taxied to its designated spot half of its occupants fought to get their things out of the overhead storage compartments and a set of mobile stairs was pushed into place by two men who looked as though they wished they were doing something else.

Once off the plane I walked across the warm tarmac towards the arrivals lounge and took in the good old familiar sight of Belize International Airport. And 'old' was the word. I once read in a magazine that when they made the film of the Frederick Forsyth novel *The Dogs of War* they used the airport at Belize as a location. A few years later the film popped up on my TV one night, and sure enough there it was, playing the part of a very run-down airport in an African banana republic. And it played it very well.

Despite a slight attack of Third World Paranoid Floyds as I got nearer and nearer to the airport buildings and all of those black people in uniform, I had no problem with either immigration or customs. I offered my passport to the immigration officer, who clocked me as British army and didn't even open it. (I felt like saying 'Hey you, I worried about this, so at least open the fucking thing and look at it.') I then queued to have my luggage turned over and once again, come my turn, they took one look at me and waved me through. Phew!

Once past customs I walked the width of a door frame and I was outside in Belize – feeling, I might add, quite pleased with myself. An old beaten-up green taxi pulled to a stop at the kerb in front of me. The bright, smiling black face of its driver leaned across the front passenger seat and asked if I wanted to go to Air Port Camp.

'No man,' I replied. 'I want to go into town.'

I then asked how much it would cost (when abroad, always ask). He came back with a figure that sounded about right, so I jumped in the back with my suitcase and said 'Let's go,' to which he replied 'Yeah, man.' And so we goed!

On the journey into town the cab driver, in between the reggae numbers playing on his radio, commented that I look like a British soldier. I replied that I was.

'Then how come you ain't goin' to APC, man?'

Good question.

'I'm not based at APC,' I replied. 'I'm at Rideau Camp, down south, near Punta Gorda. I don't have to be back from leave for another two days, so I thought I'd book into a hotel in town and party late. You ever been to Punta Gorda, man?'

'Yeah, man. Been there a few times. Nice place, if you're a crab.'

As we headed for downtown Belize City the taxi bumped up and down as we hit pothole after pothole.

'You got bad roads here, man,' I remarked.

'Everythin' been goin' downhill since independence,' he replied. Which surprised me, as I had always thought that all Belizians were in favour of the break away from British control. I pressed him to tell me if his was a rare view.

'We all liked the idea at first, man, but now no one fixes the roads, no one fixes nothin'. Nothin' gets done.' And he said that.

When we reached the Fort George Hotel I paid the driver in US dollars, hoped his roads got better for him and made my way to reception. At the desk I asked if they had a special rate for members of the British army, which was a lawyer-type question because I knew they did. I showed the clerk my ID card and booked in for two nights.

Once in my room I unpacked, had a shower and then changed into another set of clothes. I now no longer wanted to look like a British soldier. From now on, if you saw me wandering the streets of Belize City, I wanted you to see 'Yank Wanker Man' on vacation in Central America. The major drawback for me on this one was my hair, which was a bit army-barmy short. But I hadn't shaved for a couple of days, and as clean and lean British soldiers are always closely shaven, at least the surface of my face didn't look army. The major prop in my American disguise was a T-shirt that some friends had brought me back from a trip to Guatemala, which had the words 'Puerto Barrios, Guatemala' printed in nice big green letters across its front. British soldiers never ever go to Guatemala. Well, not to any of the built-up bits, anyway, and even then only because a jungle's a jungle no matter who it belongs to.

Having successfully returned to Belize, it was now time for me to face up to the bit that might prove difficult, not to mention a touch dangerous: 'Scoring the weed, man.' All of my previous bulk buys in Belize had taken place in Punta Gorda. In fact, the only times I had ever scored grass in Belize City were the three times when I'd bought dollar wraps on the street with Dave. But at least on each of those occasions it had been the same street, and what's more, it was a street that was only yards away from my hotel.

After one last check in the mirror I left my room and headed off for a stroll down Sensi-No-Seed Street. Two yards into it I spotted the man for me. He, like me, was playing the 'Let's look American' game. He wore the standard baseball cap, dark glasses and a T-shirt that informed anyone who cared to look that Coca-Cola was the Real Thing. He was sitting alone on a small brick wall, smoking what I recognised, before I could even smell it, as a cone of grass. When I drew level with him I stopped and asked if he knew where I could find such-and-such a place, which was another one of my lawyer-type questions. He replied 'Yeah, man,' got to his feet and began to explain the way. Once he had finished I repeated his directions back to him, pointing down the street and swaying my arm in tune with the song that would get me to where I wanted to go.

I might have liked to believe that I no longer looked like a

British soldier, but at the same time I wanted to be quite sure that if a military police patrol came spinning round the corner it would be perfectly obvious what I, the white man, was doing talking to him, the black man. It may seem funny ha-ha, but an off-duty British soldier talking to a black Belizian is automatically seen as suspicious. Unless, of course, said Belizian is a lady of the night. Perfectly natural, that one, even at two in the afternoon.

Right on cue, a military Land Rover carrying a brace of MPs came spinning round the corner. I almost felt like I'd willed its presence. I had a little panic inside, despite the fact that up to that point I hadn't done anything wrong bar being in Belize without Sir's say-so. Even so, I was relieved when they drove right by without so much as a glance.

End of panic and I'm cool again.

I thanked my new mate for his directions and then, completely out of the blue, asked him if he knew where I could score a couple of wraps of grass. 'Yeah, man,' he said, and from under his T-shirt he pulled out a plastic bag full of dollar wraps. This was Belize City big time, this was, because the wraps were made out of pieces of what had once been a glossy colour magazine. In Punta Gorda wraps were wrapped in bits of at least third-hand brown paper bags. Me, I panicked again and asked him pretty pronto if he would please put his plastic bag back under his T-shirt. Once he'd done that, I asked if he knew the café down by the swing bridge. 'I'd like to have a talk,' I said. Could he meet me there in twenty minutes?

Twenty-five minutes later we were sitting together at a corner table eating egg and chips. He was hungry, I was paying. Once more I gave it to him straight: I wanted to buy ten pounds of grass. Could he supply me with it?

'Yeah, man. No problem,' he said with confidence.

I then asked if it could be sorted out today, and once again with a confident tone he replied, 'Yeah, man. No problem.'

Now it was time to talk about the money.

'How much a pound?' I asked.

'Seventy dollars a pound, man.'

In Punta Gorda I had always paid just sixty, but as $10 Belizian was only equivalent to £3.30, there was little point in causing any bad feeling over what amounted to only £33 on ten weights of bush that I could pass on in England for £6,000. I told him he had a deal. 'Yeah, man.'

Then came the funny bit – and did I laugh? He wanted the money up front.

For some reason that has always been beyond me, a lot of white people consider that black people who live in what are termed Third World countries are basically all as thick as yesterday's custard. No money, no sense. At the same time, though, a lot of those very same black people consider us white folks who live in the so-called civilised Western world basically even thicker than yesterday's custard. Lots of money, no sense. And of course, my new Belizian acquaintance could see that not only was I white but I also appeared to be able to have egg and chips whenever I wanted them. But hey! You've gotta try.

Cash up front was not a possibility, I told him, and if this was an insurmountable problem, then I'd just have to go elsewhere. After all, we weren't in Russia.

He said he would have to check on it and asked me to wait for him to come back, saying he'd be gone about half an hour. He then left the café, leaving me to twiddle my thumbs and wait – something I had not planned to do. 'Marvellous,' thought I. 'Absolutely fucking marvellous.'

So me and me had another cup of tea and then racked the balls for a couple more frames of 'what if?'. And there were a few of them. Like what if he didn't come back? Or even worse, what if he shopped me to the law? After all, I hardly knew the guy, and for all I knew the idea of scoring a couple of Brownie points with the Belizian New William might be right up his street. I then wondered if the Belizian police would fancy approaching a British soldier and accusing him of trying to purchase a class B controlled substance. I fancied not. But, what if the Belizian police went and told the military police? Now that one I could believe in. It would take time, though. So how much?

Lighting up one of my prop Marlboros (and appreciating again that if the Lord had meant me to smoke them, he would surely have seen to it that I was born in New York) I decided that the guy didn't have a minute over the half-hour. If he wasn't back by then, I was out of there.

He returned well within the half-hour and as he sat back down at the table it became his turn to give it to me straight.

'Ten pounds. No problem, man. I'm goin' from town now to pick it up. It's gonna take me a few hours, so any time after seven.'

I realised that it was important that I be the one to choose the point of handover. Midday down a back alley in Torquay was not a possibility, and you could forget completely the one about a back street in Belize at midnight. On the other hand, I hardly wanted to do a handover in the centre of town in broad daylight. Despite my so-called prior preparation and planning, to prevent piss-poor performance, I found that once again I was making it up as I went along.

From my day trip to Belize City with Dave I knew that close to the back of my hotel there was a park. I also knew that the park had no fence around it and there were roads running along each of its three sides. In other words it was open. At the top end of the park there was a war memorial and four or five park benches. I thought that because of its openness and nearness to my hotel, the park was perfect. So I said so.

'You know the war memorial in the park, man?'

'Yeah, man.'

'Meet me there at nine. Be on your own. No one else. I'll have the cash.'

'Yeah, man. No problem. I'll have the herbs.'

And then he left.

Later, back in my hotel room, I counted the money out on my bed. Ten weights of grass at $70 Belizian each was $700, but I didn't have that much in Belizian currency. In fact I didn't even have $100 Belizian. But this was no problem. After all, I was in Central America and anywhere there you can spend American dollars, of which I had plenty.

By a little before nine I was waiting near the monument as arranged. Although this was the rich people's part of town, where the electricity didn't go out twice daily and everybody lived in a fenced-off house with matching dogs in the yard, the street lights weren't that bright, which suited me just fine. I sat down on one of the park benches and took in the view looking out over the ocean. Every now and then I had a slow look around, and it was all perfect – just me, the sea, the stars and my money.

Then I heard a car start. I looked to my left just in time to see a set of weak headlights come on. They pulled away from the kerb and the car slowly started to come towards me. If it was him, then clever him, because he must have watched me arrive and I must have missed him in the darkness.

The car reached me and stopped. Inside I could see that there were four men. So much for my 'no one else' instruction. The nearside front door opened and reggae music from the car's eight-track broke into the silent but not so holy night.

'You got the money, man?' a voice from the car asked.

'Yeah, man,' I replied. 'You got the grass?'

'Yeah, man. Ten pounds, just like you asked.'

With that one of the back doors opened and a large clear plastic bag was passed out.

'OK, man?'

I looked at the bag and immediately knew it didn't contain ten pounds. Five or six maybe, but never ten. So what now? Four of them in the car all guaranteed to be bladed up. Me, alone and unarmed. I didn't think so.

'Yeah. OK, man,' and I handed over the white hotel envelope that I had put the money in.

'See ya, man,' and with that they drove out of my life.

Their car disappeared around a corner and the night once again became just me, the sea and the stars. Except that now we've been joined by a big clear bag full of Mary-do-you-wanna-dance, and all I can think about this is: 'Stupid fucking me.'

For some reason it had not dawned on my limited brain to

bring along a bag to carry the fucking stuff in. I just assumed that it would come wrapped or covered or something. But no. It was in a thick clear plastic bag tied at the top with a twist of wire. Oh well, the best laid plans of mice and thick-shitted dickheads like me . . .

I looked around for other people on the streets. Thankfully there were none. Right, get a grip and be cool. I started to walk back towards the hotel, wondering what to do along the way. One thing was for sure – there was no way I could just go breezing through the hotel's reception with this thing tucked under my arm.

'It's OK. It's for my asthma.'

I needed rid of it, and I needed rid of it like now.

When I came to a clump of bushes that ran alongside the road, I stopped to make sure no one was looking on and pushed the bag into the nearest bush as deep as it would go. I then looked around again. No one.

All I could do then was give what I hoped was a good impression of a casual stroll and head back to the hotel. The clear plastic bag had thrown me. My heart was making out like it had just been through combat, my hands were visibly shaking, and just in case that wasn't enough for me, my mind had joined the mass abandonment of ship and was throwing up a mental picture of the guys who had just sold me the dope telling some policeman around the corner to 'go fetch'.

When I finally, thankfully reached the hotel I walked through reception feeling as though all eyes were upon me. When I got to my room I found a black plastic bin liner, which was going to have to do because bagwise it was all I had, and I headed off back out towards my bush within the bush.

Once outside again I hovered around for a few minutes, checking this way and that before strolling past my hiding place twice. There was no one around. On my third pass I reached into the bush, pulled out the clear plastic bag of dope and hurriedly stuffed it inside the bin liner. With that done, I once again attempted my nervous impression of a casual walk back to the hotel.

When I reached the lobby, with eyes unblinking and looking straight ahead I lasered it past reception. As I walked I tried to look completely blank so as to give no one any reason to stop me. However, just as I reached the doorway to the corridor that led to my ground floor room I heard a voice, and for a flash I genuinely believed that I was experiencing the beginning of a stroke.

'Hey, Ken! What are you doing here, guy?'

It was Larry, the tropical fish buyer from Miami.

Since my first visit to Belize City back in April I had visited this hotel four times now, and on each and every occasion I had run into Larry. Call it the old Central American paranoia if you like, but I was seriously beginning to wonder about Larry and what he might really do for a living.

'Larry!' I quickly replied, praying to Jehovah that I sounded like I was happy to see him. 'Hey, if we go on meeting like this, people are going to talk.'

Once again I found myself in a situation where I was going to have to make up my story as I said it out loud for the first time, because the last time I had seen my good mate Larry was on the night before I flew back to England, so he knew that I'd finished my time in Belize some three months ago. As my brain did a rapid search for a believable reason why I should be standing on a carpet in Belize opposite him (I couldn't use American Linda because Larry knew her), all I could do was try and avoid answering Larry's questions by asking some of my own. So I just pretended that I hadn't heard him ask what I was doing here and instead asked him what he was doing here.

Thankfully, Larry being Larry, instead of just replying 'Buying fish' he went off on a two-thousand-word explanation that began right back at his shop in Miami. This, praise the Lord, allowed me the time, while I stood there smiling and nodding away, to come up with a story of my own. I decided it was going to be that I'd had to come back to Belize to act as a witness at a court martial that was taking place the following day.

Luckily (and from where I was nervously standing with a

black plastic bag full of class B narcotics there was no other word for it), Larry was in a rush to meet someone and so all I had to do was give him my room number and agree to meet him for a drink in the bar when he got back in an hour or two.

Relieved that my torment was over, I immediately about-turned and headed straight for my room. When I got there I locked the door behind me and threw down the bag of dope as if holding it any longer would have given me syphilis. Then, for the second time since it had come into my possession, which can't have been much more than fifteen minutes ago, I started to wish that I'd never scored the stupid stuff in the first place.

I began to pace up and down my room like the caged worried trooper that I had become. My mind raced away, piling on thought after negative thought, and I soon realised that if I didn't want to have a complete breakdown, then I was going to have to get a grip. And quick. So I started by trying to convince myself that it was no good wasting energy wishing I hadn't bought the grass, because I had and that was that. All I could do now was keep my thoughts together and get on with the job of getting me and that large bag of dope over there back to England.

I guess ten minutes or so passed before I was finally able to gain the necessary amount of control to start breathing normally once more and get around to asking myself a few logical questions. The fact that I was due to meet Larry again later put him right to the top of my 'problems to be thought through' list. When I did see him I was sure to have to come up with some explanation for my return to Belize, so I started to build a few details around the court martial I had dreamt up for the morning.

The only experience I'd had of coming into contact with a military police investigation had been when one of the guys in my patrol in Northern Ireland had stuck his rifle butt into the face of an inhabitant of Forkhill. If the truth be known, all boys together, a case could be made that the local and his loud mouth had deserved everything they got, but by the time the SIB – the Special Investigation Branch of the Royal Military

Police – got around to interviewing us, we hadn't seen doodly-squat. So, realising that it's always best to construct a lie around a truth, I based my court martial story on another soldier who had hit a local in the Rose Garden Club when our company was in Belize City to do the parachute jump.

With that out the way, I was suddenly gripped by a thought that had me wondering if the dope I had just bought really was dope. After all, they'd ripped me off over the weight, so why not the quality as well? I quickly picked up the bag and began to inspect its contents through the transparent plastic. It certainly looked the business, but there again, so did that two ounces of crap that Dave and I bought that time in Punta Gorda.

There was only one thing for it – to put my mind at rest I was going to have to sample the product. So I undid the wire twist, pulled out a couple of fingers' worth of sticky green stuff and knocked up a neat one-skinner. Then I lit up what turned out to be my third big mistake of the day.

Any fears I may have held about the grass's quality had totally disappeared by the fourth toke, and by the fifth I realised that it would probably be a wise move on my part to put it out for 'Ron'. For this stuff, without a doubt, was as strong as the grass Dave and I had smoked that day by the river. I was therefore now very stoned, and I do mean very. So much so that I had once again reached a point in my life where I was wishing I hadn't smoked the joint I just did.

Checking for the third time that my hotel door was locked, I turned the lights out and lay on the bed hoping to come to terms with my new state of mental health. Outside my ground floor room the conversations between insects that take place outside every window in Belize at night started to come at me in quadraphonic sound. I felt like I was tripping. In fact I was tripping. So with nowhere else for my stoned self that wished it wasn't to go, I headed off into my own mind. And once I arrived there it wasn't too long before I was overtaken by a feeling of total panic. What was I doing lying on a hotel bed in Central America, stoned out of my mind, with a bag of marijuana in the wardrobe? I was miles away from being the highly planned military type of guy that I dreamed I was. After all, just look at how I'd handled things so far. How could I have been so stupid as to not take a bag with me when I went to pick up the dope? How could I do that? And then, when I ran into Larry, where was my prior preparation and planning in the event of ambush? I should have had stories prepared for every eventuality, but I hadn't. And what was I doing smoking a joint? I had broken the number one golden rule. I had smoked on my dope – meaning I had smoked a joint in a place where I was concealing a large quantity of marijuana. One whiff of the air in this room and my game was up instantly. I should never have smoked a joint. Never. So why had I?

The truth was, I just didn't know. That was just me. Though one thing was for sure, if was I going to make it back to the UK with me and that bag of dope over there intact, then I was going to have to seriously raise my mental game.

To achieve this I realised that the first thing I had to do was stop pushing negative thoughts into my own brain, and to this end I jumped up from the bed and threw the lights on. Then I went over to the radio and found a music station that I could bop along to. I had to change the stimuli that surrounded my thoughts, which is the thing to do whenever anything you may have taken has a go at taking over you. I took off my clothes and stepped into the shower, but as I stood under the cool running water my heart took another leap. The phone in my room had started to ring.

Who could that be? A quick working out of the odds said it had to be Larry, even if it was a little early for him to be back from his appointment. Another scenario that flashed through my mind had two military policemen waiting in the hotel's reception for me to pick up the phone. But that couldn't be. Could it? MPs would surely just come knocking on my door. Wouldn't they?

One thing was for sure – there was no way in the world that I was going anywhere near that phone, never mind pick it up and start talking into it. Before I could get around to changing my mind on this one, the ringing stopped.

Just as I had come to terms with this and dropped the burden of not answering it, my mind once again flashed a picture of a couple of MPs, only this time they were out of reception and on their way to my room. So what if there was a knock on the door? I wouldn't answer it. It was all I could think to do. I quickly sprang into action and turned off the lights and the radio. Then in the darkness I sat on the end of my bed and waited for the knock on the door. I imagined how it would sound and then imagined the noise of a master key being turned in the lock.

A good few minutes later I was still imagining and still waiting. But no knock came, and eventually I started to believe that it never would. But what should I do now? I decided to wander over to reception and ask who it was who had rung me, on the excuse that my phone had stopped ringing before I'd had time to get out of the shower to answer it. So once I'd finally managed to convince myself that I was straight enough, I left my room in search of the answer to who had been on the phone. When I reached reception my quick on-the-spot calculations in the shower turned out to be correct because there was a message waiting for me from Larry.

Ten minutes later a much relieved me finally caught up with Larry in the hotel bar. He was sitting on the exact same stool he had been occupying the last time I had seen him in the bar three months before. Larry was the only customer and along with the Belizian barman he was watching TV. Once we'd said our hellos and Larry had got the first round in, as predicted I had to explain all about the court martial I was supposedly attending the next day. All in all I think I gave a pretty convincing performance and Larry seemed to take it all in hook, line and sinker. But there again, why shouldn't he?

Playing on the TV above us as we talked was the American TV channel that was it as far as television in Belize was concerned. It came in via satellite from, I think, Chicago to Belize City and then from there it was transmitted out to the rest of the country. As a background and something that I might look up at every now and then, the TV was fine. Where I lost control with it was when Larry went off to use the little white boys' room (it's a Belizian joke) and I got involved in watching a commercial break.

The ad that did it to me, made me spit out my drink and go off on a bout of uncontrollable laughter, opened at a yuppie-type office party where everyone was disco-dancing like the Sour Grape bunch on the Banana Splits. But hold on. What's this? One man on the dance floor is hardly moving at all. And there's more . . . the sexy chick he's dancing with is none too happy about it. Oh no, she's left him for another, groovier dancer.

Just as I'm beginning to wonder what product this ad is leading up to, a caption appears on the screen, backed up by a voiceover for the illiterate: 'Are you a safe dancer?' Speaking for myself, I didn't know, but the man who had lost the girl certainly was. Then a tube appeared above the caption. 'Oh, he's using the wrong toothpaste,' I thought, 'that's why he can hardly dance.' But no, it's not a tube of toothpaste that's on the screen, it's a tube of haemorrhoid cream.

Luckily for our budding John Travolta, someone else at the party, who has noticed his 'safe' dancing, happens to have a tube of the cream on him. So it's off to the bathroom for a spot of out-of-view application, and before you know it our man is back at the party – and he's now one dangerous dancer.

I was finding the ad so funny that the only thing I could do was quickly down a couple of large Southern Comforts and use my favourite Punta Gorda ploy of getting pissed to hide the fact that I was stoned.

When Larry got back, funnily enough he said something about me that I had already been thinking about him.

'You know something,' he said, 'the last four times I've come to this place I've run into you.'

'Just a coincidence, I suppose,' I said.

'Of course,' Larry replied. 'What else?'

Though to this day I still do wonder about Larry. Was he

maybe a drug-runner himself? Or maybe a member of the CIA? After all, there were enough of them floating around Central America to start a war. Or maybe, maybe he really was just a tropical fish buyer out of Miami?

Had I been James Bond I could no doubt have turned around and asked Larry what water temperature the Belizian *Swimmis finnis* has to be kept in or something. But I wasn't, so I couldn't, and all I could come up with were a few run-of-the-mill enquiries of the kind you might make about anyone's occupation. Except, of course, the one about how do you get the fish back to the States? (In water-filled plastic bags on aeroplanes apparently.)

By the time Larry and I parted company that night I had drunk far too much, and the next morning I didn't wake up until around ten, which was much later than I'd planned. Though hey! – there was hardly anything new about me straying from the plan. My first decision of the day was to get checked out of the hotel, el pronto, and go find another one to stay in. I had three exceptionally good reasons for this. Firstly, the guys I had scored the grass off last night probably realised that I was staying here as it was only a stone's throw away from the park where we had transacted our late-night business. Secondly, Larry had said the night before that he was going to be around for a few more days, and I didn't really want to meet good old Larry again. And last but by no means least, I was now going to have to go steady with my money, which straight away made this hotel far too expensive for me.

Fortunately I did know of another, smaller hotel, which (conveniently for me and my bag of dope) was situated right on the other side of town. I knew of its whereabouts because Carol and I had had a passing drink there when she was over on holiday. I also recalled that when we were at the bar we struck up a conversation with a couple of back-packing Americans who were booked into the place for the night, which, roughly translated, meant that it was probably not that expensive to lay your head there.

I managed to check out of my old hotel without running into

Larry again (which was just as well, as he might have wondered why I wasn't knee deep in military justice by now) and caught a taxi over to my new hideout. When I got there, fortunately they had a vacant room for the two nights I required, and at a rate that was $30US per night cheaper than the last place.

Once I was booked in and comfy with my new surroundings it became time for me to face up to the task of parcelling up the dope and getting it posted up at Air Port Camp. The first thing I needed to do was go out and buy some wrapping paper and Sellotape. In itself this turned out to be not such a stunningly difficult thing to do, though I cursed myself along the way for not having had the foresight to bring tape and wrapping paper with me from England.

When I got back from my shopping I double-locked my door and immediately started to get my parcel together. Two seconds later I stopped abruptly. What a dick! I had gone off and bought paper and tape but had forgotten to buy something, a small holdall for example, to carry the parcel in once it was wrapped. I gave myself yet another mental slap and headed off outside again to purchase a bag, returning a short while later with a red holdall made out of the Chinese Republic's finest plastic.

I wrapped the dope inside a couple of army shirts and a pair of army issue boots, then taped it all up into a real neat-looking parcel and addressed it to myself in Aldershot. With that finally done, I went into the bathroom and shaved off my stubble, thereby turning myself back into everyone's image of a British soldier.

Then I did something which to this day I just don't understand. I picked up my newly wrapped parcel, tucked it snugly into its new red holdall and left the hotel. Outside I flagged down the first passing taxi, and when the driver asked 'Where to, man?' I said 'Take me to Air Port Camp, please.' Now, in itself that wouldn't have been too bad – after all, I did need to go to the camp to post the parcel – but by the time I climbed into the cab it was lunchtime and I knew that when I reached the camp the post room would be closed. And still I went.

Arriving at APC some twenty minutes later, I waltzed my way past the two Gurkhas on gate guard with a simple flash of my ID card. Just to make sure, my first port of call was the post office, whose door, just as I had known it would be, was closed until two o'clock. So, with time to kill, I headed in the direction of the NAAFI, where I hoped my presence would not attract attention. The only consolation was that APC was a large camp made up of many different cap badges, not to mention a whole pile of RAF personnel, so the chances were that half the people in the place had never seen each other before.

The good news when I arrived at the NAAFI was that there was a troop movement going on. The place was overflowing with soldiers dressed in civvies who were all, just like me, carrying hand baggage. I also concluded, since they all had skin as white as snow, that they had just arrived in Belize. I bought myself a good old mug of English tea and found a nice camouflaged seat among a group of the newly arrived who were watching a video.

Not surprisingly, at one point I did have to ask myself the serious question of why I was sitting where I was. It went without saying that by being on the camp with a holdall of dope between my legs I was at my most vulnerable. Anyone could wander over, especially one of those interfering types with a crown on their forearm, and ask me who I was and, even more to the point, what was I doing there. So why hadn't I just delayed my departure from the hotel so that I would have arrived when the post office was open? The only excuse I've ever been able to come up with is that I was just overly keen to get on with it.

Another not too pleasant reality that dawned on me, as I sipped on my tea, was that I hadn't invented a cover story should anyone start asking me questions. So what if? The best I could come up with was that I had just been released from the military hospital and was waiting for my return to unit. As I had stayed in APC's hospital for nearly a week with my bout of 'Non-Specific Tropical Disease' (doctor's talk for they didn't know what), I did know all about the hospital. And if I was pressed further, I'd mention how contagious my condition was and cough a lot over whoever was doing the asking.

I had just finished my tea and was debating whether or not to have another mug when a sergeant appeared in front of the TV and ordered my camouflage to go and climb aboard trucks that were now waiting for them outside. When the last one of them had walked out of the NAAFI, all that remained in the way of people were me and two others. Considering it was lunchtime, and late lunchtime at that, I would have thought that a NAAFI on a camp this size would have had a few more people in it. But no, and it was typical – when I didn't want soldiers about they were everywhere, and when I did, what did I get? I got two.

And then it became none. The remaining two soldiers finished their drinks and, being good lads, returned their empty bottles to the counter and then they left. Marvellous. Now it was just me.

I was probably worrying too much, but I really did feel I was sticking out like a white rabbit in a coal bunker. I had to get out of this place and like now, please. I returned my mug to the counter, because I was a good lad myself, and spent the next however long it was walking circuits of the road that ran around the interior of the camp. Eventually, finally, thankfully, I saw a corporal, who looked to me like a man who was going to work, entering the post office. When I followed him into the place a few minutes later I found out that the corporal was, in fact, a customer. I also found out why the NAAFI had been so empty: every fucker was in the post office. There was a queue of four or five waiting to be served and just as many others filling out forms and whatever around the room. Having sent a few parcels in my time, I didn't need to ask what had to be done to send one to England. I filled out a customs declaration, which ended up somewhat lacking in detail as to the parcel's complete contents, and took my place in the queue. When I reached the counter I handed the parcel over, it got weighed and stamped and paid for, and then I said thank you (though meaning thank fuck) and marched my little relieved self right out of the door.

It was done. And by the time I'd made it back out through the camp's gate and climbed into one of the taxis on hanging-around duty outside, looking back, it all seemed like a piece of cake. Easy, in fact.

Now all I had to do was get myself home. Even easier.

Miami and home

The time to leave Belize finally arrived. And finally was the word, as I really did want nothing more than to get out of the hot sticky place. My business had been done, the parcel was on its way, homeward bound, and the only way I could look at things was that the longer I stayed around sunny Belize City, the more chance I had of being asked something by someone that I'd have trouble providing an answer for.

When the plane touched down back in Miami it was late morning. Today I don't remember a single moment after leaving the hotel in Belize City right up until I found myself standing in front of a glorified burger/hot dog bar in Miami airport. In my hand I was counting out my American small change and working out if I could afford a meal or not. My connecting flight back to England didn't leave until the following afternoon, and of course I'd overspent in Belize, so I didn't have enough money left to get myself a hotel room for the night and was going to have to camp down in the airport.

Now, here's a thing that's good about having been in the army. In the army you get to spend lots and lots of time waiting for things: trucks to come and pick you up, planes to take you away, helicopters to circle and land, even people to decide 'Right, let's go' for you. Mostly, and I don't know how they manage to work it that way but they do, these times of waiting tend to take place in the rain, in the middle of a field, and normally somewhere in the middle of nowhere. So you're wet and you're cold, and chances are you don't even know how long you're going to have to remain that way. In Northern

Ireland I had spent up to six days at a time just sitting in rainy hedgerows, watching and waiting to ambush something with four walls and a roof, while eating, shitting and sleeping within the confines of a two-metre radius. All you can do when faced with such mind-numbing adversity is learn to come to terms with it, learn to accept the things in life that you have no power to change. And being in the army learns you that good.

So try as I might to have a moan about my circumstances in the warm and dry interior of Miami airport, nice coffee machine over there, hot running water in the washrooms, I couldn't really get into it because I knew that life had the potential to be a whole lot worse. Though I do recall having a five-minute mind tantrum about handing over too much cash in Belize for the grass. I could have done with it now and got real angry with me about it.

I roamed the airport for an hour or so and kept myself interested for a moderate amount of time by working out how to operate a vending machine that sold instant travel insurance, which was something I'd never seen before. The idea was that you took an envelope, filled out the form inside it with your name, rank, number and flight details, added some cash depending on how much you figured your death was worth, and then popped it all into the slot provided. If your plane then fell out of the sky – 'Bingo', it's pay day.

Just a couple of points on this one. Firstly, if your plane did crash, then who was to know that you'd filled out the form in the first place? You could, of course, make a phone call before takeoff: 'Hi, honey. Plane gets in at eight. Should be home by ten. By the way if I get killed on the way . . .' I don't think so. And unlike circulars from the Reader's Digest Company, on the machine there were no pictures of Lucky Mr X from Wyoming who'd won a cheque for $200,000 when the 747 he was riding made like a tin can into Dallas airport. So where was the proof that they had ever paid out to anyone?

I had also seen enough episodes of *Starsky and Hutch* in my youth to know that America was a place of many crazy people, who all had guns. What if some Yankee suicidal loony-tune decided do the right thing by his wife and kids, took out a million dollars in life insurance and then blew himself and me to kingdom come? No, I decided that I did not like the idea of on-the-spot vended travel insurance.

I must have got fed up with touring the airport, because by early afternoon I was sitting in a bar wondering if I could afford another Southern Comfort and Coke, and if so, how long I'd have to drag it out before I could bear to spend more money on another one. The bar, or so I gleaned from the barmaid, was unusually busy for the time of day. Heavy snow had been cancelling flights all over America and the knock-on delays had dominoed their way down to sunny Miami. Next to me on a stool at the bar was an overweight guy with a small moustache, no neck and clothes that appeared to be just a little tight all over. I would guess he was ten or so years older than me, and with nothing else for either of us to do, we started up a conversation. He was stopping over from somewhere on the way to somewhere else, and because of the snow up north his connecting plane had been delayed, which meant that he had at least another six hours to wait.

'Six hours!' I said. 'I bloody dream of having only six hours to wait. Bloody luxury that would be. When I was a lad we used to have to wait for six years just to use the toilet. Course, it wasn't really a toilet, just a bucket with a hole. But it was a toilet to us.'

'Oh, that's Monty Python, right? I love those guys,' he said. 'You're English, right? My second cousin Tony's been to England.'

No. He wasn't going to ask me if I knew him. Was he?

I extract the urine, but actually, like most Americans he was just a normal down-the-middle decent type of guy. Had played college football as well. When I told him about my financial situation he insisted on buying me drinks for us long as I was with him, which, as it turned out, and it's funny the way things sometimes do, was to be for a lot longer than I would have imagined. And to lead to all sorts of unplanned adventures.

They began, as so many twists in life do, with two women

walking into a crowded bar (in this case, the one we were in). They found a space next to us, and after they'd ordered their drinks the guy I was sitting with, who I think was called Mike, began to swap life stories with them, which again is a very American sort of thing to do. They'll talk to anyone, and the simple fact that someone else is American is more than enough in common for them.

I would say that one of the girls was in her late thirties and the other in maybe her late teens or early twenties. What they looked like I now have no memory of, although I do recall that at the time I would have been happy to have got personal with either one of them, which means that they must have been at least a little bit attractive, as back then looks were a big thing for me come pick-a-lady time.

The girls, who I'll call Maggie and May, were old friends. They had apparently just flown into Miami from two different parts of God's own country to meet up for a holiday with another friend who lived in Miami (and it starts to get a little complicated now), but they couldn't move in with their friend in Miami, who lived on a small yacht, until the following day, because he had some other friends using up the bunks that night. He was also at work right now, which was why he hadn't come out to the airport to meet them and why they were still here and in no hurry to go anywhere else.

So what were they going to do? Well, they decided to come into this bar and have a drink and think about it. And as they thought away out loud, Mike ordered another round of drinks.

Six or seven drinks later Mike's pissed (as in the English definition of the word), I'm not too far behind him, the girls are flirting like crazy, and I don't know how, but the next thing I know we're all going off to rent a car on Mike's credit card and one of the girls' driving licences for a few hours of sightseeing in Miami. The actual negotiation of the hire car I wasn't a part of, though I did explain that I couldn't afford to chip in towards the cost and if they wanted to go off without me, then I was out of here. Unfortunately, they wouldn't hear of it.

'No, guy. You're coming with us.'

The plan, as best I could understand it, was that we'd go for a spin around town, the girls would drop me and Mike back at the airport, we'd say bye-bye, they'd get to keep the car for the rest of the day and then off they'd go to meet their friend from his work.

So we loaded the girls' suitcases into the back of the car, leaving Mike's and mine in a couple of luggage lockers, and then I'm sitting in the back of the rental car with the younger May sat here next to me and we're rolling over six-lane freeways and past huge skyscrapers, roof down, rock radio on, and boy, have I landed on my feet with this one. I then wondered if the younger May sat here next to me would be up for it.

We drove around the city centre for an hour or so before Mike decided, on a whim, that he'd like another drink. Parking was going to be a problem, as was finding a bar, and so in the interests of economy, both financial and timewise, Mike decided that we'd best find an off-licence – or a liquor store, as he referred to it.

Good idea.

We drove out of the city centre and into that part of town that most cities have, which lies somewhere in the grey area between where most people work and where most people live. We stopped on a wide four-lane avenue alongside a row of liquor stores, supermarkets, takeaway food shops and used car lots. On the other side of the street was a large building that appeared to be the American equivalent of a British DHSS office (as they were still called then), all of the shops in the surrounding area displayed signs saying that they were pre-pared to cash welfare checks inside, on the street most of the people that passed were either black or Hispanic – and this wasn't fiction. All around was exactly as the mean streets of big city USA were portrayed on *Starsky and Hutch*. Right away, because I'm quick, me, I figured that this was not a good part of town for us tourist types to be hanging out in. Mike got out of the car to go to the liquor store, and me, excitement-seeker that I am, volunteered to go along with him. Mike was drunk and flash to boot, and so he got a bottle of Jim Beam for him, a bottle of Southern Comfort for me and a bottle of something brown that I'd never heard of before for the two girls.

The shop, as far as its layout and fridges and all the knick-knacks that make up seven-eleven consumerism were concerned, was fine. What wasn't was the type of customers that were skulking around its floor space and queuing at its two tills. Behind one of these was a tall, thin rake of a lad who, judging by the condition of his skin and his greasy, uncombed long hair, was either a heroin addict or a student with a bad case of acne. As for the people he was serving, they certainly didn't look or dress like they were citizens of the richest country on the planet.

Watching them, and especially those in the aisle with the rows of 'hard liquor', was a black security guard whose main eye-catcher was a large holstered pistol that hung from his right hip. At the time I don't think we had reached the point in England where it had become necessary for a guard to stand over the spirits counter on the lookout for winos trying to grab a free hit, although today all the supermarkets in my home town have either an overweight or an overaged security guard watching the legal liquid drugs. Fortunately, we don't have a constitution that guarantees the right to blow each other's brains out, so none of them are packing at the hip. Guns in Tesco's? Can't ever see it. Well, all right – in Belfast, maybe.

Mike paid for our bottles, having the quick on-the-spot sense to score a pack of plastic tumblers as well (so he couldn't have been that out of it) and we headed off back to the car. As we drove away I began pouring out the drinks in the back seat, which apparently was a highly illegal thing to do in America, as I dare say it is in England. I passed Maggie her drink, of what I think was chocolate-flavoured scotch with a coconut flake top, and as she took a hold she commented that she could sure do with a hit of grass right now.

And I thought, well, I haven't contributed much here, except of course for my good looks and witty conversation, and as it so happens I do have a small bag of Belize's finest stuck down the crutch of my underpants . . . say 'cheese'.

'You got some grass? All right!'

I knew enough about smoking dope the American way not to put any tobacco in with it, so I rolled a neat little tight one-skinner and popped a cardboard roach in the end. I got it lit up, had a couple of tokes and then passed it forward to Mike. I figured that one little joint wasn't going to go far between the four of us, so I got down to knocking up another one, which as it happens proved to be a good thing, 'cos the one that went up front never did come home again.

Now, I'd been smoking this dope every day for near on seven months, and as with most things in life that are taken in excess, I had built up a resistance to it. Even so, the gear we were now smoking had still ripped off my face when I tried it back in Belize and so I shouldn't have been that surprised when my three travelling companions suddenly developed all sorts of problems of the out-of-your-head kind.

It started when Mike turned into a stuck gramophone record that kept exclaiming 'I'm really stoned. I'm *really* stoned. I am really stoned.'

'Me too. Me too,' chirped Maggie and May.

Now me, I'm feeling a bit that way myself, but I ain't going on about it. And more to the point, I'm having a great time with it. Unfortunately Mike wasn't, and after mumbling something about not being able to handle it any longer, he slammed on the brakes and we came to an abrupt halt in the middle lane of what now appeared to be a hundred-lane freeway.

Oh fuck.

As if that wasn't enough, he then hung himself out the window and vomited the contents of his more than oversized guts on to the road. Maggie and May's reaction to all of this was hardly helpful. As the people in the cars behind began tooting their horns and shouting out words Paul and Arty never heard in the bible, Maggie and May just fell apart. While Maggie turned into another stuck gramophone record that kept praying 'oh my God, oh my God', May turned on me, demanding to know what it was I had slipped into the smoke.

'It's just smoke,' I said, though I could tell she didn't believe me.

Something inside of me realised that we had to get out of here and quick. Stopped in the middle of a motorway, stoned, pissed and with booze bottles on the floor, was not a good place to be. Mike came back from hanging out of the window and promptly slumped his head on to his chest and passed out. My first thought was that he was dead, but after a quick feel of what went for a neck on him I found a pulse and realised that he was only sleeping. Fucking only.

I asked Maggie if she could drive. Her helpful answer to my desperate question was to get out of the car and start walking away upstream against the oncoming traffic. In five words, I couldn't fucking believe it. Today I think I should have done the exact same thing and just got out and walked, leaving Mike to face Crocket and Tubbs when they turned up, as turn up they surely would. But I guess it was an army-type thing that wouldn't allow me to leave a wounded buddy. I knew I had to sort it out.

By this time the ever-helpful May is curled up into a ball next to me, accusing me of spiking her dope with LSD and crying like a baby: 'Why me?'

Outside, vehicles were beginning to pile up behind us and the chorus of horns and verbal abuse was growing louder with every new arrival. I just had to do something. So, hero that I am, I leaned over from the back of the car and somehow managed to pull, push and threaten two-ton Mike into the passenger seat. I then climbed in next to him and started up the car. Something I hadn't noticed from the back was that the car was an automatic, and of course I'd never driven one before. As it turned out, and thankfully, my guess that 'D' was for drive proved correct and once I'd got going it was easier than I expected, though I still kept reaching for the clutch and still kept wishing it was a manual.

Another problem to add to the day's growing list – and come

on, pile 'em on – was that I had never driven on the wrong side of the road before either, and what had by now grown into a thousand-lane motorway in America didn't appear to me to be an ideal place to start. The only thing I seemed to have going for me was that in America they drive a lot slower than we do back home, although, stoned as I was, it was still far too fast for my complete appreciation.

Twenty seconds of me trying to drive calm, breathe calm, think calm and be calm later we drew level with Maggie, who was still walking up the freeway bound for where only her out-of-it brain knew where. I would have tooted the horn, but I couldn't find it, so I slowed down and shouted her name. She stopped and I pulled over, and then May immediately flung open the back door and darted out to be with Maggie. So now I'd got both of them out of the car, and even worse, both of them were not prepared to get back into it with me, the madman who according to them had put some kind of herbal Mickey Finn in with the smoke, causing Mike to die and them to freak out. No way, Mr Englishman. They weren't stupid. (Oh yes they fucking were.)

Now what I had on my hands here, and I knew full well because I had been to that place a few times myself, was two irrationally paranoid people of the stoned kind. Of course I wasn't some sort of crazed killer who went around doing whatever it was they thought I was going to do, and anybody could have seen that. Anybody who wasn't out of it, that is.

Well, by this time I'm not happy about anything and I'm starting to imagine in great detail a cop car coming along and us all getting busted, and the paranoid sisters screaming that I tried to date-rape them, and us being hauled off to the jail and then up before a judge, and then on and on and on all the way up to me being back in battalion trying to explain what I was doing on leave in Belize and Miami over Christmas.

Fuck 'em. I pressed the petrol and left them to it. If they wanted to walk, then they could walk. I had to get Mike here to a coffee and then me and him back to the airport.

About a quarter-mile up the road I came upon a large gas

station attached to a small city that went by the name of Hypermarket. I had read somewhere, and please don't take this as gospel as it might not be true, that the best thing to have when you're out of your head is fresh orange juice. Since Mike was certainly out of something, I found a parking space in the garage forecourt and headed off inside in search of bottled vitamin C in liquid form. I found it in Falls Road Catholic family-sized containers, which thankfully still only cost about 3p, and lugged one of them back out to the car and the waiting lips of Mr Sleeping Blubber. (I should point out that by this point I really didn't go a lot any more on Mike, the fat American civvie wanker who couldn't handle his narcotic intake.)

I was just starting to slap him awake so as to try and pour some orange juice down his throat, when lo and behold, who should I see coming over to the car but Maggie and May. Before I could get so much as a syllable out, Maggie started screaming at me that if I didn't give them back their luggage that I'd stolen they were going to call the cops. And then I'd be in trouble, mister.

To say the least, I was now finding all of this somewhat frustrating. Looking back, we'd had a big problem when we were stopped in the middle of the freeway with Mike passed out in the driver's seat, but that nightmare was over and we should rejoice. We'd moved on to here and all we had to do now was get Mike back to the land of the conscious and then ourselves back to the airport. So I tried to reason with the girls.

I said this and I explained that, I asked them to think about it, and then I said: 'Would I be talking to you here now if I was the crazy guy you think I am?' What won the day for me, though, was showing them my passport . . . and my army ID card . . . and my plane ticket back to England for the following day . . . and saying: 'Look, why don't you phone your friend at his work, tell him where you are and who you're with, give him my name and passport details, and then if anything did happen to you he'd be able to tell the police exactly who you were with. Now would I let you do that if I intended to hurt you?'

(Strangely enough, by this point I wouldn't have minded hurting them, so maybe the safety clause was just as much for my benefit as theirs.)

Maggie and May put their silly heads together and finally said OK, and off they went to phone their friend. I went back to slapping awake Mike, who by now was definitely coming around in a groggy sort of way (and who I could quite happily have knocked unconscious again). By the time the girls returned Mike was half-awake and asking what had happened, and the girls' phone call to their friend had done the trick and they were both all smiles again.

'Ah gee. We're really sorry about that,' they said.

I told them I understood and said that was OK – I didn't mean it, of course, but anything for a quiet life. Mike was still ten light years away from being able to drive, though, so it was still going to have to be yours truly at the wheel if we were to get him back to the airport in time to catch his flight.

Now where was the airport?

It was a good question, and one that I knew I was going to get no help in answering from either Maggie, May or the Comatose Kid. The international language of sign came to my rescue with a silhouette of a white plane on a green background that told me to get my butt off the freeway at the next junction.

And then we were at the airport. Mike, bye-bye, fuck off and I hope we never meet again, and as for you girls, likewise. And I'm out the car and off in search of the luggage lockers. Five minutes later I find them, get my baggage out and turn around in search of a place to wait, when lo and behold again, it's Maggie and May again. And 'oh look' they were sorry for what happened 'all right?' but 'gee, guy' they had both been tripping, and well, they got scared and 'kinda freaked out'. But whatever, they were really, really sorry, and to make up they said that if I wanted to I could come and crash in their hotel room for the night.

Normally I don't need a lot of make-your-mind-up time when choosing between comfort and discomfort, and let's face it boys, a night in a hotel room with two good-looking girls, even if they are loonies, is better than sitting in an airport chair tick-tocking the seconds away. But then that was the problem, they were both top-of-the-class grade A certifiable loonies. And American as well.

But you know what? So was I. Not American, of course (I'm no mongrel – pure English/Polish/Irish/Scottish, me), but I could match loony with the best of them.

Before we went anywhere the girls wanted to phone their friend again to see about meeting up later. As we headed towards a row of phone boxes, there across the way, being guided by an airline employee, was Mike. And 'cos I'm a nice guy who can never hold a grudge for long, I was glad to see that he had acquired a chaperone.

The loony twins made their phone call and the plan now was for us to pick up their friend from the marina where his boat was moored (see, I did learn something from hanging out with all those sailors) and from there we'd go find a hotel.

'Do you mind driving again, guy?' asked Maggie.

Well I did actually, but as the only alternative was to have one of them behind the wheel, I could live with it. (Although maybe this was the real reason they'd invited me along?)

How we ended up finding the marina I can't today imagine, let alone remember, but somehow we did, and waiting for us when we got there was their friend Carl, whose name I still remember today because the only other Carl I'd ever met was one of my best friends/worst enemies at infant school.

Carl was dressed appropriately in plimsolls, jeans, a turtle-neck jumper and a bright yellow waterproof windcheater. Well, lived on a yacht, didn't he? He was about thirtyish, and one of those types who's very laid back to the point of being annoying. He hardly ever said a word, and when he did it was so quietly that you missed half of it, even if you strained to listen.

Carl was going to join us for the night and stay with us in the hotel room. I did wonder just how crowded this hotel room was going to be, and even more so when we got to the chosen hotel and May, Carl and me were instructed to hide out in the bar while Maggie checked into a single room.

Single room? Well, they do say everything's bigger in America, and if hotel rooms are anything to go by then they ain't lying. It was huge, with two beds that could have slept four apiece.

By this time it had become apparent, and I am quick, that Maggie and Carl were boyfriend/girlfriend. I had thought so when they greeted each other with a deep-tongued snog at the marina, and I really knew so when they jumped into the shower together as soon as we reached the room.

And boy, were they loud about it. Or at least, she was. I like to think of myself as a man of the world, someone who's been to a few places – hey! – slept with a few chicks, but I'd never heard anything like it in my life. Talk about talk to the animals. She was a whole jungle. So much so that because I'm really English at heart, it got to be embarrassing to hear. What made it worse was May, who spent the whole performance sitting in a chair, quiet as a mouse, reading a magazine. Oh, American girls. And they are, they're terrible. Pick you up in bars, take you home, have their wicked way with you, and the next day they never phone.

When the noise coming from the bathroom finally ended in a stunningly abrupt and even more embarrassing silence, the water was turned off and I turned to May, popped on my best ironic break-the-ice smile and asked if she'd like a shower now. Which was a joke, right? Wrong. Not to May it wasn't. She made it perfectly clear in fluent Feminist that she was not available and did not appreciate my sexual harassment, which I thought was a bit strong coming from the girl who had been all over me back at the airport bar. Desperate for it back then she was, and now it turns out that she's a Lesbian.

So I told her straight that she had been getting me wrong all day and I had no wish whatsoever to 'go to bed with her', and that her opinion of me was, frankly, not only an insult but hurtful as well. Poor me. (Wouldn't have wanted to shag that anyway, unless of course she'd let me).

When Maggie and Carl returned to the room from their water sex they got dressed again and then left me alone, which was perfect by me, while the three of them went for a quick walkabout around Miami. They did say before they left that they would be gone for a couple of hours, but as it came to pass, they were hardly gone for one.

While they were away Maggie must have told Carl all about the grass I had, because as soon as they returned he asked, all laid back, if he could see it. Sure. Why not? By the way he examined it and smelt it and ran it through his fingers, I figured that May's hallucination about it containing LSD had been passed on, and when I asked the two girls if they'd like another smoke, they both said that they were never going to smoke grass again. So no, thank you.

'What about you, Carl? Would you like a smoke? Do you think you can handle it?'

Like a red rag to a bull that was and Carl said 'Sure,' though he insisted on rolling it himself. Chicken.

So Carl and me had a spliff of THC and then we got stoned.

And do you know what? With a smoke inside him he was a much nicer guy altogether, and I dare say he'd say the same about me. He had obviously done a bit of toking in his time and he was smart enough to take it slow and enjoy it while it lasted, which in the case of this grass was for hours. We all ended up later that night in the hotel's version of a McDonald's, and I can recall that I had enough money left to buy myself something to eat but couldn't afford a beer to go with it. But that was OK, because my new buddy Carl got me a couple, and when we got back to the room I gave him what was left of my grass.

When it came to lights out and nighty-night time, Carl and Maggie stripped off and went loudly at it again in the darkness while I lay on the other bed. May slept on the floor, which she insisted on doing even though the bed was big enough for us both to be in it and neither of us know the other one was there.

The next morning I had to be up and at 'em early. When we all said our goodbyes before I set off to drive back to the airport, I offered Maggie, who had paid for the hotel room, my Walkman and the tape that was in it as a thank-you gift. Unfortunately she accepted it, and I don't know why I should remember, but the tape I lost was Lou Reed's Greatest Hits, which I had bought from a Britannia Music catalogue when I was serving in Northern Ireland. Easy come, easy go.

Like the flight from Belize I don't remember a thing about my return journey to England beyond handing in the car keys at the rental desk at the airport.

When I found myself once again walking the polished floors of Heathrow Airport (I'm back! I've done it!) it was Sunday morning. My plan had been to go straight home to Aldershot, but by now I had virtually no money at all, so the only thing I could think of to do was telephone Mo. My call woke her up, and hey-hey-hey! Good-looking boy that I am, she was happy I'd called and eager to see me, which was 'Funny you should say that . . .'

After confessing that I was broke (as predicted), I asked Mo if she could drive out to the airport and pick me up. But she had an even better idea, which was that I jump into a taxi and she'd pay for it when I arrived. She said she would have to pop out and visit the cashpoint (God bless them and all their buttons and screens), but she would be back well before I arrived. Not being a complete idiot, I told her I'd call her back in half an hour to make absolutely certain that she'd got the money, as nothing else has more ability to throw up a disappointment in life than a cash machine.

Good girl that she was, and impatient swine that was me, when I phoned a mere fifteen minutes later she was already back with the cash and had even bought me a pack of cigarettes because she thought that I'd probably run out. Aren't girls great?

I left the terminal and caught the first black cab I came across. Carol was still away at her folks' house for Christmas, so a night with Mo in London would be great. And it was. I guess I didn't feel bad about what Carol might think either, because I wasn't going to hide it from her. I still felt I held the moral high ground because of her own affair. Even though I'd been at it ten times worse when I was away in Belize, I was still decent – because when I had slept around with other women, I hadn't left her for them.

I spent the night with Mo and the next day, before work, she drove me to Waterloo to catch the train back to Aldershot (at her expense). Well, some of us did have a country to defend, you know.

When I finally got back to the flat I could see that Carol had visited while I'd been away and opened a card that Mo had enclosed with the fifty pounds I'd asked her to send me. When I went away Carol had known nothing about me and Mo – although as she was living in London and had left me, what did it have to do with her anyway? But she knew now all right, because Mo had written in her card some witty, truthful remark about me being a sex god, which would have left Carol in no doubt as to the nature of our relationship. Another thing the card did was welcome me home from my travels to Belize, which would straight away have let Carol know that I'd gone back there, and she would no doubt have worked out why.

Two days after I returned from Belize I went back to work, not letting on to a soul where I had been over Christmas. Because of my experience of the corporal in Belize whose wife had left him, I also didn't tell a soul that Carol had moved out, so although I was still pining in my spare time, in barracks everything was normal.

When I did finally get around to speaking to Carol again it was because she phoned me – which was different. She was in a phone box at the station, about to catch a train to Aldershot to see me, and was just checking that I was going to be in.

I don't know why, because I was overjoyed to speak to her again, but I was very curt with her. I told her that I would prefer not to see her again and that she had started all of this, and then I hung up. Two minutes later the phone rang again and Carol was back on the line, only this time she was crying. Me, I tried to hold out and to keep on being mean (though like I said, I don't know why), but I just couldn't, and an hour later Carol was on the doorstep and in my arms.

Since I'd last seen her she had dumped the boyfriend, moved

out of the house she'd been living in and moved in with another girlfriend in another part of London.

Five minutes after she arrived at the flat we were upstairs and in bed. After that it was like the break-up had never happened and she agreed to return to Aldershot and me.

There was of course the small matter of Mo to deal with, and the only way I could think of to do it was phone her up at work and just tell her the truth: Carol and I were getting back together again and I couldn't see her any more.

A few days after Carol moved back into the flat the parcel arrived from Belize and I made another phone call to Manchester. On the following Friday after work I caught the train up, sold the grass and then returned the next morning to Aldershot. And that was it. All the dope I was ever going to sell was gone and I'd got away with it.

We could now return to normal transmission.

They're coming to take me away, ha-ha!

They came on a Saturday. I was on guard at the time. In fact I was second in command of the guard at the time. At one point late in the morning I had gone off to the NAAFI to buy some cigarettes, and as I walked around the outskirts of the battalion parade ground on my way back to the guardroom I spotted the three of them, two men and a woman, and I knew right away that they were police. I also knew that it was me they had come to see. I did try telling myself that I was wrong. OK, yes, those three over there in the smart civvies were police, but that didn't necessarily mean they had come to talk to me. After all, the civilian police of Aldershot paying a visit to the in-town parachute battalion was hardly a rarity. But it was no good. I had this inner uneasiness that told me different. Guilt, I guess.

We had mounted guard (i.e. turned up for it) as per normal at zero eight-hundred hours. We went through the normal song and dance of coming to attention, and then being inspected, and then someone being bollocked for something they'd forgotten to do, and then being told 'Thank fuck we've got a navy and air force,' and then finally we all fell out and headed for the guardroom.

For the soldiers who did the stages, i.e. either stood on the camp gates or patrolled its perimeter with pick-axe handles, guard duty meant two hours on and four hours off. But not for me, mate. The guard commander and my good self covered the twenty-four-hour period with stages of six hours on and six hours off, which was an easy life. All we had to do in that time was answer the phone, wake up sleeping soldiers in time for their stages, whine to the cookhouse about the quantity and quality of the tea and sarnies provided for the guard, and occasionally tell any prisoners who might be banged up in the battalion cells that we were not welfare officers and would they please just shut the fuck up. As I said, compared to freezing your balls off outside it was an easy life, and God bless my stripe.

As it was Saturday the television in the guardroom was switched to Saturday morning kiddies' TV, which led to the normal level of intellectual debate on the subject of sex education for pre-pubescent children (and certain members of Noel Edmonds' studio audience in particular). There was also a video recorder in the guardroom, and once the topic of discussion had turned to sex it wasn't too long before somebody asked the question, 'Has anyone got any porn?' The answer was an all-round no. So, next question: 'Does anybody know where we can get some?' Answer: 'I do.' Les, the manager of the local snooker club had some. At the time Dave and I had been putting in more hours at the snooker table than most professionals at the game do, and Les had only a few days before rented us a couple of porno tapes 'under the counter'.

'All those in favour of me going off to pick one up, say "aye".' The ayes had it.

The snooker club was situated in Aldershot's town centre and although it wasn't too far away it was still a bit of a hike. Uphill on the way back as well. Thankfully, though, the army had been kind enough to provide us with a Land Rover for the day, and as we were on a mission to get the porn, no one had any objection to us borrowing the duty vehicle for half an hour or so. As was pointed out, if the commanding officer ever wanted to use it to pop into town, did we ever say no? No, we did not. So fair's fair, and me and the duty driver were on our way.

Naturally, this being real life, when we got to the snooker club it was open and Les was sitting behind the counter, but, sod's law, he had no porno tapes. They were all out. But surely he had one? There was always one.

'Do you not know,' I said, 'that the men who await my return with a tape of porn are heroes of this great nation of ours?'

'They signed on, didn't they?'

'Men who stood as one in the face of an evil South American military dictatorship . . .'

'They all got paid, didn't they?'

'Men who answered the call of our great leader Margaret (Les loved Maggie) in our nation's hour of need. Men who . . .'

Les had heard enough. If I was really that desperate for some pornography (well I wasn't, but the troops, you understand) then there was one up at his house. He would phone his wife, and if we could go and pick it up we could have it for four quid ('Give you three.' 'OK.'), but he had to have it back by six (eighteen hundred hours) or I would never pick up a snooker cue in his club again.

With that sorted, we handed over the cash, drove around to Les's house to pick up the tape, and then, later than advertised, headed back to base. When we reached the guardroom we got the expected 'Where the fuck have you been?', but as we had a tape the moaning soon petered out once the play button had been hit.

The video was a 1970s American full-length porno feature, with a plot that revolved around an occult group that had found a magic spell but needed a virgin for the ritual. As virgin-type ladies tend to be a rare commodity in porno films, the group struggled somewhat to find one. Their luck changed, however, when one day one of their number ran into, the way you do, a set of incestuous bisexual twin sisters. Luckily, one of the sisters had only ever had anal and oral sex before and so technically, apparently, was still a virgin.

Just as we settled down to watch the twin in question being buggered for the third time that morning, while her sister looked on approvingly, the guardroom door opened and in walked the duty officer with the three dressed in civvies in tow.

'Please just ask for someone else' was all I could think.

But they didn't.

After a brief round of introductions, from which I learned that the two men were Special Investigation Branch, Royal Military Police and the woman was a civilian drug squad officer, I was led upstairs to the battalion orderly room. When we got there they sat me in a chair and the policewoman, with a smile and very nicely, asked me their very special first question.

'Do you know why we're here, Ken?'

There were only two possible answers to this: the one my head Lego was falling apart over, which was 'Too fucking right I know,' and the one my lips instantly replied with.

'No. I've got no idea.'

'No idea at all?'

'No. No idea.'

'Funny, you wouldn't think that to look at your face.'

And I knew she was right. No matter how hard I tried, I just couldn't stop my pulse from racing. Couldn't stop my mind from rushing through thoughts like how should I now be looking and acting and talking.

With no immediate confession forthcoming from me, the policewoman told me what they had. And they near enough had it all. All, that is, apart from one small detail which, come courtroom time, would make one huge difference. In her version of 'Marijuana, Belize and Ken Lukowiak', Marijuana was played by Cocaine, a class A illegal substance carrying fourteen years for the importation of. Although, as one of the kindly military policemen pointed out, with my good war record from the Falklands I'd probably only be looking at ten.

I continued to deny all knowledge. What else could I do?

They then mentioned the names of two other ex-soldiers who, according to them, were involved in it with me. The two men they referred to had been in the same platoon as me in Northern Ireland, and if I remembered correctly they had been discharged from the army just before we got back from there, for beating up a 'crow'. Apart from once, when they had both come back to Aldershot to pick up their discharge papers, I hadn't seen or heard from either of them since, so I couldn't work out how they had come to be involved.

236

Then one of the policemen asked me two questions that I actually had prepared answers for: 'Why did you return to Belize over Christmas leave?' and 'Why did you not seek permission before you left?'

I spun back the line about going to see Linda and pleaded that I hadn't realised that 'one' needed permission to 'holiday abroad'. I could see them think it: 'Oh, a smartarse.'

And then I knew they had me.

They asked, which was polite of them at least, if it would be all right for them to go and search my flat. As I was in the army they had no real need to ask permission. The military police-men could have just gone and done it. I maybe could have denied access to the civilian drug squad officer, but what was the point? Under my sofa there was a serving tray with a pile of grass on it that I'd been smoking from the night before, and upstairs, in the wardrobe in the spare room, there was half a pound or so of Belizian marijuana. Stevie Wonder could have found it. And when they did find it, in would be invited the civvy drug squad officer, happy, no doubt, to meet again the arsehole who had kept her waiting in the car while all the fun was going down inside.

So I gave in. Just like that. I ran up the flag and walked forward with my hands up. The first thing I did was put them straight about the cocaine. There had been none involved and would they please just drop it as a subject. Funnily enough, or so I've thought many times since, they did. Never mentioned the word again.

As they were leading me away to their car the duty Land Rover pulled into its parking space. Seeing the driver again reminded me that the porno tape that was out in my bad name had to be returned to Les by six. I explained this to the policewoman, substituting war movie for skin flick, and asked if I could go over and have a word with the driver before we left. Surprisingly, she didn't mind, though I wasn't bright enough to realise why at the time. So I called out to the driver, he stopped and I walked over to him. When I reached him I would guess that I was a good twenty metres or so away from the police. I was certainly out of earshot. I explained to the driver that I had to go away with those nice gentlemen over there and their ladyfriend, and asked him if he could please make sure that the video got back to the snooker club on time. He said he would, I said thank you and then I started to make my way back.

I had taken no more than two steps when one of the MPs called out for the driver to stop. He came over, and then, right in front of me, asked the driver to repeat what I had just said to him. The driver said something that included video tape, snooker club, Land Rover and return by six, and the MP said 'Fine' then thanked him and sent him on his way.

Many times since that moment I've wondered if I missed my chance there. If I'd had the quickness of thought, I could have asked the driver to phone my wife and let her know I was on my way home with the police. If Carol had then cleaned the place up, by the time we turned up there would have been nothing for them to find. No evidence, no case. Of course, I had already confessed nearly everything there was for me to confess, so I doubt if it would have made that much difference to the final outcome.

On the other hand, if I had held on to the very last bullet, kept my mouth closed until they actually put their hands on some grass and showed it to me, then maybe it could have turned out to be my last-minute arrival of the cavalry. Though again, that would have depended a lot on what answer the driver had given when asked what I had said. I can't say I knew the guy very well, but at least I knew him, and ironically enough he had been a policeman himself before joining the army, which must have meant that he knew the score. I believe that, had I asked him not to say anything about my request for a phone call, he wouldn't have. If nothing else, the unwritten code of fellow paratrooper against military police would have seen to that.

Either way, though, what does it matter any more?

SNLR (Services No Longer Required)

The police drove me from the barracks to the flat, and when we got there the four of us went up in the lift, walked along the landing to my front door and then – well, I don't really remember. I don't recall whether I opened the door with my key or rang the bell. Today I just hold this picture of Carol standing in the hall and the horror that was that moment. I don't even remember if I introduced the police or if they introduced themselves. Either way, in seconds Carol had worked out what was going on.

And then we were in the lounge (though I think I still called it the sitting room then) and lying on the floor was the dinner tray with my dope from the night before on it. There was some comment from the policewoman about how open it all was, but there was no malice in the way she said it. She then asked if I had any more on the premises (which was one of her lawyer-type questions) and said if I did, would I please lead the way to it. I took them upstairs to the spare room, pointed to the box with my grass in it and left them the pleasure of opening it, which they did.

'How much is in here then, Ken?'

I didn't know. A pound or so maybe?

'A pound or so, Ken?'

I didn't know.

'And this is it, is it Ken? You've got no more?'

Again I didn't know. Though I knew I didn't have 'more' as in by the pound. As for the odd smoke or two that may or may not have been lurking in a jeans pocket or a bedside drawer, I truly didn't know.

And then came the worst bit so far. They searched the house. At the time I liked to think that I knew a little more than the average bod about searching a property, simply because I'd once done a two-week Northern Ireland search course, so, as I was led from room to room to witness their more than legal invasion of my privacy, I could tell that their hearts weren't in it, that they were just going through the motions. Or, to put it another way, that they had believed everything I'd told them. What fools, eh?

Well, no – because everything I had told them so far had been the truth.

Nevertheless, it's still not nice to have strangers going through your drawers and wardrobes and cupboards and pockets and books and mail and diaries . . . even underpants (though not the ones in the laundry basket, I noted). They dug out my passport, which confirmed all of the dates of travel, and they also found my old airline tickets, which right away told them the name of the bucket shop in London where I'd bought them.

After the searching was done (and maybe it's country and western songs I should write) we were led back downstairs and both formally arrested. And once again it was all just like I'd seen it a hundred times before on the TV.

'You have the right to remain . . . etc.'

After the items they had gathered from our home had been placed in plastic evidence bags we left the flat and (altogether now), with a feeling that this wasn't happening, were driven the short distance to Aldershot police station.

When we got there the two MPs said their goodbyes – though don't be sad, they said, because they'd probably come and visit me again some time and we could all have a nice chat then. Inside the station Carol and I were both booked in with the desk sergeant and then we were led away to separate interview rooms.

Naturally enough, my new acquaintance the policewoman

wanted to know the whole story, and when she use the word 'whole' she meant it. From the first joint I'd ever smoked, right up to the last piece of dope I'd sold on the streets. Streets? What streets? I didn't sell anything on the streets.

'So where did you sell it, Ken?'

I could see no harm in telling them that I'd sold all my dope in Manchester, but as to who I'd sold it to, I wasn't prepared to say. Now, in the films at this point the copper normally says something like: 'Make it easy on yourself, son. Give us a name and it'll look better for you in court.' But there was none of that. When I told her that I wasn't prepared to name anyone else, all the nice polite police lady said was OK, and that in truth she hadn't expected me to. (There again, what I didn't think of at the time was that she still had plenty of stuff to ask me in the future.)

The questioning went on for the rest of the day and we even stopped at one point for a meal in the police canteen. By the time the policewoman started thinking about the closing theme to Andy Pandy, I'd near enough given them all of it. Except that I could see no need to confess to the exact number of parcels I'd sent and so I kept it down to two: one when I was in Belize and another when I went back at Christmas. When she did finally put her papers away for the day, the policewoman wondered out loud why I'd done it in the first place. I seemed like a nice sensible guy, with a lovely wife and a very good army record, so why had I done it?

I said I didn't know. And the policewoman said that she could believe that.

I was led back to the desk sergeant, who gave me the news that Carol was not to be charged with anything. Which if you ask me (though no one did) was only fair, since she hadn't done anything in the first place.

So Carol was free to go, but I was to be kept in a cell below Aldershot police station for the night. And no, sorry, I couldn't talk to my wife before she left, though they would be kind enough to pass on any message I might have.

'Oh, right. Thanks. Well, could you just ask her to phone my mate in Manchester and tell him I've been busted, so would he let everyone I sold dope to know? And in case she hasn't got the number, it's . . .'

I didn't have a message.

The cell I ended up in was already occupied by another prisoner. Now, it's funny how certain bits of information that we pick up along the path we all must walk that is called 'life' (no, come on – I'm locked up here, all right, so I'm allowed), but on the voyage down to the Falklands War we were shown films on how to go about things if we should end up a captive. Because the films were American, in black and white and dated from the Korean War, we struggled to find any real significance in them. And who was ever going to be taken prisoner anyway? But do you know what? One of the films had this American PoW being locked up for the night with another prisoner, only this other prisoner, he wasn't really an American. Well, he was, but he was a spy who would pass on anything he heard. So you see, those information films they showed us did work, because as soon as I saw my cellmate lying on his bunk under a blanket and looking all H-Block, the first thing that flashed into my mind was the Korean War.

I was very suspicious of him, although I did keep trying to tell myself to stop being so stupid. I mean, for starters why would they bother? I was hardly the Mr Big of the Hampshire drug scene. All the same, I was careful about everything I said.

After about an hour a policeman arrived at the cell and the man I'd been locked up with was told that he was leaving. If he really was a stool pigeon – and today I seriously doubt it – he was a nice one, because he left me his cigarettes and wished me luck with the judge. The judge! I hadn't even thought that far ahead.

When the cell door had been closed and its locks turned, I sat back on my bunk and tried to take in everything had happened. And who wouldn't? Since the police had lifted me in the morning, this was the first time I'd been on my own, and so, I guess, the first time I was really in a position to start thinking things through.

The big question (in fact, make that the fucking big question) was how did they know? As far as I could tell, none of the parcels had been intercepted. But then, maybe they had? Maybe they'd been discovered and let through anyway so that the chain could be followed. There again, it was hardly a ton of gear and therefore, or so you'd think, the chain was hardly worth following. Besides, if anything had been intercepted then it must have been at Brize Norton. Unless, that is, one of the parcels had split open. Which hadn't happened. Or had it? No it just couldn't have, because I'd checked each one on arrival, and such are the qualities of army issue masking tape that you'd need the cast of *Mission Impossible* to wrap it all up again without giving the game away.

So, if they weren't discovered en route, then somebody, somewhere, must have talked. After all, they hadn't pulled my name out of a hat, that was for sure. But who knew to talk? There was only Dave. He wasn't involved with the parcels, but he had known about them and could have accidentally opened his mouth to someone.

And then something came into my mind that until then I had completely forgotten about. About a week or so before, a policeman had come knocking on our door carrying out routine door-to-door questioning regarding an incident that had happened on the estate that day. While I was standing on the doorstep telling him that I'd been at work all day and didn't even know there had been an incident, I couldn't help but notice the overwhelming smell of the joint that I had going in the lounge. After I'd closed the door on him I did wonder if he had noticed the smell as well, but then I just thought that if he had he would have said something there and then. He could have passed his suspicions on to the drug squad, though. But even so, what did it have to do with parcels of dope from Belize? I turned this over and over again in my mind for the rest of the night, and when I awoke in the morning it was again the first thing to come into my head.

I was brought breakfast on a plastic plate, and once I'd eaten it (I just love plastic) I was led back up through the police station to the desk sergeant, who turned out to be another of those people in life who are just going through the motions. He was pleasant enough, though, and, like all the police I'd met so far, he called me Ken. I don't know why, but there was something about his manner that made me feel like I was twelve and top of the class. Which was strange, as I was in fact twenty-four and standing in the corner with a cone on my head. The kindly sergeant told me that I'd been granted police bail, which meant (and I'm glad someone knew) that I was free to go and a swipe of a credit card wasn't required.

Although, for me, everything had changed, outside the police station it could have been any early Sunday morning in Aldershot. On the short walk back to the flat through the army housing estate I hardly passed a soul. The British army slept.

When I got back to the flat Carol was still in bed and all I could think to do was join her. You'd think we would have had a few urgent matters to discuss, but I guess we both knew that it would get us nowhere. So the first thing we did was make love – which even at the time struck me as a bit strange. Over the course of the past twenty-four hours our lives had been turned upside down. For one, I was now absolutely, definitely out the army. For two, we could start packing, because out the army meant out the flat. And for three, unless a miracle of the proportions of water into wine happened, I was also definitely headed for a term in prison.

I tell you, give me Goose Green any day. Though you know something? Not really, really.

When we did finally manage to pull ourselves out of bed, I made a few quick telephone calls (from a phone box in town) and passed on the news of my downfall to everyone I thought needed to know. The list included no one from either of our families. There would be plenty of time for that in the future, once we had discovered what, exactly, our future was going to be. At least, that was my excuse.

The next day, surreally enough, it was back to barracks as per normal, although there was nothing normal about the way I was feeling. I had imagined that I'd walk into shit like I'd never known it before, but in fact what had happened, and what was going to happen to me, as in bye-bye army, was hardly mentioned. And if it was, then the term used was always that I had a 'civvy case pending'. As for me, if I say so myself, I handled being in barracks quite well. There again, what I had done was so serious that there was no chance of salvation. I was out, and until the day the paperwork was signed and sorted, the best thing anyone could do was try not to mention it.

One thing that did change (and I didn't mind one bit that it did) was that people started to avoid me. I was now a dangerous man to know as far as army careers were concerned. After all, if I smoked dope, then maybe my friends did as well?

Oh well, at least things couldn't get any worse, eh?

Go on then.

Well, three days after the police had busted me Carol arrived home from work and said that she was pregnant. And oh, what joy! Or it should have been. Or it was. But how could it be, with what we were going through? The Dick and Jane books had this as one of the happiest moments of our lives, but because of me – and let's face it, it was me – how could this be good news?

When we finally put the lights out that night and I lay my head on my pillow, all I could do was be scared, so scared. At first I couldn't even begin to understand how it had all ended up this bad. Though when I looked at it, it was simple. Somewhere in Belize I had lost not only the plot but the whole darned allotment and done something stupid.

And then, naturally enough, I put myself through a whole lot of 'why did I do it'? The only thing I could blame, help share some of the shame, was the dope. Every day I had smoked it, and that cannot be good in anyone's books. But boy, did I wish I had a joint on me now.

True to their word (and don't you just love people that keep their word?), my two pals of old, the SIB detectives of the Royal Military Police, paid me a visit at battalion one morning. It was obvious that they'd already been busy playing twenty questions with various members of my battalion, and once they'd got me all lonesome and given me a quick run-through of my confessions to the police, they kicked off by asking me how many parcels Dave had sent back. Not *if* he had sent any, mind you, but how many.

Now to be frankly honest, to the best of my knowledge I've only ever been A-grade cool – and I mean really cool, to the point where a penguin would want to fuck me – twice in my whole life. The first time was during a night parachute jump when I was number one in the stick. The door was open, the wind was rushing in from the darkness outside, and me, I looked liked an emotionless rock. Behind me in the stick at numbers two, three, four and five were four new boys to the company, just up from basic training. In front of them, believe me, I looked cool. And the second time I was ever really, truly cool was just after the two MPs asked me how many parcels Dave had sent back. Word for word I replied: 'I mean no offence [or something like that], but you can fuck off.' (It's the fuck off bit that's word for word.)

Even then I realised that as far as the army went they could do nothing to me now except throw me out. If they had so wished, they could, I guess, have charged me with something and probably locked me away until the civil courts wanted me. But the thing was, I knew they did not so wish. All the army really wanted from me was a nice quiet bye-bye with no ripples. The MPs may have wanted to know how many other members of my battalion had been smoking in Belize, but as for the army, and especially the regiment, it was the last thing they wanted to know.

Even so, I sort of hoped, and would even have bet my shirt on it, that on being told they could 'fuck off' the two MPs would have lost their rag completely and come back at me all nasty. But I was wrong. (Surely not you, Ken?) Yes, I was, because all they did was apologise for the inconvenience, pick up their files and leave. And do you know what I realised? To these people, me, now, I was no more than paperwork. And where I was surely going, I could offend them? Get real.

The subject of Dave was to be raised again by the civilian police the next time they popped into the barracks for one of their 'chats', as they liked to call them. They had obviously been liaising with the two MPs because they'd brought them along with them. What's more, they'd now turned all their attention towards Dave. According to them – and, incidentally, the photocopies of certain pages from the guardroom check-out book at Rideau Camp (You haven't got them? We have.) – near enough every time I'd signed out of camp Dave had signed out with me. So why not make it easy on myself . . .

Much as I would have liked to tell the civvy police that they could get 'fucked' too, although I stuck to my line that Dave knew nothing, I was definitely slightly more polite about it. Unfortunately, or so it was to prove, when they got around to talking to Dave himself, who knew that they had absolutely nothing on him and never would have, he was not so polite. After the police had finished with me that morning we left battalion headquarters together and by chance came across Dave in the car park outside (and before you even think it, there are lots of inside ones in the army). One of the MPs, who had obviously had the pleasure of Dave's company before, stopped Dave and told him they wanted another word with him. Dave's reaction to this was to tell 'em it like it was. They had nothing on him, so they could get fucked. He wasn't answering any more of their questions, and if they did want to talk to him then they'd have to go through the proper channels, *and* he wanted an officer present. So fuck off. And off he walked. A bit over the top, if you ask me, but good for him.

Well, not really, because some of those policeman types, you can't get four of them into a Mini. Many moons later Dave was on the piss one night in one of Aldershot's many para pubs. He's shooting pool, getting drunk and getting on more than nicely with these two civvy tarts who are all over him. Towards the end of the evening one of the girls asks him if he wants to come back to their pad and party for a while. Dave naturally agrees and says he'll get a few cans in. The girls then ask him if he has any dope on him, which he hasn't. Well, does he know anywhere that he could get any? Does he *know*? So they give him five pounds and Dave runs around the corner and scores a fiver's worth from a man in another pub. When he returns to the girls, they all have another drink and then leave to go off to their orgy of sex and drugs.

Two seconds after they walk out on to the pavement outside, one of the girls pulls a Military Police ID card from her purse and Dave is nicked. He's just thinking that these two don't really know him from Adam so maybe he'll just run, 'cos they're only girls after all, and if it comes to it he'll take his chances in a battalion ID parade, when round the corner walk two MPs in uniform accompanied by two civilian police officers.

So the next scene in Dave's life is that he's at Aldershot police station getting booked in for selling drugs. But those civvy police, they're not all daft, you know. Because when the MPs told the story of their great bust and got to the bit about the two short-skirted female officers asking Dave to buy drugs for them and then giving him the money to go off and do it, the desk sergeant asked if they were joking. Had they never heard of a thing called 'entrapment'? And did they not think that it was more than possible that by giving Dave money they might have been 'encouraging crime'? Without another word, he cautioned Dave for being in possession of a class B controlled substance and sent him on his way.

Unfortunately, though, the army had no need to be so understanding. When it got around to them dealing with Dave he was sentenced to sixty days in Colchester military prison and then discharged from the service. And do you know what? They didn't once thank him for all those Argentines that he'd killed for them. But then, why should they? They'd paid him, hadn't they?

As for my own discharge from the army, it was now a definite, and the only questions still to be answered were when and under what part of Queen's Regulations. At first I had asked if I could buy myself out, which as a solution to the problem (and my discharge was a problem) would have been perfect for everyone. As yet the army hadn't charged me with anything and they were now unlikely to do so, as the civil

248

police were going to hit me big time, so if I bought myself out there would be no need to write the word 'drugs' on anything before I rode off into the sunset. The problem with this solution was that before I could hand over the money I would have to hand over the army flat, which was not possible.

In the end I was discharged under Queen's Regulations paragraph lots-of-numbers: 'Services No Longer Required'. It meant that I went quietly, and because I hadn't been charged by the army for anything, my conduct during service was marked as 'Exemplary' and I was allowed to keep my medals.

On my last day in uniform I handed in all of my clothing and equipment (so my last day wasn't in uniform after all) and completed the final paperwork at battalion headquarters. I guess that if I had been getting on a train and leaving Aldershot that day then I would have had a walk around and said my goodbyes, but I wasn't leaving and would no doubt see people around town.

On my last walk from the barracks to the flat I couldn't help but feel sad. As I skulked along my mind flashed through the past five years that had been my life in the army. From basic training, on to Northern Ireland, through to the Falklands War, then Belize, of course, and now this, my discharge. Like I said, I couldn't help but feel sad.

In any other circumstances the first thing I would have done now was look for another job, but as everyone was convinced that I would be going to prison, what was the point? Though I did do something I hadn't done in five years and signed on down at the employment exchange. Once I was officially unemployed I also went along to the nearest solicitor's and applied for Legal Aid. According to the nice policewoman, the first thing that was going to happen to me on the legal front was an appearance at Aldershot Magistrates' Court. More than likely the magistrates would think my offence too serious for them to deal with and so would pass me on and up to the Crown Court in Winchester. Either way, even though I was going to plead guilty, I was going to need a solicitor.

As the days passed and Carol's stomach grew bigger and

bigger, every now and then our lives were interrupted by house calls from the police, who nearly always had something they'd forgotten to ask. I can remember that on one such visit they wanted me to draw a map of Punta Gorda (and remember, this would look good for me in court) and mark the house of the man I'd bought the grass from. This was a new one on me. In fact, so surprised was I that I replied by saying that I really didn't know Punta Gorda that well, and besides . . . 'I only ever went to Demas's place twice.'

'Whose place?' they asked.

Without thinking, I'd given them Demas's name, and all I could do was hope that it was not passed on to someone in the army who would in turn pass it on to someone in Belize. To this day I don't know if my big mouth caused Demas any harm, though when I think it through I can't really see what they could knock on his door and do if he simply denied that he knew me. Even so, it just goes to show what an unthoughtful tongue can do.

Four or five weeks after my discharge from the army we still hadn't told either of our families the real reason why I'd left, and it was now time to go to the Magistrates' Court. I wore the grey suit I'd bought with the first money from Manchester and left the flat knowing that I'd be back again within two hours (or so everyone had told me). At the court, after a half-hour wait my case was called and right away the prosecution lawyer stood up and said that so serious were my offences that he wanted them and me to go to the Crown Court. Then it was my solicitor's turn. He replied that there was no need to go to Crown Court, because what I'd done wasn't all that bad and they could deal with it themselves then and there. It would save the taxpayer a lot of money as well. As per everyone's predictions, though, the magistrates adjourned the case, kept me on police bail and booked a date at the Crown Court in Winchester: 21 August 1984, to be precise.

And the truth of it is that by the time it did come around to my appearance at Crown Court, I was quite looking forward to being locked away. All I wanted was to escape. Run away.

250

Leave my pregnant wife to sort out the mess of where to live and where to have the baby and how to pay off the overdraft, and please, just leave me alone.

Judgement day – hey-hey!

The day to face the legal music finally arrived. Dave turned up at the flat at eight to give me a lift to Winchester Crown Court and, God willing, back to Aldershot again later. I kissed Carol goodbye on the doorstep and we hugged tightly and both whispered 'Who knows?', we might get to see each other in the afternoon. Not that deep down, though, both of us didn't know it was unlikely.

I remember not a lot of the drive to court, or how I felt on it, but I do recall that we smoked a joint and I do remember taking a final, so human look back at Carol, six months pregnant and crying on the doorstep. I hated me then. For a minute or two.

Then I'm sitting on a chair in a small cell-like room and talking to my QC, the man who was going to defend me, or at least speak up for me, as I was going to plead guilty. And I'm thinking there's something not quite right here, because I'd never met the man before in my life. I would have needed money to do that. More than anything he was interested in my war record from the Falklands: where I had been on the islands, what battles I'd fought in, the names of any of my friends that had been killed.

Once his questions were over he hit me with a piece of fair dinkum realism, which was that I was 99.9% sure to be given a custodial sentence.

'Which is?' I asked.

'A term in prison, I'm afraid,' he replied.

And the good news for me? Well, there wasn't any.

And then I'm in the dock of a Crown Court that's absolutely, precisely, just like the ones that used to be on ITV on weekday afternoons, only now I'm the one who's being referred to as 'the accused'. Once the judge had entered and the court had gone through the 'All stand' and 'All be seated' routine, the counsel for the prosecution (boo-oo!) got the ball rolling by reading out a list of my crimes: importation of a class B controlled substance, supplying a class B controlled substance, and last and by all means least, possession of a class B controlled substance. With that out of the way, he gave a quick run-through of the events of my arrest at Bruneval Barracks and what was allegedly said by me at the time. And allegedly was the word, because technically what he said was untrue. He said that when I was first interviewed by the police I had denied my crimes, which I hadn't. All I'd denied was the false accusation that I had smuggled *cocaine* back from Belize. At this point I felt I should jump to my feet and say it ain't so, Joe. But I sometimes do know when it's best to keep my trap shut, and from what I knew about authority, this was definitely one of those times. So mum I did keep. The counsel for the prosecution then called a police officer to give evidence, and once again (surprise, surprise, chuck) just like the QC who was defending me, I had never seen the man before. And talk about formalities.

Once the policeman had said all he wanted to say, it became time for my counsel to speak – my one hope of saving the day. In my defence the only thing he could do was present the mitigating circumstances of me having been at war for my country the year before my crimes. And a fine account of my actions he gave as well. In short, Colonel Jones VC and me got dropped at San Carlos Bay, from there we marched together to Goose Green, he got killed in the battle and I went on to take Port Stanley all on my own. Not quite the way it was, I admit, but at the time that version was fine by me.

And there was more. For twelve months I had served my country in Northern Ireland, on a tour of duty in which twenty-one members of my battalion were murdered (I liked that, good word) by Republican terrorists. (He didn't mention that twenty of those members had been killed before I even joined the battalion. There again, and I'll defend him now, I hadn't actually told him.)

And there was even more. So good had been my behaviour during my five years of service that I had never once been charged, and I had left the army with an 'exemplary' conduct record.

'Yes,' interrupted the judge, 'I find it somewhat confusing that a soldier who is dismissed from the Parachute Regiment for the self-confessed crime of smuggling cannabis can walk away with an exemplary conduct record.'

He had a point.

Once all the hoo-ing and ha-ing was over with (and really, we could have done it all by post) we reached the part of the proceedings that really mattered. Double jeopardy time: the judge's summing-up and, after a short intermission for coffee and cake, the sentencing.

What the judge's name was I don't now recall, and in fact, if you had asked me it two minutes after I'd left his court that day I probably wouldn't have been able to tell you. But oh, he really was everyone's stereotype of the old grey-haired fuddy-duddy. Didn't know what a Sony video recorder was but looked like he could have told you all about the 'Lovely Lucy' blow-up doll with real hair and three holes. And boy, did he waffle on.

The highlight of his summing-up was when he said that he had heard through the grapevine that soldiers were smuggling marijuana back from abroad, wait for it . . . in the barrels of their rifles. I couldn't see Dave in the court, but at this point I heard him from somewhere above and behind me. Just how much grass did his honour here think you could get down the barrel of a rifle? You'd need a whole brigade at it just to get enough back home to make two good joints and a half-dozen hash brownies.

When the judge did finally stop rambling and get to the bottom line, I wished he'd rambled some more, for I was stunned. He gave me eighteen months for the importation, six months for the supplying and another six months for the possession. I didn't need a calculator. That came to two and a half years. In fact, make that two and a half fucking years. Like I said, I was stunned.

Of course, he had taken into account my brave service for my country, but I had been trusted to handle Her Majesty's Mail and I had abused that trust by posting herbal cannabis through it.

Well, was he right? He wasn't wrong. But there again, not one letter that passed through my post room in Belize was ever addressed to The Queen, Buckingham Palace. Not one.

Two and a half years, though. I felt terrible.

But then, believe it or not, only a few minutes later, after I had been led from the courtroom to the cells below – hey-hey-hey! – things started to look up, and in a big way. I was locked into a cell with two other men who had also just been sentenced up above, and when we started to talk, after we'd all answered 'What did you get?' like we'd all been fishing, one of them, after checking my figures with one of the 'screws', said that I'd had a right result.

A *what*?

'Two and a half years may be many things, mate,' I said, 'but a right result is not fucking one of them.'

'But it ain't two and a half years, is it?' he replied. And then he broke it down for me.

Firstly, what I'd really been given was only eighteen months, because the two six-month sentences were to run 'concurren- tly' (and no, I didn't know what it meant) with the eighteen. Well, I was feeling a little better already. And it got even better, because secondly, eighteen months really meant twelve, as you automatically got a third off for good behaviour. And thirdly, if I was to get parole – which, as a first-time offender with a pregnant wife, not to mention a good war record, I was more than likely to – then the twelve months would be reduced to six. Which was a long way short of two and a half years.

Eighty per cent off. Good discount, boss.

It turned out that both of my cellmates had been in prison before and so I was keen to ask, listen and learn. More you know, less you fear. I became pretty much like I'd been when I first joined the army. Back then I could sit and listen to old soldiers (ones who were maybe twenty-two, twenty-three) telling tales of army life for as long as they cared to talk. With prison, though, it was different, because I never reached the point of comparison where the mere sight of a paratrooper, in red beret and with Para wings up, would make me want to become like him. At no stage did I ever, ever want to end up like one of these guys. Right from the off I decided that going to prison was like parachuting: it's the second time around that really counts.

I stayed in the cell below the courts until the day's proceedings upstairs were over, and then I was handcuffed to one of my cellmates and we were loaded aboard a prison van that was to take us to HM Prison Winchester.

When we got there we were uncuffed and locked up, one by one, in a row of small cubicles. Inside they were much like public toilets only without the plumbing and somewhere to sit. I had a feeling that there must be some deep psychological reason for right away confining us in such a small space. To let us know that our lives now had boundaries, I guess.

Again one by one, we were let out of the cubicles, told to strip and then taken to another room where a row of baths already filled with water awaited us. After taking a bath we were each issued a prison uniform: blue-and-white striped shirt, blue jeans and black slip-on shoes that had gone out of fashion some time in the 'sixties. All in all, it was pretty much like the day I got issued my army kit in basic training. A long line of men on one side of the counter, with two men on the other side handing out the clothes.

When the administration was over we were led in single file through a labyrinth of vinyl-tiled corridors that seemed to have locked gates and bolted metal doors every ten yards. Lots of keys, there are, in a jail, and lots of men walking around with oversized bunches of them hanging from their hips. Which I guess, not surprisingly, was one of the very first things I noticed about my new environment.

If along the way we passed any points of interest, such as the medical room or the library or the gate that led to the workshops, say, then they didn't point them out to us. When we reached the wing that held the reservations for our first night banged up, our presence was announced by a prison officer who shouted aloud 'Six on!' (though it may have been seven).

As we walked through the wing, another mild surprise for me was the way the majority of the prisoners in my new intake seemed to be not so long-lost pals with the prisoners already there and the men in uniform who guarded them. It was all: 'Hello Joe! Oh, all right then, Mr Andrews.'

'Heard you were on your way back, son. How long did you get?'

'Two years.'

'Two years? Sounds a bit steep. Oh well, I'm sure you'll manage.'

'I'm sure I will, Mr Andrews.'

That first night I was locked in a cell with seven or eight other prisoners, all of whom had arrived at the prison in the past few days. And crowded was the word, to say the least. Although when I turned it over a little in my mind, I realised that I had lived in far more confined and uncomfortable conditions when I'd been in the army in Northern Ireland. And looking on the plus side, at least in prison there were no crazy Irishmen trying to blow me up into unrecognisable little pieces.

I guess most of us tend to think that anyone who's in prison must be a hard man of the desperately evil, violent variety: murderers and bank robbers, villains from London's East End. But as I looked around the cell that night I couldn't see one man who fitted into that category. Small-time petty criminals was more like it. Though just like the two men I'd been locked up with in the cells at the courts, nearly all of them had been to prison before.

Lying back on my bed, gazing up at the springs and wire meshing of the bunk above me, I tried to get my head around the idea of where I actually was. Six months suddenly seemed like six years, and yet all I could do was shut up and get on with it, learn to accept a situation that I couldn't change. And once again it was something for which the army had prepared me well.

My thoughts were interrupted by the smell of burning hashish. No, it couldn't be. After all, we were in prison. I sat up in my bed to look around the cell, and sure enough, there were three of my cellmates sitting around a bedside locker smoking hash. And the way they were smoking it was a new one on me. You could say that they were 'hot-knifing it', except that instead of picking up the hash with two heated knives, they had cut it into pieces not much bigger than a matchhead and were picking them up with the end of a lighted rolled-up cigarette. Once the roll-up had set the hash alight, they would suck the resulting smoke into their lungs using an empty Biro tube.

One of them noticed me noticing them and asked if I wanted a hit. Well, why not? So I went over, and three small pieces of hash, which wouldn't have made a quarter of a joint, were pushed in front of me. I was passed the lighted roll-up and empty ball-pen case and off I went. Apparently the name for what I was now doing was 'spotting it', and as a way to make your hash last longer I can recommend it, although it's not quite the social thing that passing a joint around is.

I can remember thinking, as the smoke started to take hold, that it was just like that scene in the movie *Midnight Express* where the young American is at the courts on a hash-smuggling charge, for which Turkish justice is just about to throw the book at him, and in one corner of the court are a group of men quite openly sharing a hash pipe.

The irony of me smoking that first night in jail certainly wasn't lost on me.

Kitchen duties

Not surprisingly, I woke up to my first morning in prison feeling a tad depressed. For that tenth of a second I wondered where I was, and when I remembered, well, I just felt depressed. The first thing on the day's agenda was 'slop-out'. The cells had no toilets, and if you needed to go in the night you had to use a small plastic potty with a lid that was standard issue to every prisoner. Slopping out meant pouring the contents of your potty down the toilet first thing in the morning, or last thing at night, and then washing it clean again.

After slop-out, and with our beds made, we lined up to get our breakfast, much like you would at a motorway service station – except that here we didn't need a second mortgage to pay for it and there were no steak knifes available. Once breakfast was out of the way we were yet again formed into a line and once more marched off through the jail. We were brought to a halt outside a small office on one of the wing's upper landings, where we were to wait our turn to be interviewed by the prison's work placement officer. When it became my time to be interviewed I marched in, stood to attention in front of the 'suit' sitting behind the desk and then answered every question he had for me like I was addressing a general. At the end of every sentence I called him sir, which having been in the army was no great hardship for me, and I could tell right away that he liked me. He obviously thought me a cut above the normal undisciplined riff-raff that passed through his door. The result of my disciplined and obedient

259

performance (and if the truth be told, that's really all it was) was a job in the prison kitchens.

'Kitchens?' exclaimed one of my fellow convicts when I got back into line on the landing. 'Who do you fucking know then?'

'Why? Is that good, is it?'

'Best place to be, mate. All you can eat.'

After the job interviews we were taken back to our cells and told to grab our towels for a trip to the shower rooms. When we got there we had to wait in the corridor outside for the group of prisoners ahead of us to finish their bathtime. Where we were told to queue was right outside the prison shop, which apart from its tobacco and Bic razors was a dead ringer for a school tuck shop, right down to the hole in the wall that acted as a serving counter. Behind the counter was the oldest prison officer I'd so far seen, checking a stock list and barking orders to two prisoners who did their time working for him. At one point he left the small shop to go into the storeroom out back. He had been gone for no more than two seconds when suddenly one of our number broke ranks, darted to the counter and leant across it into the shop. He grabbed a few half-ounce packets of tobacco and quickly stuffed them into his towel. With that the stampede was on and people were fighting for space at the counter to reach in and grab some goodies. Me, I stayed where I was. There was no way I was going to get involved in any of this.

Within half a minute the shop's shelves had been stripped almost bare, and I couldn't help but think that as soon as the prison officer returned he'd have to be a near-sighted bat not to notice that he'd been robbed. I further figured that it would also be more than a little obvious who had robbed him, and after a quick search of our persons the game would be up. But hey! Not for me, because I hadn't got involved.

When the prison officer did finally reappear, it took him the best part of half a second to notice that some thievery had taken place. He look at the shelves where all of his tobacco had once been, then he looked across at us, where all of his tobacco now was, and then – well, then he did nothing. And I guess he had worked out that he just had to swallow, because as sure as night follows day the next scene in the movie would have had him up before someone higher in the pecking order who was asking him: 'You did *what*? With *how many* convicted thieves standing outside?'

The more I thought it through, the more I realised that he couldn't say doodly-squat, because it was his fault. And remember, a mistake only becomes a bollock of the dropped variety when others find out about it.

I wished I'd grabbed a few packets for myself now.

After our shower session (during which I'm glad to report that no one tried to bugger me like they do in all of those prison films) we were marched off back to our wing. At one of the many metal gates that we passed through along the way, we were stopped for a quick body search. The guy in front of me was the one who had been first across the shop counter and because of this he had three ounces of tobacco on him. He turned to me and explained that it was an offence for prisoners to have more than two ounces in their possession at any one time, and then asked if I'd do him a favour and carry an ounce back to the wing for him. I really didn't want to get involved, but as our queue drew nearer to the search and the guy began to plead with me, I couldn't be the one to drop him in it, so I took the tobacco from him.

I passed through the search – which was more like a laying-on of hands by a reluctant healer than a thorough examination of my clothing – with no trouble, and when we arrived back at the wing I found my peer the tobacco thief and gave him back his booty. After saying 'Thanks, mate,' as he bloody should have, he ripped opened one of the packets and gave me half of the tobacco inside. Again, as he bloody should have.

Later that day I was told to pack up what few personal belongings I had into the shoe box that had kindly been provided for them and was led away to a cell on another wing, where the overspill of the kitchen workers lived. The kitchen was below what I took to be the ground floor of the prison and had its own set of steps leading down to it. Opposite the kitchen were five or six cells that accommodated the cooks and bottle washers, but these were all full, which was why I was being put on a different wing.

The cooking bit of the kitchen was exactly like the kitchens I had seen in the army, with large fryers and large boilers and large tea urns and large everything. There was one prisoner, who I'll call Lofty, even though he wasn't particularly short or tall, who was the kitchen 'number one'. I guess he was the equivalent of a concentration camp 'capo' in that he had a certain authority over the other prisoners when it came to work around the kitchen, and as the number one he got extra privileges, which included no less than his own black and white portable television in his cell. Talk about luxury.

The rest of the prisoners came down for food three times a day. On one side of the kitchen there were serving hatches and at mealtimes a constant line of men walked by them for us to dollop the day's menu on to their metal trays. Normally, before the general prison population came to queue for their meals the men on what was known as 'the rule' were brought down to collect theirs separately. The rule referred to was Rule 43 of the prison code, which allowed for certain prisoners to be segregated from the rest of the prison population for their own protection. The majority of the men segregated in this way were sex offenders, men who liked children and rapists, but you could also find ex-policemen amongst their number, as well as convicts who were known to be grasses.

When I first saw the men on the rule – or the 'nonces', as they were collectively known – the first thing that struck me about them was that they were a fucking ugly-looking bunch. The majority wore thick black-rimmed National Health glasses and had buck teeth and greasy skin, and they all had a shifty look about them. Although protected from the other prisoners in general, they still came into daily contact with the kitchen staff, whose opinion of them was no better than anyone else's. As they shuffled past with their trays, my fellow kitchen workers would spit in their food or tell them we'd cooked some shit into their pies, and all in all just give them a hard time. On the whole the prison officers guarding the nonces just ignored the abuse, but on the rare occasion that a nonce would maybe spit back, and violence broke out, they were soon in there breaking it up. Even so, no further action ever seemed to be taken.

Having only ever cooked in mess tin-sized quantities before, in true hotel catering fashion I had to start on the bottom rung of the culinary ladder. And once again all of that army experience came in useful, for I had prepared vegetables and washed dixies in abundance in my khaki days. Not everyone was entrusted with the job of peeling vegetables because you got to use knives, which as you can imagine are something that no one is permitted to have in the nick. At the end of each day we had to return our knives to their lock-up and the safekeeping of the prisoner whose job it was to count them all out and then count them all back in again.

Most of the other prisoners in the kitchen were all right. Everyone else around the vegetable table with me had also recently been banged away, and it passed the time of day to stand there and peel and listen to other people's tales of failed crime. As with the guys I'd spent my first night inside with, my fellow helpers in the kitchen had all been inside before and all fell into the category of 'petty criminals'. It was a label they had been all to happy to have attached to them in court, but were not quite so keen on when found cutting cabbage at Her Majesty's pleasure. Boy, did some of them bullshit. If someone described himself as a 'burglar' and claimed to have spent all his time robbing country homes and stealing from the rich, chances were he was really a spotty-faced unemployable twat who broke into granny flats stealing pensions from the poor and valuables from the defenceless. Prisoners who called themselves 'pickpockets' in reality tended to be men who just snatched purses and ran, and again did all of their stealing from the poor. In fact, if you took your statistics from what was said by the inmates of prisons, you'd believe that no crime in this country ever occurs to anyone over fifty or to anyone who couldn't afford to be robbed in the first place.

263

As for me and my crimes, I had no need to tell porkies. I had smuggled dead plants from Central America and that was it. At first, however, no one believed that I had been a paratrooper.

'You, you cunt, you couldn't get a job as a bouncer at Mothercare.'

It was the kitchen mouth and hard man, who right from day one hadn't taken to me at all. I'll call him Dipshit, because it's how I remember him. He was exactly the same guy I'd first met in the infant school playground and kept bumping into in bars and clubs and platoons in the army ever since. It got to the point with him that every time we passed he just had to say something that would end in a threat or an insult. Of course, as we know from our father's knee, the only thing to do with bullies is smack 'em in the face as soon as they start. 'Even if you get a hiding, son, if you hurt them they'll think twice about doing it next time.' Right from the off the thought crossed my mind a thousand times, but I had two very sound reasons for not whacking him one and fuck the consequences. The first was that good old carrot, parole. If I got into trouble in prison I would add days, maybe even six months, to my sentence, whereas Dipshit, who had been 'on the in' on and off since he was six, had no chance of parole and therefore little to lose. The second reason I didn't whack him straight away was that I was scared. Big ex-para that I was, I'd never seen myself as a hard man, and certainly not by Parachute Regiment standards, but Dipshit was a big guy and strong to boot. He was one of those weightlifting fanatics you'd see in the prison gym, bench-pressing weights that I'd have trouble just getting off the floor.

The gym was a popular place, and one of the perks of working in the kitchen was that you could visit it every day. The fact that there was a gym at all surprised me, because if I'd been in charge of a pile of villains I don't think I would have provided the facilities for them to all get trained up and return to the streets fitter and stronger than they'd been when they were sent in. By the time the police got to meet them again, and with most prisoners it was a definite that they would, it stood to reason that they'd be more dangerous to catch.

On my first Sunday in the kitchen any doubts my fellow inmates may have had that I'd been a paratrooper were washed away with that day's edition of *The Mail on Sunday*. 'Falklands Veteran In Drug Bust Scandal' made a few inches on one of the inside pages, and after that there was no longer any doubt that I was the ex-para I'd always said I was.

(Twists and turns of life . . . when I later became a writer, my first journalistic assignment was for *The Mail on Sunday*, when I was sent off to cover the civil war in Bosnia. Which, incidentally, was one of the few trips I've made since that included moments when I would gladly have settled for being back in the prison kitchen in Winchester.)

So, I really was an ex-para. But Dipshit was not the least bit impressed and continued to give me nasty verbal whenever he could. I just kept walking away and trying to laugh it off, but inside I fumed and spent many a twisted hour in my cell at night fantasising about hospitalising him, to the point where it was becoming unhealthy.

Things finally snapped one morning around the veg table as I was telling my fellow peelers a war story about Northern Ireland and a friend of mine there who went on to be killed in the Falklands. Dipshit was passing, and of course he just had to say something about all paras being queers, and how he could kick the shit out of any one of us, and how he'd like to shag the wives of all the ones who'd been killed at Goose Green.

That was it for me. I don't know why, but I knew straight away that he'd crossed the line with that one. Losing parole, getting filled in, none of it mattered any more. So I let him know it. His response was to invite me out to the storeroom, which was where people always went to be out of sight of the screws when there was an argument to be settled.

'Let's go,' I said.

And do you know what? The stupid, stupid dipshit replied 'Fucking right,' and then he turned his back on me to walk off to the storeroom. Thank you, Lord.

He didn't know what had hit him, though for the record it was an industrial-sized egg whisk. Holding it by its springy wire head, I whacked him over the back of his head with its heavy metal handle. And a fine whack it was as well – though fair play to him, it didn't put the boy down. But from there on in all he could do was protect himself from the fists, knees, head butts and kicks that were raining in on him.

In all the fight lasted no more than thirty seconds before other prisoners jumped in and broke it up. By that point it was me who needed the restraining and Dipshit who needed the saving. As I was pulled off him I noticed that it was a couple of white-shirted uniforms that had done the pulling, so I relaxed and adopted a position of submission. With hardly a word, never mind a bollocking, one of the screws who had instantly appeared from the cracks in the wall led me away, out of the kitchen and back to my cell. When we got there I was asked politely to step inside and the door was locked behind me.

Trouble, eh? But boy, did I feel fucking fantastic. My big smiling body was a little tired and a little achy from its half-minute of violence, but apart from that, and a few marks on my knuckles, I had suffered not a scratch. As for Dipshit, he was no doubt in need of more than a couple of aspirins by now, and his face just had to be marked.

I was left to stew in my cell for an hour or so before the screw who had led me from the kitchen reappeared and told me to pack up my things. Apparently I was moving house again. I asked where I was going and was told I'd soon find out, so I didn't press the subject, taking it for granted that I was headed for some kind of punishment cell. Not so. I was led to another wing (I think it was B Wing), marched up two flights of steps to the second landing and put into a cell identical to the one I'd just left, except that this one was a single.

Another hour or so passed and then two prison officers dropped in to hear my side of the events in the kitchen. Dipshit, in true honest con fashion, had refused to say anything, but when I was asked who started it I replied that I did. Or that I'd thrown the first punch anyway. I'd long since learnt that with uniformed authority it's always best to come clean if you can. They like you for it. Stand up straight, tell it like it was, and tell it like a man. If you do this, you're then more likely to be given the opportunity to run through the circumstances, mitigating. So I told them that he'd been pushing me since I arrived, and that his last crack about wanting to shag the wives of dead mates from my days of service to our country was one time too many, and I went for him.

I assumed that I was now destined for a trip up before the governor, but I wasn't. The two prison officers both knew Dipshit of old and the only thing they couldn't work out was why it had taken so long for someone to give him a slap. So they let it go. No names, no pack drill. And good for me.

Of course, the fight meant that I wouldn't be returning to the kitchen, and the next day a new place of work was found for me. I had thought that sewing mailbags was an activity that only took place in prisons depicted in Giles cartoons and Ealing Studios films, but no, they really did sew mailbags in one of the prison workshops, and a needle and thread had now been reserved for me.

Working in the shop was much like I imagined it must be for members of a women's sewing circle. We sat on wooden chairs lined up in rows, like they would be in a classroom, with a screw up front playing teacher, and as we sewed and stitched we nattered amongst ourselves. The work was basically easy and untaxing, and when all's said and done I was much happier with it than I had been at any time in the kitchen. In the kitchen the day had been longer, as we had to get up at five-thirty to get breakfast on the go, and it had finished later, after dinner was over and everything had been scrubbed and put away. True, we did get to eat a lot more than the other prisoners did, but even that wasn't the gift it first appeared to be, because we always had to eat after everyone else had finished, by which time the food was at best lukewarm, anything that had once been crisp had turned soggy, the tea was always stewed, and chances were the custard and pie was all gone.

For the first few days after the fight my new accommodation included room service. I guess to avoid me trying for another round with Dipshit, all of my meals were brought up to me from the kitchen. When my first meal arrived on its tray, as the prisoner who was carrying it handed it to me at my cell door he quickly whispered for me to check the bottom of the plastic mug. Then he took a quick look around and slipped me a note. As it happens there wasn't a screw within twenty yards of us, so there was no need for him to go all secret squirrel at all. But hey! He seemed to like it, so why not? Underneath the mug was taped a piece of hash. Sizewise, if I spotted such a piece on the floor today I probably wouldn't even bother to pick it up (well, all right, a slight exaggeration maybe), but to me back then it looked like a rock. The note accompanying it just said: From the boys in the kitchen.

Aah, they liked me.

In all I spent well over a week in the cell on my own, and during that time I began to visit the prison library, go to the gym and meditate in my cell every morning and night. I had never meditated in my life before and only started after finding a book on the subject in the library. At first I found it hard to sit in one place for twenty minutes keeping still and thinking about nothing, but after a few short days I got the hang of it and felt better for doing it. I was more relaxed in myself, and better able to handle the boredom that is basically the bottom line of life inside.

On the whole, I would even say that I was beginning to enjoy my time of solitary, and I would have preferred to keep it that way. But, prisons being the overcrowded places they are, I knew it couldn't last for long. And sure enough, on my return from the mailbag shop one day, I found that another bed had been moved into the cell.

My new playmate was a man much older than myself who was apparently in for fraud, as in cheque books and other people's bank accounts. I no longer remember what his name was, but he was all right, and he must have been getting money in from somewhere because he always had plenty of tobacco and didn't seem to mind sharing it with impoverished me.

I would have been happy to stick with my new cellmate

(though purely, I have to confess, for the free supply of tobacco) if it hadn't been for one major drawback that eventually wore me down. In terms of decibels, he was to snoring what Maggie in Miami had been to sex. I tried to put up with it, I really did, but it got to the stage where I just had to get a good night's sleep, so I put in for a move. My request was answered almost immediately and I was moved along the landing to another cell on my own.

The wing screw I put my request to had been a Royal Marine before joining the prison service. He said that he'd known a good few paras when he was in the marines, and that they were all good men who would be ashamed of me and what I had done. I don't know why, and at the time I really didn't, but that got to me. It hurt like the truth. I remember saying in my defence, 'Yeah, but at least I didn't choose to come here, like you did.' And do you know what? I think that got to him.

After a couple of weeks, with no explanation, I was told I was leaving the mailbag shop and being moved to 'Plastics One', which sounded to me like a course at a technical college. In fact, it was the workshop where inmates assembled plastic switches for the dashboards on, I think, Czechoslovakian cars. Each switch was made up of four parts that had to be collected in bulk from the storeroom in different plastic buckets and then clicked together to make the complete unit. The more switches we put together, the more we got paid, although there was a limit to the number of switches you could be paid for in any one day. I forget the exact figures of it all now, but I know that when I first started I couldn't reach even half the daily maximum, and I quickly came to accept that I would never reach the giddy heights of the top rate of pay. Which was a bind, because this wasn't a Japanese factory floor, so when people did reach the daily maximum they stopped dead and did nothing for the rest of the day.

The funny thing with the switches was that the work was so fucking boring that you couldn't help but start racing yourself to make them. At first I had been putting them together as I'd been shown, one at a time: take an A, then it's B–click, C–click,

D—click, done. But then I changed to an assembly line method, putting fifty of the Bs into their As before adding all the Cs and then the Ds. This system proved quicker, and I rapidly got quicker still, until within a week – to my amazement, because I really hadn't thought it possible, folks – I was reaching the daily quota with time to spare. Which only goes to show what practice can do for you.

While working in Plastics One I received my first prison visit from Carol and my brother Lou. The system for visits worked by invitation only and each prisoner was restricted to two visits a month. To be granted one (and you were granted them, because visits were seen as a privilege), you had to send out a piece of paper called a Visiting Order to the person you were inviting, and in turn they had to contact the prison to say when they were coming.

On the appointed day a screw came into the plastics workshop and informed me that my audience awaited me. I was led from the shop across a yard I hadn't walked before and into a large prefab building that could have doubled as a temporary classroom. In what would have been a small cloakroom, my name was ticked off a list and a prison officer gave me a quick pat-down search (in case I was smuggling out plastic switches, I guess).

It had been nearly a month since I'd said goodbye to Carol on the doorstep in Aldershot and in that time her bulge had grown to double its size. If I did still have any capability to feel sorry for myself and the predicament I was in, it soon disappeared when I saw Carol. By then she would have been over seven months pregnant, and we both knew that I wouldn't see her again now until after the baby was born. She had so much to worry about – having to move out of the army flat and in with her parents, sorting out an overdraft in our joint bank account that she'd had no part in building up, being pregnant while her husband was in prison, no longer working so having to live off Social Security . . . It was just horrible for her, and yet she still found the soul to worry about me and how I was doing. And in truth, compared to her I was doing fine, relieved to have run away from all the trouble I'd caused. As for actually being inside, and the prison itself, after five years in the Parachute Regiment, it wasn't that hard.

Since I'd been in prison an unemployment giro had arrived for me, and as Carol could do with the money she had brought it along for me to sign. And here's a lesson for you. Instead of just signing it, which I could have easily done in the crowded visiting room without a screw clocking me, like a good boy I chose to ask if it would be all right for me to sign it.

Well, it wasn't. Apparently, and they weren't wrong, because I was in prison I had lost the right to sign anything. And as for saying 'But hey, man, she's pregnant and she's broke,' don't even bother. Rules is rules. In the course of the visit I asked my brother if he had any money on him, and if he did, could he please sneak me a note. Although cash couldn't be spent in prison and it was an offence to have any in your possession, it was a highly prized commodity on each wing's black market. So Lou slyly folded up a £20 note, which would do very nicely thank you, and slipped it to me under the table. I stuffed the note down the front of my trousers and prayed to the god of right that I didn't get on the receiving end of one of those strip searches I'd heard so much about.

After half an hour or so had passed, a screw came to our table and said sorry, but our time was up. I shook hands with Lou and asked him to watch out for Carol, and then I kissed her goodbye and told her to take care. We both still managed a smile as she watched me being led, like the convict I was, out of the room and back to my sentence. Hers as well, I guess. Bye-bye!

The search on the way back from the visit was as short and sweet as the one on the way in, so the £20 note that Lou had slipped me made it back to the cell with no problem. Now all I had to do was work out what to do with it. Though I needn't have bothered, because others had already being doing that for me.

That night, on wing association (which was like a free period every evening, when you could wander around the wing for an hour or so and enjoy the pleasant company of the establishment's other guests), I was approached by a man I used to work with in the kitchen. I'd never had much to do with him myself, but I knew he was a bit of a wheeler-dealer, and he somehow knew that I'd had a visit that day.

He asked if I'd managed to 'bring anything in' off my visit, and when I said that I had and that it was twenty big ones, he offered me some tobacco and/or hash for it. The deal was that I gave him the money now and tomorrow night he'd come back up from the kitchen on association and give me the smoke. So I handed over the money.

And I'm not so quick, me, after all, because I didn't get to see him again for another week. He didn't come up from the kitchen on wing association the next day and I wasn't allowed to go and visit him in his wing. In the end I got to talk to him again when he was dishing out the stew at dinner one lunchtime. And I told him straight, either I got paid tonight or I was going to cut him. With what I don't know, as the nearest thing I had to a blade was a disposable razor, but I was pissed off and he was out of order.

My attack on Dipshit had presumably left the guy with the impression that I'd carry out my threat, because that night one of his mates appeared at my cell and delivered the overdue amount.

And they say violence doesn't get you anywhere.

Incoming spoons (part 2)

I knew from the first day of my incarceration (Latin for having your balls caught between two bricks?) that I wouldn't be spending the whole of my time inside at Winchester Prison but at some point would be transferred to another jail – though heaven knew when. Apparently, where I would end up was another one of life's little lotteries, though as a first-time offender, and one who had committed a non-violent crime, the word on the wing had it that I was odds-on to end up living under a less harsh regime than the one at HMP Winchester.

One evening, while minding my own business on association (well, who wants to associate with a bunch of criminals?), I got an unexpected call to visit the wing's office. When I got there the duty prison officer informed me that he was doing the final paperwork for my transfer to another prison and asked me if I wanted anything to be taken into account before the decision was made.

By this time Carol had moved out of the flat in Aldershot and gone back to live with her parents. They lived in the Midlands, not far from Wolverhampton, so if I did have a say in my transfer then I wanted it to be to a prison as near to there as possible. After the prison officer had told me that he'd see what he could do and then dismissed me back to my cell, I did wonder if I hadn't made a mistake. After all, if they asked you that sort of question in the army and you replied, say, 'Somewhere where it's hot, please,' chances were you'd end up working in the laundry room at Camp Arctic Circle.

A few days later I was again called to the office and handed a piece of paper which confirmed that a reservation had been made for me at HM Prison Shepton Mallet. Now if I remembered rightly, Shepton Mallet was not a million miles away from Bristol, though whether north, south, east or west I couldn't quite recall. Either way, it was nearer to Wolverhampton and Carol than Winchester was, so I had to be content with that. Once I'd worked that out, the next item on the thought agenda was to find out how many stars Shepton Mallet rated in the Convict's Guide to British Prisons. Was it an open one? Did it have snooker tables like the prisons rich people get sent to?

When the day arrived for me to pack up my old kit bag and leave HMP Winchester, it was hardly heartbreaking. In fact, all that saying bye-bye left me with was a feeling that if I never, ever saw the place again it would be too soon.

Before boarding the coach that was to take us to our new prisons we were handcuffed together in pairs. While the cuffing was going on and I was waiting to find out which mass murderer I was going to be chained to for the next five hours (and what if we smash into a train carrying nuclear waste or something?), a prison officer carrying a clipboard appeared on the scene and asked which one of us was Lukowiak (which he pronounced something like Luck-Ow-Wee-I-Ack). At last! The Government must have discovered that it was all a KGB fit-up. So I took one pace forward march. I was then, without explanation, handcuffed to a prison officer. Well, at least he was clean.

Now I took my being cuffed to a screw as no more than one of those things. After all, if we had an odd number travelling, then somebody had to get cuffed to Postman Pat here. However, on the way, the coach that had picked us all up at Winchester dropped us all off again at Bristol Prison, where we were to wait before travelling on in smaller groups to our various holiday destinations. I was uncuffed from my escort (promising that I'd write and that it wasn't just a holiday romance) and put into a room with seven other prisoners who were also waiting for the transport to Shepton Mallet. After a cup of tea and a quick round of introductions, during which I teamed up with a black guy from Lewisham called Tony, who was also in for smuggling herbs, we were called forward to be cuffed for the onward journey. Once again I was asked to show myself and then handcuffed to a prison officer. Because we were an even number, this meant that one of the other prisoners would also have to be cuffed to a screw – so there went my 'one of those things' theory. Also, when it came to who they were going to handcuff to another prison officer, it didn't seem to matter who it was. 'Any volunteers?'

So why me, eh? What the fuck was I, a colonel in the IRA or something?

On the short journey to Shepton Mallet I did have a go at pumping my very own prison officer as to why somebody somewhere should have decided that I needed to be attached to a handler, but he just kept shrugging his shoulders and coming out with wise, wise remarks like 'I don't make the rules, son' and 'I'm just doing my job'.

When I thought about it (and let's be honest, who could help but think about it?) I could come up with two possible explanations as to why I had been singled out for such personal attention. It could be that the powers that be knew my wife was in the late stages of pregnancy and therefore saw me as odds-on for doing a runner to be there at the birth. There again, if I got parole I only had another four months to do, so why would I put that at risk by running now? No, what I thought was more likely, if only because on paper it would have seemed outrageously far-fetched, was that they knew that I'd been in the Paras and had spent many a happy hour (I'm sorry?) being trained in behind-enemy-lines escape and invasion. And come to think of it, having the local police ring your mum to see if you'd popped in unexpectedly for tea had to be better than having the bastards I'd played grown-up hide-and-seek with on mountains in Wales after you.

After Winchester, strangely enough arriving at Shepton Mallet was a bit like the first day at a new school. There were the 'big boys', the older cons who between them were inside for just about every crime you could think of, and then there were the new teachers and the headmaster and deputy head, played by prison officers and the prison governor and his number two (battalion 2i/c, as we would have called him in the army).

All new inmates to Shepton Mallet were accommodated for the first few weeks of their stay on A Wing. From there, once you'd been processed into the system and whoever it was that made such decisions had decided where you were going to work, you were moved over to either B or C Wing to finish your time.

What wing I would end up on (and for those of you who just can't stand a mystery, it was to be C) was settled for me on my first night 'on the in' in 'the Mallet', when I was wise enough, for once, to take some good advice. I was sitting on my bed and minding my own business as per normal, when a prison officer appeared at the cell door and asked if I was Lukowiak. As this was the third time that day that someone in uniform had asked me if I was me, I did begin to wonder why the world suddenly seemed to have developed an unhealthy interest in my identity. Oh well, get it over with and handcuff me, baby. But no, this screw didn't want to handcuff me. He merely wanted to know if it was true that I'd been in the Paras.

Well yeah, it was true. So what of it? It turned out that he had been in the regiment himself and had served his time in the same battalion as me: '2 Para, mate.' In fact, our days in battalion had overlapped briefly in early 1980, just before he got his discharge, though I had never seen or heard of him before.

The prison officer then went on to ask me things like what platoon I had been in in depot, who my platoon corporals and sergeant had been, what company I was in when I first joined the battalion, and did I know so-and-so. Because I was who I'd said I was, I had no difficulty in answering any of his questions, and midway through my replies, just in case I hadn't worked out that he'd been interrogating me, he said, 'Fuck! You really *were* in 2 Para, weren't you?'

Then he asked me how I'd ended up at Shepton Mallet. It

said something in my file about drug smuggling? So, in a no names, no pack drill type of way, I explained about Belize. And in true, compassionate Parachute Regiment Senior NCO fashion, as I related my tale of woe he laughed all the way through it. Once I'd finished, though, he did come out with one of the best summarisations of my crimes that I was ever to hear.

'Well, what a cunt you were, eh?'

He then went on to give me some tips about life on the inside in Shepton Mallet, like what and who to look out for and how best to make sure that I got that magic time-wiping parole. Firstly he recommended that instead of wasting my days in one of the prison workshops, making either donkey jackets for the Coal Board or toy soldiers for our nation's little children, I should use the time to learn a trade.

'Like what?' I asked.

'Painting and decorating's a good one,' he replied. 'You don't kill yourself, and it's not a bad little skill to have in Civvy Street.'

Not only that, but it would also look good on my parole papers if I could show that I'd been putting my time inside to good use by looking towards the future and preparing to support my family on my release.

So that was it, I decided to book myself on to the painters and decorators' course right away. In fact, don't bother, because he'd do it for me when he got back to the office. And it's funny, isn't it, how life goes, but really, years later, what a big part of the final jigsaw learning to paint and decorate was to turn out to be. And it's all the more strange that it should have been an ex-para who pointed me in that direction.

Another suggestion the prison officer had to help the old parole along was that I start to attend church every Sunday. Now he was joking? No, straight up. Apparently the types you got on parole boards tended to be of the Christian persuasion, and a good attendance report from the prison chaplain had never done anyone any harm. So, Onward Christian Soldiers – and where's my hymn book? And with all his advice given, my fellow ex-para wished me well and left.

Later that first night banged up in Shepton Mallet, while I was sitting at my little junior school-sized desk eating dinner out of a multi-compartment silver tray, I somehow managed to knock my spoon on to the floor. I leant over to pick it up, and as I reached out for it – whoosh – I was zipped back to an earlier moment in time when I had dropped another spoon. Which funnily enough had been identical to my prison spoon, right down to its embossed government issue crow's foot.

That first spoon had been dropped by my I'm-still-breathing self some two and a bit years before, and it had been dropped, almost, into a waterlogged trench on the Falkland Islands. I say almost, because as it slid towards what looked like a certain muddy end I somehow managed to dive down, all gazelle-like, and catch it. Howzat?

And here's the real funnily enough . . . When I got back up again, spoon in hand, smile on face and quite chuffed with it all, I took one look around me and saw that everyone else was now lying down. In a panic that lasted a fraction of a second, it dawned on me that they must have heard something (as in incoming, loud and potentially flesh-ripping) that I had not. So I joined them face down on the ground. And quick about it.

As it turned out, no one had heard anything. As it turned out, everyone had been hugging the ground because out the corner of his eye someone had caught my swift downward movement as I dived to rescue my spoon, and from there he and then everyone else had all fallen down like a row of camouflaged dominoes.

And how we laughed.

So, two and bit years later – from one dropped spoon to another, uniformed paratrooper to uniformed prisoner, if you like – it kind of made a nice point-to-point story and I couldn't help but have a little think about the gap in between.

Then, just like the words in that 'one word, sounds like Wong', I had to ask myself: 'How did I get here?'

By behaving like a fucking dickbrain, mate, that's how.

Which was quite right.

Best not thought about though, eh? Look on the bright side. At least here there are no mad Argentinians trying to kill you.

Which was quite right again.

Prison, though. Not a good place to have ended up, was it?

In all I think I spent about three weeks on A Wing, during which time, while I waited for the next painters and decorators' course to start, I was given a job in the prison tailor's shop and quickly stepped into the pace of my Shepton Mallet routine. And fucking boring it was too. In fact, I think that was the whole idea.

Life, though, no matter how bad or boring the circumstances (and at least banged up for six months in a British nick ain't four years chained to a Lebanese radiator), does have a way of throwing little victories our way. And it's life's little unexpected victories that keep us going, give us hope. Especially when they come like they do in *Cinderella*, bringing you down one minute, up the next, then down again, until finally the slipper fits and it's happy ever after.

On A Wing one night I was on a downer because I didn't have any tobacco to smoke, when, just before bang-up, a con appeared at my cell door (for we were in prison) and offered to lend me a quarter-ounce of Old Holborn and some cigarette papers until pay day. Well right on, and thanks, my old mate. Such was the timing of my good luck that no sooner had my fairy godmother handed me the tobacco than a screw turned up, shooed him away to his own cell and locked me and my cellmate Tony up for the night. Just made it. Hey!

And I tell you, sitting on my bed holding my newly acquired tobacco, boy, was I chuffed with life. Like the kind of happy you get when you drop your very last coin into a fruit machine (or a one-armed bandit, as they used to call them, and at least you couldn't accuse them of not giving you a clue as to the odds), press the button and immediately hit the jackpot: Pay Me Now. One second you've got nothing, the next you're flush. What a result, eh? Yeah, what a result.

But then . . .

'I–can–not–fucking–believe it!'

Do you know what? I had the tobacco and I had the papers, but I didn't have a light. What a dick. And Tony didn't smoke – well, not tobacco anyway – so he didn't have one either. If only I'd had time to think when I was loaned the tobacco I would have realised, but it all happened so quick. What a bastard!

I wouldn't say that I then lost it completely, but boy, was I pissed off. And what didn't help was Tony, who, as a non-smoker and an Afro-Caribbean one to boot, couldn't help but enjoy seeing the weak-willed white boy moaning and weeping just 'cos he couldn't have a smoke. He really thought it a joy to watch.

Eventually I stopped my moaning, sat down on my bed and said: 'Right, let's have a little think about this.'

Now, when you're at home and you haven't got a light what do you do? Well, I use a bit of rolled-up newspaper and light it on the cooker or an electric fire or something. Unfortunately, my cell didn't come fitted with household appliances, so that was out for a start. OK, so instead I go to the corner shop and score a box of matches. But once again, being in prison and all that, this was not really an option without an escape committee and a tunnel. So, what else? Sunlight through a piece of broken glass? Nope, sorry, it's nighttime. Have a go at rubbing two sticks together? Now that's just not possible, full stop. Or . . . er . . . and that was it. I was clean out of ideas.

So I got pissed with life again, and, to the accompaniment of Tony's laughter, started to pace up and down the cell like a caged animal out of one of those petroleum company TV ads.

A fresh idea finally came into my limited brain when someone in the cell above dropped something that made a loud bang. I'd forgotten all about the prison equivalent of borrowing a cupful of sugar off the neighbours.

The window in our cell was closer to the ceiling than the floor and to look out of it you needed to stand on a chair, grab hold of the bars and then pull yourself up. With that done, I managed to open the window and call out to the cell above, which I knew housed a guy called Bill, who I'd spoken to a few times in the exercise yard. Bill was in for murder, as in stabbing his uncle to death during a little family affray one Christmas. Still only in his late twenties/early thirties, he'd already been inside for seven years, which as a stretch in prison I couldn't even begin to imagine.

After I'd called Bill's name a few times a reply finally came and I asked him if he had any matches. As fate would have it he did, only unlike me he didn't have anything to light with them. So a deal was struck and a few minutes later, dangling from the end of a length of cotton (which was apparently kept by everyone for just such occasions), a box of matches arrived at my window. Once I'd untied them and pulled them safely into the cell, I attached a bit of tobacco and a few Rizlas to the thread and sent it back up.

I was going to the ball after all.

The African connection

A surprising thing about Shepton Mallet Prison (well, it surprised me anyway) was just how many Nigerians they had locked up there. And that wasn't all that was surprising, because all of them seemed to have been locked up for attempting to do the same thing, in the same way, at the same place.

The place was Arrivals, Terminal Two, Heathrow Airport and their 'thing' was having a go at walking through the green channel with a suitcase full of compressed African marijuana.

On my landing alone there were three Nigerians, all of them decent, likeable men who went out of their way to cause no offence to anyone. None of them were the bushmen that a lot of the white folks in prison assumed them to be. In fact, as with so many cases of bigotry, the exact opposite was the rule. Nearly all of them were city boys, Lagos born and bred, who on the whole possessed a better education than most of the rest of us — especially when it came to languages. Even so, their English was spoken in a very correct manner, so much so that when they did talk they sounded very incorrect. In my early days in Shepton Mallet, after bang-up at night my cellmate Tony and me would pass many a hysterical hour playing back some conversation we'd had that day with a Nigerian. They really were a hoot to talk to.

I had never been to Nigeria, and still haven't, but from the things I was told by the Nigerian inmates, it sounded like one of the most corrupt nations on the planet. Some of them had been in British prison before, but once their sentences had been served they'd been extradited home, where they apparently had no trouble buying a new passport in a new name. And then it was back to England for another go at the same thing, in the same way, at the same place.

They also all seemed to have some scam or other for making money back home, which, to be successful, needed an accomplice in England. Most of them seemed to involve a pile of traveller's cheques and a relative who worked in a bank. Personally I could never work out where the profit lay in these schemes of theirs, but even I could, there was no way I'd have wanted to get involved.

One night, while passing the time away dreaming up imaginary crimes in our cell, Tony and me came up with a scam of our own involving the Nigerians, which had nothing to do with traveller's cheques but had the benefit of being very heavily loaded in our favour. It figured, we figured, that for every Nigerian that was banged up in here with us there had to be at least twenty who had walked through customs untouched. So when we were 'on the out' we'd meet up in London one day and, dressed in our best suits, take a trip out to Heathrow Airport. When we got there we would head for Arrivals, Terminal Two and wait for incoming flights from Lagos. All we had to do then was clock the people with the appropriate baggage labels, pick out the one who wouldn't look out of place on B Wing and prepare for action. Once we had chosen our man we'd follow him down to the underground, catch the same tube as him into town, then simply walk up to him, flash a bus pass and ask if he was carrying anything that he shouldn't be.

From what we knew of the Nigerian drug-running fraternity from the tales they all told of their arrests, if our man *was* carrying anything he would instantly break down and confess. And how. ('I am guilty' – that's how.) So much so that if someone were to do a true-to-life impression of a Nigerian come 'fair cop' time, it would sound like a piss-take.

If it turned out that our man was on his first trip to England, then he might also hold the mistaken belief (as some of our Nigerian friends had told us they did at first) that he would now be taken away and shot. Therefore, it could be argued, he might just breathe a huge sigh of relief when all we did was to put him off at the next stop, minus his suitcase.

One day, during morning exercise, I heard a Nigerian tell the tale of his first grass-carrying trip to England (he was walking circles with us that day for his fourth, by the way), and it all sounded pretty much par for the course. He had flown into Heathrow direct from Lagos, of course, and been fortunate enough to breeze through customs untouched. From the airport he had caught the tube to Brixton, where he had heard, from a close friend back home, that he would be able to sell his grass.

When he reached Brixton he walked into the first café he came across and had the good fortune to meet a gentleman of Jamaican extraction, who said that he would be able to help the Nigerian move his weed with no problem. The Jamaican guy took the grass and told our Nigerian friend to wait, saying he would be back in one hour with the cash.

'But do you know?' the Nigerian said, still able to look wide-eyed and shocked after all these years. 'He did not return.'

'No! It cannot be,' we all replied in disbelief of the mocking kind.

'But it is true,' he insisted, pinching the skin on his left forearm as he added, 'yet he had the same colour skin as me.'

Of course, on the wings the majority of homespun criminal opinion said of the Nigerians that they were so well fed and looked after in prison in England that they were better off than they would have been back home in their own country. 'Paradise for 'em in 'ere it is.'

It's true that they certainly smiled a lot, but given the right day they could find it all just as miserable and frustrating as the rest of us. There was one Nigerian guy, named John, who lived two doors along the landing from me. John was a real gentle giant of a man who was also very religious, and each night he would pray on his knees, surrounded by the pictures of the Virgin Mary and the Pope that decorated the walls of his cell. He was married with three children and had last seen his family nearly two years before, when they had waved goodbye to him and his suitcase at Lagos Airport.

John lived every day, as did most of us, with the lottery of parole. The bottom and worst line with parole is that you can reach a point where, for instance, you don't know whether you have only one month still to serve or (as in John's case) two years and one month. There were hard and fast rules governing who got parole and who didn't, though just like the supposedly hard and fast rules surrounding anything in life, there were always exceptions. If your offence had been drugs, the running of, then the chances were that you wouldn't get parole. But there again, that tended to apply only to drugs as in heroin and cocaine. When marijuana was involved it was by no means a negative certainty. Sometimes people got parole, other times they didn't.

The Nigerians, though, were nearly always granted parole, followed by a same-day deportation. After all: 'Do you know how much it costs the British taxpayer to keep all of those foreign criminals locked up in 'ere?' Well, lots.

John was therefore pretty sure that he would get parole, and one day he got back to the wing after work and was called into the office . . . only to be told that his fellow Christians on the parole board had turned him down. In a stroke, John's strong hope of seeing his wife and children the following month had turned into no hope at all, and all that night everyone on the wing could hear him weeping with despair.

'Shut up and do your bird!'

Promise for a new life

It was the 2nd of November 1984. And I had no tobacco – I remember that. My transfer to the City & Guilds Painting and Decorating course had not yet come through and I was still stitching together sleeves for donkey jackets in the prison tailor's shop. I used to hear people say of my job, 'Stitching sleeves? Nice work if you can get it, pal,' but it never seemed that way to me. I hated it and would much rather have passed my time in the 'Noddy shop' below, which was so named, I was told, because it was the sort of place you could just imagine Noddy heading off to each morning, packed lunch in hand.

The prisoners who worked in the Noddy shop below passed their time making battalions of miniature plastic soldiers. As these fall into the category of 'war toys', it could be argued that working alongside Noddy rated very low on the politically correct work scale, but it did pay all right, and everyone who worked in the Noddy shop said they did good old fuck all when they were there.

In the prison tailor's shop the donkey jackets that we made were for Britain's coalminers, who, as I sat stitching sleeves, were all out on strike, doing not a lot and earning bad old fuck all.

With the miners on strike, their donkey jackets began to pile up at one end of the shop, but that didn't stop us from putting yet more together. So I kept stitching away, and as I stitched I couldn't help but think that given a couple of left-wing agitators, or better still a couple of right-wing infiltrators posing as left-wing agitators, the workshops of Her Majesty's Prison Shepton Mallet could be brought to a grinding halt. Up with the miners! Down with war toys for our children!

My sleeve-stitching for the donkey jackets for the Coal Board for the miners who didn't need them was done on a piecework basis. The more I stitched, the more I got paid, and the more I got paid, the more tobacco I could buy. However, by whatever day of the week it was on the 2nd of November 1984, my stitch rate had not yet reached a level where it could feed my need-to-smoke rate.

(On a Wednesday morning nearly nine years later, while being interviewed for a radio station in Cornwall, I was asked what had been the most noticeable improvement in my life since my writings were first published. I replied: 'Every morning now, when I wake up, I open my eyes and see a pack of cigarettes waiting for me.' And I wasn't joking. I am a very serious nicotine addict.)

So on the 2nd of November 1984 my lack of nicotine was causing me many different-coloured types of head problem. And just in case that wasn't enough, just to add that Mogadon touch, the speakers on the walls around the tailor's shop were playing elevator-type music that was only interrupted by the voice of Jimmy Young. I can recall thinking at the time that my mother would have liked it very much. As Jimmy chattered away and the elevator of my mind went up and down and then up again, I was getting very pissed off, and I do mean very. With life, the prison, me and everything. I really could have done with a fix of nicotine.

My inner ranting only stopped when a fellow prisoner came up to me, bringing a message.

'The screw in the office wants to see you.'

I knew why.

I got up from my sewing machine and walked across the workshop towards the office. And it's a funny thing (though there's no laugh in it for me, not even today), but I really do remember that. If I close my eyes I can still feel my black slip-on shoes stepping on the vinyl floor tiles and my fingers pulling down the hem of my jumper. But when I revisit this time from the past I can't recall what I was thinking. I can't quite manage that. I know I wasn't thinking happy thoughts, as there was no way my shame would have allowed me to. But I must have wondered if I now had a son or a daughter. I must have wondered that.

When I reached the office I tapped politely on the open door. The prison officer was sitting at his desk reading the morning paper. On the desk next to his paper was a large tin ashtray that was almost filled with half-smoked cigarette butts. The cigarettes had long filters – I remember that. I also remember that when I saw them I wished that I could have them, so that I could break them down and re-roll them to smoke.

The prison officer looked up from his paper, smiled and said that the prison had received a telephone call from my mother-in-law. Carol had given birth to a baby boy in the early hours of the morning.

Besides saying thank you, I don't think I said much in response to this news. I don't remember. What I do remember is that I thought of asking the prison officer for the contents of his ashtray. In the circumstances, I thought, I stood a good chance of him giving it to me. He might take pity on me. But then I thought about one day standing in front of my son and telling him about the day I had heard of his birth. How I was in prison at the time, and how just after learning of his arrival I had asked for the contents of another man's ashtray. After that I thought no more of asking. And good for me.

Before sending me back to my sewing machine, the prison officer gave me some well-meaning advice. He said something like 'You have a son now. In future you want to try hard to keep out of places like this.' And good for him.

I once again thanked him for the news and then made my way to the washrooms. I could be alone there. I could have a go at thinking things through.

In the washroioms I found a space on the floor, sat myself down and started to think. And as I thought I started to look. I was in prison, not a good place to be. So I looked for people to blame, but could only find me. I forced into my mind memories of the war, of the dead men I had seen, and I tried to blame them for where I had ended up. And still I could only blame me. Then I tried to tell myself that everything was wrong, the world was upside down. Travel thousands of miles away from home and kill people, and they give you a medal. Travel thousands of miles away from home again a year later, bring back a few dead plants, and they lock you up for months. But I knew that in thinking that I was just being naïve – even though it was the truth. So still I blamed me.

Finally I realised, plainly and simply, that I *was* to blame, that what I had done was wrong. Not necessarily because the law said so, or because God might disapprove, or even because it was against Queen's Regulations paragraph lots-of-numbers. It was wrong because it had caused pain to others, shame to others.

And with that thought I felt so helpless. My mind filled with thoughts of my sweet wife and our new life, and I hurt so much that I broke down and cried. Poor me.

Then, as the tears fell from my eyes. I began to make promises. I promised that I would turn things around. I promised that I would do my time, leave prison and become a good man again. I would find work. I would find somewhere for us to live. I would become someone my wife and our new son could feel proud to call husband and father. This I swore. And this time I meant it. Truly.

My tearful self-pity was interrupted when another prisoner entered the toilets. I looked up from my sorrow, thinking that he would just ignore me – not so much because he didn't care, but because sometimes it's best to leave a crying man to himself, especially in prison. But he stopped and asked me what was wrong. So I told him about the birth of my son and how sad I was to be where I was, and how stupid I had been, and how sorry I was for my actions.

'Life's a bastard,' he said, and all I could do was nod in agreement.

Then he asked me what I was in for. So I told him. I told him all about the army and Belize and my marijuana smuggling.

'You wouldn't believe the high,' I remarked at one point.

'Good, was it?'

'Unbelievable,' I said.

Then, before you could say something you might feel like saying, the two of us were up and running in the two-thirty in the dooby-fillers' stakes. Lots of 'I had this stuff one time in Africa . . .' and 'Well, this gear I smoked in Mexico once . . .' and so on.

And here's the good bit – he had some on him.

So I said, 'Skin up.'

And he said, 'It's already rolled.'

Then we sat together on the washroom floor and smoked his joint. It was some kind of squidgy black – I remember that. And it got me very, very stoned.

'How did you get it in?' I asked. 'Did you swallow it and then shit it out, or did you make yourself throw it up?'

'I swallowed it and shat it out the next day,' he told me.

Then he said something which, in my stoned state, I found very, very funny: 'That's put me right back in my tree, that has.'

I laughed so hard I couldn't stop.

Today, as I sit back in my own tree, I no longer laugh at this. Because, only a short time before I laughed so hard that day, I had supposedly been overcome by true sorrow. I had supposedly felt shame for my crimes, and in my remorse I had made promises for the future. Promises which this time I intended to keep.

But then I smoked a joint. And my true sorrow and true shame and true remorse and true promises, they all hit the ceiling with the smoke. For if I had been caught smoking and toking in the washrooms that day I would automatically have lost my parole. I would instantly have added another six months to my sentence – a sentence shared by my sweet wife and our 'new life', the very people I had supposedly just been weeping truth for.

Today, when I recall that time in the prison washrooms on

the 2nd of November 1984, the day my son was born, the day I sat stoned on the floor next to a prison urinal, I realise me. And I don't think much of me.

And now I don't feel like writing any more. Not another word. So I won't.

Because I'm a free man now.

Even if I have written another word after I said I wouldn't. Poor me. Fuck me!

Bend over . . .

When the day finally came for me to see my son, in the morning I went to work in the decorators' shop just like on any other weekday. Because I knew Carol would be visiting with the baby that afternoon, the time dragged. As of course it would. I did attempt to lose myself in my work, but no matter how I tried, I couldn't stop myself from looking at the clock. Do your head in that sort of thing can.

But eventually the morning passed. And after lunch, when everybody else returned to the workshops, I remained in my cell, polished shoes and best jeans and jumper on.

When you're waiting in a cell on an empty prison wing you can't help but hear all the palaver that goes on every time someone either comes on to the wing or leaves it – doors being unlocked, keys being rattled, bolts being thrown, the call of 'One on' – and, like a child waiting for the school tuck shop to open, every time the rigmarole started I wondered if it heralded the start of my visit.

And then finally my name got called and I was led off to face a horrible/joyous mix of emotions. To cut a long walk short, he was like a little teddy bear, dressed in his one-piece fluffy suit. And Carol looked just beautiful. Holding my son for the first time, and going 'goo-goo', the way you do, I really did feel so happy and yet so ashamed at the same time. Because this was not the way it was supposed to be. Never mind for me, but for them. It was not the way it was supposed to be for them.

Time now flew at treble speed of course, and when it had all gone I sat in silence as I watched Carol turn and smile one last time before they both disappeared out of the door. Bye-bye, eh?

After the visit I was escorted back into the small room in which the searches were carried out, where, sad as I was and ashamed as I was, I expected no more than a pat down. After all, the game was that sometimes they would search you and sometimes they wouldn't, so they didn't have to. But, to my horror, for the first and only time after a prison visit I was told to strip.

You should have seen me then. Fucking jailbird drug-runner, mate–ex-para–been to war–know the score. As I began to undress I felt so humiliated. And it got worse, because once I'd stripped and lifted my feet and had my hair and my fingernails searched, I was ordered to bend over and spread my cheeks. To this day (not surprisingly) I can remember wondering, and then praying: 'Oh God, no. They're not going to put on rubber gloves?'

I thought about the two men who were doing this to me, and what I thought was: 'You, you fucking pair of screw arsehole bastards. Do you think I would allow my wife to come into this jail with my son carrying drugs? What do you think I am, you fucking pair of key-holding scumbags – a convicted drug-runner or something?'

It was clear that what I had here was a pair of bullshit bastards who could see how upset I was and were taking the opportunity to give me a bit more grief.

'But I'll tell you what, son.'

'What, dad?'

Out of everything in prison and about prison – the being locked up, the lack of freedom, lack of sex, lack of food, lack of space, lack of all life's little comforts – that strip search was by far the greatest deterrent to me *ever* committing a crime again.

And do you know what? Today, when I look back, I wonder if those two prison officers weren't actually doing me a large favour, and maybe even knew what they were doing. But there again, when it comes to drug-takers, especially those needle-in-the-arm types, there are some who would smuggle smack in their dead mother's ashes if they thought it would help get it through the green channel.

You take my word for it. You 'just say no' – even if it is years since Nancy Reagan first coined the phrase.

'Who, dad?'

Gambling back to happiness

For a time back there in Shepton Mallet, my three cellmates and me (God bless us) were the richest convicts on the wing. Of course, on the other side of the prison walls we still had absolute zilch between us, but inside we never lacked for tobacco or hash or sugar or powdered milk, or even, can you believe it, cornflakes. Now that is rich. If credit's to be given where credit's due, then it has to be said that it was me who had the accident of fate that put us on the road to such riches (though likewise, I would never have got there without the others aboard).

It all began on the walk over to the workshops one morning, when I happened to notice three different prisoners approach the same man, say something to him, and then pass him some tobacco. Having not quite been born the day before yesterday, I had a pretty good idea what was going on here, but just to make sure I sought a second opinion from the man walking next to me. And sure enough, the prisoner taking the tobacco was a bookie.

With that piece of knowledge shelved away, it wasn't too long before I decided to have a little punt on the horses myself. So the next day after pay day I scanned the exercise yard in search of the bookie. But I couldn't see him anywhere. Eventually I spotted one of the men I'd seen placing a bet with him on the way to the workshops that time and asked him if he'd seen the bookie.

'He's gone,' he told me. 'Not released, either. Just disappeared before opening up this morning.'

That same evening I passed this information on to my three cellmates and asked Malcolm, because he had been to prison the most, where he thought the bookie could have gone so suddenly. Having seen it all during his years inside, Malcolm had several possible explanations for the bookie's sudden departure – the big favourite being that someone had found out that he was not the sort of honest-to-goodness everyday wholesome criminal that the rest of us were. In other words, he was either a child molester, a rapist or even, God forbid, an ex-policeman.

If that was Malcolm's odds-on favourite, then his three-legged outsider put into the starting stalls facing backwards with a blind one-armed jockey aboard was that the man's disappearance had anything to do with his sideline as a turf accountant.

'If they sent him to another prison for that, it would be like admitting they couldn't control what goes on in their own nick.'

So then I said, more thinking out loud than anything, if he was now gone, why didn't we replace him? It stood to reason that it had to be a good business to be in. After all, apart from a couple of the Nigerians, who could name one single prisoner on our wing who didn't like a bet?

To set up our bookmaking business, the first thing we had to do was pool our capital and get a bit of payout money behind us. In prison the main everyday currencies are tobacco, hashish and cash in note form. On top of these, there were a number of other items which, given the right day, could be exchanged for tobacco. Most of these items came into circulation because they had been purchased with prisoners' 'private money', which meant any cash they may have had on them when they were sent down, or any that had been sent in to them by friends or family since. There were various restrictions on the use of private money – for example, you were not permitted to buy tobacco, food or sweets with it (which just about covered everything you might have liked to buy with it) – but you could use it to buy radio batteries, newspapers or bags of matchsticks for modelling.

I had a few pounds of private money my dad had posted in to me, so the next morning I put in an order for a large EverReady battery and a bag of matchsticks. When they arrived I swapped them for tobacco and added it to the pot. We also, just at the right time, had me come first and Jock second in the wing's weekly pool tournament. So, when we added the two ounces of tobacco which that had brought in, our start-up pot stood at nine ounces.

We agreed that to begin with we'd have to go steady and be careful what sort of bets we laid. If someone was to put an ounce on a twenty-to-one shot and have it romp home, then we were sunk. To avoid this happening we decided that to begin with we would take no single bet of more than half an ounce, and we would only pay up to odds of four to one. This meant that if you bet on a horse with us and it came in at four to one or less, we'd pay you those odds, but if it came in at, say, six to one, then we'd still only pay you fours. In a way this was unfair, although on the positive side it did say that we wouldn't take any bet we couldn't pay out on.

We also agreed that we wouldn't take any bets from prisoners who didn't live on our wing, and that all bets had to be placed with the tobacco stake up front.

For our first couple of days' trading, business was slow to the point of being non-existent, but that rapidly changed come the first Saturday afternoon and live racing on the television. In short, we took in six separate bets totalling two and a half ounces and didn't have to pay out on one. Which was a great start. Out of the winnings the four of us took a dividend of a quarter-ounce of tobacco each, leaving the payout pot up at ten and a half ounces.

Our next action came the following day, when there was a live football match on the TV between Sheffield Wednesday and Arsenal. As a bet, a football match is a three-horse race: it's either a home win, an away win or a draw. Even though

Arsenal were the away side, they were big favourites to win the game.

Since I was the one who had once worked as a croupier, it was left to me to calculate our odds for the match. I knew that all three of the people who had so far enquired whether we were going to take bets wanted to place their hard-earned tobacco on Arsenal, so I made Arsenal our two-to-one on favourites. This meant that if someone bet half an ounce and Arsenal won, then we'd have to give them their half-ounce back plus a further quarter-ounce in winnings. With Arsenal at odds of two to one on, I should have made Sheffield Wednesday at least four to one, but hey! – we weren't Ladbrokes. So I made them six to four to win, with the draw at even money.

By the time the game kicked off we were in the enviable position of being guaranteed to end up in front no matter the result. If Arsenal won, we would be one ounce up. If it was a draw, we'd be up three and a half ounces. And if Sheffield Wednesday won, then we'd be ahead by the fantastic sum of five ounces.

If there was one thing I'd learned as a croupier, it was that when you're taking people's money off them you should do it with grace. Don't get loud, never brag, don't ever tell anyone else about the person's loss. Just do it quietly and with grace. Before we all settled around the TV to watch the match, I passed on these words of wisdom to the others. 'And don't let *anyone* know that we're in front no matter what happens,' I warned them.

Ninety minutes of football later, as the final whistle blew and Sheffield Wednesday had won the contest by one goal to nil, it was me that was having trouble behaving with grace. Between us we now had fifteen and a half ounces, which in terms of hard currency in one cell made us fairly wealthy men.

Unfortunately, it also made us illegal men, as no prisoner was allowed to own more than two and a half ounces of tobacco at any one time. What's more, according to Malcolm there was now a strong chance of our cell being searched, because he was sure that by the end of Saturday's racing there wouldn't have been a screw in the prison who didn't know that we now ran a book. Someone somewhere would have just had to give away our little secret. As Malcolm would often tell me, 'Your worst enemies in 'ere, mate, are not the key-carrying screws but the other prisoners.' And he was right, because after all was said and done, at least you always knew exactly where you stood with a screw, and there were very few prisoners you could say that about.

To get around our problem, for the time being at least, we had two choices: we could either give our surplus tobacco to other people to hold for us or we could hide it somewhere. Like most choices in life, both of these options had their drawbacks. If we gave it to someone else to look after, we would probably have to pay them. On top of that, there was always the possibility that they might not want to give it back. Hiding the tobacco was not as easy as it sounded either. The obvious place to stash it would have been in one of the workshops, except that they were always being searched by people and dogs.

In the end, we settled on getting other people to look after it for us. I managed to pass two ounces on to Tony, in exchange for two straight cigarettes on pay day, and in the interests of goodwill to all men we loaned out the remaining surplus to the men who had lost it to us.

As the days passed and our payout pot grew larger and larger, we started to convert our tobacco into other currencies. The one we were always on the lookout for was hashish – though in truth, when we did get hold of some it wasn't so much a case of currency conversion as a spending spree, because we always smoked it. After hash, our next love was cash in note form. Cash was not only far less bulky than tobacco, so it could be concealed easily, it was also the preferred currency of the prisoners who sold the dope. In most cases it was their wives and girlfriends who were passing the hash over to them on visits, so it was always nice for them to be able to hand some cash back. And it was very profitable, because hash increased in price tenfold once it had made it past the prison gates.

Another way we got to exchange our wealth was in the

prison shop. Of course, we couldn't just take five ounces of tobacco along and say 'Can I swap this for Bounty bars, please?', but we could get the people who owed us tobacco to buy us other things in its place. As prison is a 'no free rides' type of establishment, this naturally always cost us a few pennies, but it was still very appealing to us.

During the third week of our bookmaking operation Malcolm's prediction of a cell search came to pass. I was papering a ceiling in my decorators' class at the time, and just as I had finished pasting two pieces of woodchip and was about to hang the first, two prison officers came into the shop and made a beeline for me. Because I'd never had the pleasure of having my cell 'spun' before, it wasn't my obvious choice for why they were leading me away. They wouldn't say where they were taking me, so at first I thought maybe there was some bad news from home waiting for me up at the governor's office. I discounted that one as soon as we walked on to the wing and up the stairs that led to my cell. Standing on the landing outside it, awaiting my arrival, were Bob, Malcolm and Jock and another two prison officers.

The first thing they did was strip-search us on the landing. Then, once we'd dressed again, they led us one at time into the cell and went through everything. It was obvious that the screws had all done this a thousand times before, but by the end of it, bar a couple of extra jumpers, they didn't find anything we shouldn't have had. They did, however, comment on what rich convicts we were, what with each of us having two ounces of tobacco in our lockers, plus powdered milk and sugar, and even, can you believe it, four whole boxes of cornflakes.

The screws, of course, knew perfectly well where our wealth had come from (and we, of course, knew perfectly well that they knew). But they asked us all the same. We just replied that people had given it to us – because they liked us.

If I was the one who had been responsible for leading us into the bookmaking business, then it's also fair to say that I was the one who was responsible for taking us out of it.

It all fell apart one night when I lost a load of tobacco at pool to Woody from the kitchen. As I passed it over to him pack by pack, I did say aloud: 'I don't believe it!' – but inside I replied: 'Oh yes you do.' I may have been a far better pool player than Woody and normally would have had no trouble in beating him, but not tonight. He was shoving it up me sideways. And really, I should have known better, not allowed myself to go in so deep.

As a teenager in Kalgoorlie I had once played pool with the Australian snooker professional Eddie Charlton, who said to me on the subject of 8-ball that it didn't matter who you were, on the right day your blind grandmother could take a frame off you. Added to that, I knew more than enough about gambling to be aware that when Lady Luck turned against you it was with a vengeance. Yet still I bet on.

By the time I reached the point in my life where I was shooting pool on a table in prison for large amounts of local currency, I was well past being able to fool myself that I would never do it again. I was even well past just saying it. All I could do was try and live with the fact that Jesus or drugs or psychotherapy or any other mind-changing experience that might jump out and say 'I can stop your self-destruction' could, in fact, not.

Not only did I lose to Woody what I had on me and what was in my cell, I also went into debt. By the time the bell finally rang for the end of association I had gone from being one of the four richest people on the wing to one of the poorest. Though once again, credit where credit's due, in the pool room at least I showed little outward sign of all the 'stupid fucking me' thoughts that were ripping up my brain. Again.

When I got back to the cell, instead of just saying 'Hey guys, I've done my whack,' I sat on the end of my bed and said nothing. And then I retreated into a black and silent mood that lasted for nearly a week.

Over that time the atmosphere in the cell became unbearable. To pay off my debt I withdrew my share of the payout money and said that I didn't want to be a part of it any more. Then I stopped talking to the others, and so – 'Fuck him' – they stopped talking to me. As I withdrew deeper and deeper into my silent mood, the worst of it for me was that I could see what I was doing, what I was becoming, but I couldn't stop myself.

If I was somewhere, then the air around me was tense. Soon the other three began to blank me completely. They would sit talking in Malcolm and Bob's half of the cell and I would sit quietly in mine. In my mind I got angry about everyone and everything, inside and outside of the prison walls. Which was stupid and illogical and not right and I knew it.

Things finally came to a head one night after lock-up. The lights were out and in the darkness Malcolm and Bob were having a conversation about cars. At one point they were both trying to remember the name of the car plant outside their native Oxford. So I interrupted.

'Crowley,' I said.

As I received no reply, I forced the issue and asked if they had heard me. Malcolm, refusing to talk to me directly, told Bob to tell me to shut up. Then he told Bob to tell me what would happen to me if I didn't.

'Why can't you tell me yourself, Malcolm?' I asked him.

In reply, once again via Bob, I was told one more word from me and Malcolm was going to come in there and cut me up. I knew enough about Malcolm's past to realise that this was no idle threat. I also knew that he had a Stanley knife for matchstick modelling tucked under his bed and wouldn't think twice about using it.

Even though it was dark and there was a wall between us and we were lying in separate beds, we were now eyeball to eyeball with teeth bared.

So I got scared, because I knew that I either had to just shut up and learn to live with having backed down, or I could carry on talking and prepare myself for violence.

I had to say something. I just couldn't stop myself. Halfway through whatever it was I did say, Malcolm let out a 'That's fucking it' and the lights in his part of the cell flashed on. I immediately jumped naked from my bed, pulled my spare blanket out of my locker and wrapped it around my left arm. I had been taught in military unarmed combat lessons that if an opponent has a knife, then you need to get something between you and its blade. And I must have been taught this well, because I just did it without thinking.

The doorway between our two halves of the cell had a small locker blocking it, which Malcolm had placed there one afternoon as a physical sign of the divide between us. He kicked it forward and it crashed into my side of the cell, spilling two pisspots full of urine over the floor. Malcolm appeared and lunged at me with the blade. I lifted the blanket and deflected the blow. The blade missed my face but caught me just above my left elbow. I saw a spurt of my blood shoot through the air. I began to lash out at him with my right fist and managed to trip him over backwards on to my bed. Then, and I don't know how, I was sitting on top him, pinning him down, and I was holding his blade against his throat. I was just about to start stabbing it into his neck when I realised what I was doing and stopped myself.

'You fucking had enough?' I shouted, and then I held the blade against his left eyeball. If he had said 'Fuck you' at that point, I don't know what I might have done, though I do know I wouldn't have stuck the blade into his eye. I was past animal reactions like that. Thankfully, though, Malcolm *had* had enough.

Our fight had been a noisy one and it wasn't too long before we could hear the never-to-be-mistaken sound of screws, with their keys a-jangling, stamping along the landing. I climbed off Malcolm and he darted back into his part of the cell and turned the lights off. I threw the blade under my bed and stood, naked, staring straight ahead of me at a point on the wall. In my head I imagined prison officers dressed in riot helmets and carrying batons bearing down on our cell.

The spyhole in the door lifted and a voice asked: 'What's going on in there?'

'Nothing, it's over,' I said.

The key turned in the lock and the cell door swung open. Standing there were two unarmed night screws, both of them in their sixties and neither of them a match for me, never mind all four of us.

'Who were you fighting with?' one of them asked.

'No one,' I replied. 'I wasn't fighting. I've had a son born. I'm doing bird. I just got angry, that's all.'

'So what happened to your arm?'

I looked at my left arm and saw that the bottom half of it was covered in blood.

'Nothing. I slipped, OK? I'm sorry, and it's over.'

They thought about this for a few moments and then one of them asked: 'Are you sure it's over?'

'Yes. It's over.'

I thought that they would then lead me away to 'the Block', but no, they must have been happy with my explanation because all they did was close the cell door on me. Its locks turned and they headed off back to their newspapers and tea.

I sat down on the end of my bed and inspected my battle wound. The cut was a short one but it had gone in deep and could maybe have done with a stitch or two. Then I got around to thinking what I should have thought as soon as the night screws had closed the cell door. Malcolm. He might come charging back in for round two. I retrieved the blade from under the bed, put it by my side and said to myself 'Just let the fucker try.' But I didn't want him to.

The silence was eventually broken by Malcolm saying to Bob: 'He handled that well with the screws, I thought. Didn't you, Bob?'

Bob grunted agreement in his West Country accent, then the lights were turned on in their half of the cell and Malcolm asked me if I was all right. I said I was OK and in return asked him if he was. He apologised for attacking me and I apologised for the time I'd spent being a moody wanker.

Then Malcolm wandered into my part of the cell and offered me a smoke, for which I was more than grateful because I was still broke. Then the two of us got down on our knees and began to wipe up the piss he had spilt with our towels. And boy, did it stink. But as we mopped, we laughed, and as we laughed, the atmosphere that I had filled the cell with over the past few days evaporated.

Later that same night, when the lights were finally turned out and life in our cell resembled the closing scene from an episode of *The Waltons*, it felt so good not to be in a bad mood any more. Which only made me wonder all the more why I had ever got into one in the first place.

The next morning I was called to the wing office, where, to my surprise, I found the prison governor himself sitting behind the desk. With a screw on either side of me, I was marched in front of him and brought to a halt. Although I had never been hauled up before the governor before, I had been in very similar circumstances in the army a hundred times, i.e. up in front of someone of higher rank who knew full well what had gone on. So I came to attention and treated the governor as I would an officer of the Parachute Regiment.

His first question was who had I been fighting with last night? To what I imagine was his surprise, I told him, though I didn't mention that it was Malcolm who had attacked me first, or that a Stanley knife had been involved. While telling the governor about the events of the previous night I stood to attention, chest out, stomach in, looking straight ahead. When I came to my punchline – 'It's over now, sir, and it won't happen again' – I looked at him, in a decent, manly sort of way, straight in the eyes. And as he looked back at me I could tell that he was wishing he had a prison full of well-disciplined convicts like my good self.

Aah, if only . . .

He then became all decent and manly himself, saying that he would take my word for it. No names, no pack drill.

'Prisoner dismissed.'

When I got back to the cell I told the others that I had said nothing, just kept denying that there had been any fight. And because Malcolm never got the call to the office that he thought might come after I'd been in, they all took my word for it. And why not?

The night before my release from prison, Malcolm confessed

to me that after our fight he had stayed awake all night worrying that I be might thinking it was my turn to attack him now. As for me, all I could remember of the aftermath of the fight was just how glad I was that my black mood had lifted and we were all talking again. I really was happy with the way things turned out.

One man's poison is another man's food, I guess.

And now for the real sentence

Just like I had always known it would, click-clunk, my release day arrived, and as with most of the major events of my life, except maybe parachuting and the Falklands War, it all turned out to be pretty much of an anticlimax. Which was a bit surprising, really, as I'd been the sort of prisoner who quite literally scratched away the days like the Count of Monte Cristo (though I did it on the back page of an exercise book). I had therefore always imagined that when I awoke on release day it would feel like there was one big joyful morning ahead of me, like the ones Welsh choirboys and Cat Stevens used to sing about.

The night before, I had walked the wing for the last time (thank fuck, eh?) and said my goodbyes to what pals I'd made since being locked up in Shepton Mallet. Though to be honest, and this really was nothing personal, I had no particular wish to meet any of them again. I'd already decided a long time ago that this was a portion of my life that I didn't ever want to revisit. When lights out finally came, I lay back on my bed and thought what I imagine every prisoner due to be released the next morning must think: 'This is for the very last time.' Of course, then I couldn't sleep for the rest of the night. For you see, inside I wasn't entirely sure that I was looking forward to my release. Yes, I couldn't wait to get out of these four walls that surround me and go back to doing things when and where I liked again, like go down the pub, watch TV late, even just eat whenever I fancied. But as for the domestic situation that awaited me when I got out, that I wasn't looking forward to.

Carol and our son were now living back with her parents and the only plan we had was for me to join them there. I hadn't seen my in-laws since the summer of '84, or to put it another way, for about eight months, and the first they had heard of my crimes, arrest, dismissal from the army, appearances in court and – for after-dinner mint – eighteen-month prison sentence was when Carol had phoned them on the day I was locked away. Which was brave of me.

One reason why we hadn't told them as things went down was that maybe, just maybe, I might have walked from court a free man or at least got away with a sentence of only a couple of months, which, as a period of absence, we could have invented some story to cover up for. Of course, another reason (and, if I'm honest, the main one) was that I was scared to tell Carol's parents. I mean, how do you put something like that? Anyway, whatever, however . . . tomorrow I was going to have to face them.

Also, I now had a three-month-old son who I'd only seen once, so I should have been overjoyed at the thought of seeing him again tomorrow. And I was. Yet at the same time I wasn't, because again I was scared. And the reason was that I didn't know if I'd be able to handle it all, or in other words, live up to my responsibilities. Well, it would be a first.

On release day morning, after breakfast ('I'll skip today's if you don't mind') and one last round of people wishing me 'Good luck on the out,' while everyone else set off for the workshops I was called from the wing and led down to the storerooms. At a counter not dissimilar to the type you might find in a quartermaster's store in the army, a prison officer confirmed my identity and then passed me a clipboard, on which I signed for a long, flat cardboard box containing the clothes that I had last worn in Winchester, six months ago to the day.

My 'civvies' in the box consisted of my two-piece grey suit, white shirt, maroon tie and burgundy-coloured slip-on shoes.

Naturally, as I put them on I couldn't help but remember the day in Manchester when I'd bought them, and that it was money from the first parcel of grass that I'd bought them with. So, two elephants falling off a cliff, boom boom ... what a fucking outrageously expensive set of clothes that turned out to be.

Once I'd done a Clark Kent (only quicker), and was back into my old identity (only thinner), I was given a small amount of cash, a giro cheque for about thirty pounds and a one-way rail ticket to Stafford. I was then led through a door opening on to a courtyard that was to be the no man's land between me and my freedom. And then (most disappointingly, I might say), I was released into the outside world through a wire gate that wouldn't have looked out of place on a tennis court. It was a bit like being the last kid let out of the park before the park keeper locks up for the night. I really had been expecting the big double wooden gate business, with a small door in one corner that had to be stepped through. And they did have one of those at Shepton Mallet, but for some reason I wasn't returned to the outside world through it. Oh well, at least I was out. Hey!

I shook hands with the prison officer who had opened the gate and, with no malice intended on either side, we both hoped out loud that we would never meet again, not around these parts anyway. As I walked away from the prison I couldn't help but stop and do a Lot's wife (can airlines be married?) and as I took a last look over my shoulder I found myself thinking of, and then comparing the view with, the time I had stood on the deck of the *MV Norland* taking my last look back at the Falkland Islands.

Oh, and that Mary Hopkins was so right.

Like that time on the *Norland*, this was a final look at something that would stay with me for life. So what had I learned? Well, that I had fucked up with a capital everything. And although I might like to think that it was all over now, because I was out now, I knew that it probably wasn't. I then thought yet again, for the Lord knows how many-eth time, how grateful I was to have spent five years in the Parachute

Regiment before having the pleasure of six months in one of Her Majesty's prisons. For the having eaten food off stainless steel trays before alone.

I walked up the hill that led away from the prison and made my first contact with the outside world when I stopped at a small newsagent's. And how fitting that my very first act of freedom should be to rejoin the consumer society and spend some cash – on a newspaper and ten cigarettes (oh, the luxury). I knew that when I was 'on the in' I'd said to myself that once I was 'on the out' I'd carry on smoking roll-ups, 'cos they weren't quite so bad for you and didn't cost as much, and here I was only 'on the out' for five minutes and already buying Benson &Hedges. But hey! I was celebrating.

From Shepton Mallet I had first to get to Bristol, where I was planning to call in at my sister's before going on to Stafford by rail later in the day. Ideally, thinking of the money, I would have liked to have taken a bus to Bristol, but I'd just missed one and the next one wasn't due until much too late in the day for me to catch the Stafford train.

So, making sure (just like when abroad) how much the fare was before I got in, I took a taxi. On the way, the way you do, I asked the taxi driver how business was, and he, the way cabbies do, gave me a rough breakdown of his fares in a week. According to him what was good about the town of Shepton Mallet from a taxi driver's point of view was the prison. Visitors coming and going, normally from Bristol railway station, and prisoners being released made for good regular business. And then he said something, I don't remember what exactly, but it was something about the prison that I felt he wouldn't have said if he had known that I'd just been released from there. Which was good, eh? It showed that I didn't look like a con, at least.

I was just wondering whether to tell him or not when he asked what had brought me to Shepton Mallet. Well, I wasn't going to lie, so I did tell him. And not that I thought about it at the time, but he was fated to be the very first person I ever told that I'd done a bit of bird. He then asked, as everyone since has asked, how long I was in for and what it was that I'd done. When I told him that I'd *only* smuggled marijuana and had been given eighteen months, though had only served six, his response was to go off on a rant about child-killers, paedophiles, thugs who mug grannies, and of course the human scum who park their cars in taxi ranks, all of whom deserved hanging without trial but usually got off with a slapped wrist and a few hours of community service. Like he said, though, who did I ever hurt with what I'd done?

I could name a few.

When we reached my sister's house I paid the fare and said my goodbyes to my first confessor. And who knows? Maybe one day they'll put a blue plaque in his cab.

There was a note on my sister's front door saying that she'd popped out and would be back soon. I rang the doorbell anyway, but she obviously wasn't home, so to kill some time I took myself off to the row of local shops. When I got there I found that not one but two of them were betting shops and I really was tempted to go in, just to have a look, get off the street for a bit. I didn't, though, because I knew I had to stop all of that now. Had a family, couldn't afford it. So I told that bit of me that just loves to self-destruct to forget it and took myself off to the Kentucky Fried Chicken instead. I've met him, by the way.

With the devil defeated and my chicken eaten, I returned to my sister's to find that she was now back. She made me a cup of tea and we sat together in the kitchen and talked about what I was going to do next. The first thing would be finding a job, though doing what I didn't know. The only two types of work I had any experience of were serving as a soldier and working in a casino, both of which, with a criminal record, I could now forget about completely. The only hope I could see was that I would find some work doing what I'd been learning to do while in prison, i.e. wielding a paintbrush.

The journey from my sister's house to Stafford railway station I don't remember a thing about (even though, apart from my taxi ride, I hadn't moved that fast for six months).

Time started again when I stepped down from the train and there to meet me was . . . no one. I walked to the street outside the railway station and took a look around, but I still couldn't see any sign of Carol. After five minutes of shuffling my feet on the spot, the sensible thing to do would have been to phone the house to find out if she was on her way, but being the coward I was when it came to talking to Carol's parents, I decided I'd rather just hang around a bit longer.

I waited at Stafford station for about fifteen minutes before Carol finally arrived (though really, she could have taken as long as she liked) and right from the off, once we'd had a welcome-home kiss and a nice-to-see-you-again hug, there was a clue there for me as to the real hurdle I now had to overcome. Because as soon as we had said our hellos I was hanging my head with the shame of it all. And the 'it all' was where we were now standing in time and space, right now, right here on planet Earth, with me just out of prison, not a job between us, no place of our own to live and our newborn son waiting for us at his grandparents'. Maybe physically I could still walk six-foot-two above sea level and look the world right in the eye, but inside I was cowering like a beaten dog.

On the drive to Carol's parents' house I realised that in prison I had been working in the wrong timescale whenever I'd looked forward to my release. Instead of seeing the days I had left to serve as a long drag towards freedom, I should have looked at them as the days still to go before I saw Carol's parents again. Time would have flown. Because make no mistake, and you can ask anyone who knew us, when Carol married me there was absolutely no doubt that she was marrying beneath herself, in every sense of the word. Although her parents never once said as much, or even gave me cause to think it (so shame on me), I couldn't help but believe they felt that way about it. And if the truth be told, if Carol had been my daughter and had married me ('That'd be incest, mate,' but you know what I mean), I'm sure I would have been a bit disappointed with what she had ended up with. And that was before I left her pregnant in Aldershot while I went off to do my 'bit of bird'.

(You're still the man, Ken.) In short, I felt ashamed to face my in-laws again and didn't have a clue what to say to them or how to even begin to apologise.

But of course, as sure as night follows day, and just like the moment when I saw my first dead body in the Falklands, not to mention the moment when the judge had said 'Do not pass Go,' the nightmare I'd been dreading arrived, and just like that (although it had taken six slow months) there I was standing in front of Carol's mum and dad again. It must have been just wonderful for them both.

And do you know what made it worse? They did. Or to be more precise, how they were about everything did. Because how they were, and I'm not exaggerating here, was just perfect. Oh, I know you might think Ken's gone a shade soft here, knows he owes them more than he could ever repay and so is being all sweetness and light in their direction, but really, what I say is true. As people, and even more importantly as family, they were perfect. Over the next few weeks I would often try to think of a fault in either of them, but the best I ever came up with was that Carol's dad used to have a quiet moan whenever I changed his radio over from Radio Four to Radio One and forgot to put it back again. (If you'd asked me at the time, I would have said he was getting wound up about nothing. Ask me now, though, and I'd have to admit how annoyed I get whenever my girlfriend's son does exactly the same thing to my radio in the kitchen. Which explains why I now keep the lead in my dressing gown pocket.)

Carol's mum and dad greeted us at the door, and once I'd said a somewhat shy and embarrassed hello (see, it wasn't all that bad, was it?) I went upstairs to where my son lay sleeping. I entered the room just in time to catch him waking up, so I lifted him into my arms and sat on the bed holding him. Of course, as I began to tell him how sorry I was that I hadn't been around for his first months of life, I started to cry. And when Carol's mum came into the room and saw me cradling her grandson in my arms, all she could do was join me in my tears.

From that moment on, all I could do was just try and get on

with life, though today, as I write this, I don't know if I ever did really tell Carol's folks how sorry I was for everything. For when I did get in among the family again, the subject of my crimes and imprisonment was never mentioned. It was like none of it had happened – and I'll drink to that.

I was fortunate enough to get some labouring work only a few days after my release from prison. This gave us a little money, at least, and it also helped me to hold my head up in the company of others. But such was my guilt complex that each night after I'd finished work I would insist on carrying out any odd jobs that needed doing around the place, to the extent that in the end I did myself no good at all. Of course, what I really wanted was for us to be able to move out of Carol's parents' house. Not that they were making me feel unwelcome, it was just that being around them made my feelings of guilt all the worse. There was also, I think, the question of class. Again it was all my problem, but the fact that they were so middle class had always made me a bit uncomfortable in their presence.

My upbringing had been very different from Carol's (and if you do have some sad violin music available, then now's the time to pop it on). Oh yes. For starters, by the time I met her my mum and dad were already divorced and remarried. (Which was a total hoot at our wedding, I can tell you.) Carol's mum and dad, on the other hand, were without a doubt each other's first and last and everything. And the Motown didn't stop with them. The same went for Carol's brother, her two sisters, her aunts and uncles, all of her cousins, and approximately two thousand more of her relatives. Whereas with my clan (and violins up a notch or two, please) at any given time there was always someone who wasn't on speaking terms with at least one other member of the family. Which, as my mother used to say, didn't mean that we didn't all love each other. It was just that sometimes we didn't like each other all that much. Carol's lot, though – with them it was always love, love, love. And genuine love at that. Which, when all put together, meant that I couldn't help but feel that I would never fit in.

But despite my uneasiness, life did go on. And although I

didn't realise it at the time, things, as in life in general, did improve to the point where they got as close to 'normal' as they do for most people. My work on the building site became regular (it wasn't quite painting and decorating, but it was a start) and we managed to save a deposit and rent a small Barratt-type house on a new estate near Wolverhampton. The sort of place where the church was built from the same brick as the houses and nearly all the roads led to roundabouts whose only exit was the road you'd come in on.

This meant that we were finally able to move out of Carol's parents' house, which was a relief for everyone, though from their point of view I'm sure the real joy was not so much getting rid of us as regaining their independence. After all, mum, dad and baby makes three. Like the good ex-con that I was, I was regularly popping off to see my probation officer, and, as she said to me at the time, 'Well done, Ken,' even though it was really a case of well done Carol and well done Carol's family. Either way, I guess things did get as normal as they do for most people.

So there I was, and there we were, and considering how things had been for us not so long ago, you'd think I would have been happy with our new circumstances. Or if not happy, then at least able to realise that life had the potential to be a whole lot worse. Like I so often reminded myself, at least no one was shooting at me any more. And now, of course, there was the new one: at least I could leave the room any time I liked. So all in all, I should have been counting my blessings. Trouble was, I couldn't even see my blessings, never mind count them.

And why not? I didn't know why not. The only thing I could put it down to was that the part of me that had once walked on beaches in four continents, and lived under the southern stars in the Australian outback, and patrolled the hostile streets of Northern Ireland, and witnessed the worst and best of everything on the Falklands . . . oh, and jumped out of aeroplanes, and smuggled dope, and spent six months in prison . . . that part of me was never going to be content with struggling to make ends meet on an estate near Wolverhampton.

By the time we'd paid the rent and the bills and bought all our food and stuff, I could forget about going to the pub (though of course I didn't forget), and even though I was working hard, the whole of my income was being taxed at the basic rate. One day, apparently, we'd get a lot of the money back, but we didn't need it one day, we needed it now. Some days I would stand in the rain on site, taking a break from digging a hole or pushing a wheelbarrow full of dirt, and I would try to feel proud of myself. I mean, I might have been working up to my knees in mud, but at least I wasn't down on those knees begging for food to be put into my family's mouths. I know it all sounds a bit like *The Waltons* again, but it was how I tried to look at things at the time. And when all's said and done, I hadn't gone back to crime, had I? (Mind you I hadn't gone back to Belize, either.)

Financially, things really hit rock bottom when I went and got myself injured and so couldn't work for four weeks. My injury came about, and there ain't no doubt about it, as a direct result of me being a dope-smoker. (So if you do have children to whom you'd like to pass on the dangers of getting involved with drugs – go fetch.)

Carol, son and me had gone to Bristol for the weekend to visit my sister and her family. Halfway through the first evening my brother-in-law remembered that he had a small piece of hash in an old tobacco tin somewhere, and once he'd dug it out, the two of us decided to have a smoke. Neither Carol nor my sister were interested – but that's girls for you. The problem was that Bob didn't have any cigarette papers and neither did I. (Come to think of it, it's not the first time that's happened in this tale, is it?) But hey, rock 'n' roll! Not to worry, because I might have some in my car, and if I don't then I could always run round to the nearest off-licence and buy some.

It was cold outside and all I had on was a T-shirt, so I ran full speed along the garden path and leapt like the athlete I still was over the sixteen-foot-high garden wall (I like to add a few inches each telling). Trouble was, my legs didn't jump quite as high as my brain had told them to, and on the way over my back foot caught the top of the wall. I twisted in mid-air and then hit the pavement like a wet rock, landing very badly on my right thumb. I knew straight away that I'd done something serious to it because not only did it hurt like period pains, it didn't look like it used to.

I then did a very strange thing, something I can't imagine I would ever do in the same circumstances today. Despite the pain I was in (and believe me, I was in tears), I got to my feet, walked back into the garden via the gate, turned around and took another flying leap at the wall, clearing it this time. Still in considerable pain, I then did a quick one-handed search of the car, though I didn't find any fag papers.

Of course, at this point any normal human being would have gone back inside the house and got his thumb seen to. But not me, mate. Me, normal? I was an ex-para. And I know it sounds like a joke, but that's all I could put it down to. Like I said, my thumb was really painful, but I had come out to get some fag papers and some fags papers I would get. 'Do you think a little thing like a sore thumb would have stopped us from getting to Port Stanley?' And with teeth clenched, off I ran in search of the off-licence to complete my task.

When I finally got back to the house, my sister, who was a nursing sister at a local hospital at the time, took one look at my thumb and told me to put my coat on. Twenty minutes later we were sitting in Casualty at Frenchay Hospital. After only a short wait (and it helps to have connections, 'cos guess which hospital my sister worked in), the long and the short of my thumb was that in America it would have cost me a whole lot of money. After I'd been X-rayed a female doctor appeared and did the old sneak attack on me by talking about flower arranging one moment (it's a passion of mine) and then snapping my thumb back into place the next. She then strapped me up and sent me on my way armed with a note for my local hospital in Wolverhampton. Apparently, what I'd done could have serious consequences in future years and so I would need to visit a specialist.

When we got back to my sister's house the others had already turned in for the night, and once we'd had a good old cup of tea my sister did the same. Me, on the other hand (literally), I hadn't broken my thumb for nothing, so I decided to sit in the lounge and roll myself a smoke. And here's a great party game for you: try rolling a spliff without using your right thumb – only please don't try it at home with a three-skinner. Shit, it was difficult. But you know me, the old para. I managed to get a joint up and puffing all the same.

Which makes me wonder if maybe it wasn't the ex-para in me that needed to run off to the off-licence despite being in pain, so much as the far from 'ex' dope-smoker.

'Yeah, but what about all that getting back up off the floor and jumping the wall again? A bit like basic training, that one. And besides, you didn't need to do that to get a smoke, did you?'

He's right, you know.

If I had been unhappy with my lot before I did my thumb in, then life after it was much the same only with even less money and long, long periods of boredom thrown in for effect. There was also the small point that although, by the time of my release from prison, Carol and I had been married for three and a half years, what with me being away while in the army as well, when you added up all the time we'd actually spent together it didn't come to half of that. Which I think is a roundabout way of me saying that I wasn't really used to married life.

By the time my thumb did eventually heal up and I was able to return to working my shovel on building sites, inside I was climbing the walls with frustration, plus ten. The way I saw it, the only way things were ever going to improve for me and Carol was for us to have more money, and the only way we were ever going to have more money was if I got a better-paid job.

At the time my elder brother Lou was still living in Western Australia (all right, calm down, I didn't go there), but his work as a deep-sea diver meant that he had to spend at least six months of every year working in the North Sea oilfields. Because he was away from home for such long periods, he had rented a small flat in Aberdeen, and after one quick evening phone call, just like that I had arranged to go to Scotland to search for work offshore. Though not over the moon about the idea, Carol raised no great objection to it, so the next day, which was a Sunday, I phoned my boss to say that I wouldn't be coming in for work in the morning. And using the last of our meagre savings, on the Monday I caught the train up to Scotland.

In Aberdeen I was met at the station by my brother and as soon as we'd dropped my bag off at his flat, out on the pop we did go, big time.

In Act Two we're back from the pub, I've had a flaming row with my brother about nothing important, and then for some reason (well, all right, too much of that old ignorant drug called booze again) I've gone all emotional and stormed out of the building.

Once outside I burst into a sprint that lasted until my legs would carry me no further. Finally, exhausted, I stopped and sat down on a large granite doorstep. As I sat there panting and trying to get my breath back, out of nowhere – or at least, from the depths of a soul that felt utterly blank at the time – I started bawling. Not sobbing, not even crying, but really bawling. I wasn't loud (more squeaky than anything), but tears were streaming down my face, my teeth were clenched and I was curled up like a little child.

After a few minutes I was joined on the step by my brother. Seeing that I was in pain, he put his arm around me and told me that everything was going to be all right. At that I cried some more, and then I sobbed, 'I didn't want to kill anyone.' Which was a strange thing to come out with, considering that I wasn't even aware the war was in my mind at the time. My big brother just said, 'I know,' and then he walked me home.

The next day (and oh, what a headache) I went about the task of finding work. Not just any work, but work offshore. It was only then that I realised just how much self-confidence I'd lost, because whenever we got to one of the many job agencies there were in Aberdeen, like an infant on his first day at school, I didn't want to go in on my own. I filled out I don't know how many application forms and on each of them I lied about my six months in prison, accounting for the time by making out that I'd been working as a labourer on building sites.

There was also a Catch 22-type situation with getting work offshore that I would need to overcome. To work on an oil rig in any capacity you had to be in possession of a current offshore survival certificate, which required a two-week training course costing £250. Normally your employer would pay for you to go on the course, but as I didn't yet have an employer I would either have to pay for it myself or forget the whole idea. Fortunately, my brother was taking home the sort of pay packets that wouldn't miss a mere £250 and so he put up the cash for me to attend the next course, which started in just under a fortnight's time. Interesting it was as well. Lots of climbing out of mock helicopters in swimming pools and pulling sand-filled dummies out of smoke-filled rooms.

Just before starting the course, as I had no money I signed on at the Aberdeen employment exchange and eagerly awaited my first cheque. During the second week of my course, my brother went offshore again for a month, leaving me the keys to his flat and enough money to get by until my first dole payment came through. When the course was over I collected my certificate proving that I was all genned up on offshore survival and then went back to the task of looking for work.

With my brother gone I was now going to have to face the search for work on my own, and once again I found myself having to constantly fight my lack of confidence. Before walking into any job agency I would get so nervous that all I could do to snap myself out of it was try to think about the war. I would stop at the door and stand there shaking on the spot as I actually said to myself, 'Listen mate, after the Falklands, walking into this place is nothing. These people ain't got guns.' I used to carry around with me a photo of my son in which he was sitting on the floor smiling right into the camera, so I'd also look at that picture and say something like 'For him,' and then I'd walk on in.

My search for work continued without success, and the more I failed, the more my confidence slumped. In the end I was spending most of my days just sitting around in my brother's flat waiting for the phone to ring. I was literally penniless when the day arrived on which my first unemployment benefit cheque was due to drop through the door. The post came late morning, so around that time I started peering out of the window in the hope of spotting the postman as he approached the house. When he did turn up I ran down to the street to save him the trip up the stairs and to get me nearer to the post office and cashing my much-needed giro. (I'd smoked my last cigarette the night before.) But, not for the first time in my life, or the last, the postman didn't bring the giro I was expecting. After I'd got over the disappointment of still having no money, I walked myself into town to try and find out why.

When I reached the employment exchange I took a number and then had to wait for more than an hour and a half. I was eventually told that I wasn't entitled to unemployment benefit after all, because I had left my last job of my own free will. I explained to the lady who had passed on this wonderful news that I had no money whatsoever and badly needed some, if only enough to get a meal. All she said was sorry, no can help, but . . . if I liked I could apply for social security instead, which was apparently something quite different. So she brought me some more forms, and I filled them out, and when I handed them back to her she told me that if I got lucky I might just receive a giro in a week or so's time. Once again I explained that I had no money whatsoever and knew not another living soul in Aberdeen, but still the answer was no can do. So what option did I have but to ask to see someone above her? With that she smiled wearily, gathered up her paperwork and left me sitting at the counter.

Waiting there on my plastic chair for the someone above to appear, the thoughts going through my head were both logical and irrational at the same time. My leg started to shake up and down and I found myself thinking yet again about my time in the Falklands. And the thing was, this time I was not only thinking about the war but I was doing it intentionally – running memories of it second by second through my mind and deliberately trying to slow them down to real time to make it like watching a film.

As I sat and remembered I got angry, and the reason I got angry was that these wasters working here, with their fucking counter and their self-importance, when I was up to my existence in blood and bullets and all of that bollocks, these fuckers had been where they were now, doing what they were doing now. As for me, they couldn't give a fuck. And I'd fucking fought for them?

In fact, of course, I hadn't fought for them and I knew it. The population of Argentina had never had any wish whatsoever to hang their national flag from a pole outside Aberdeen's employment exchange. All the same, I still felt I deserved something. Even if it was just enough to get some food.

I waited for about another half-hour until finally a man appeared on the other side of the counter with my file in his hand. Without so much as acknowledging that I was there, he sat down on the chair opposite me and opened my file. After half a minute or so he looked up and asked, 'What can I do for you?' So once again I explained my financial situation and, just about short of begging, asked if it would be possible for him to make me some kind of emergency payment. Please. He looked back down at my file and flicked through a couple of its pages. Then he looked up again and said no. He was sorry, of course (though he managed not to sound it), but rules were rules.

In desperation more than anything I blurted out something about the Falklands War, to which he replied that if I was looking for 'charity' then I should try the British Legion. And right there and then I truly understood why it was that they had these people sitting behind two-inch perspex. Because believe me, if that hadn't been there, I would have had him. It would have been wrong, because after all the man was only doing his job, and having served in Northern Ireland for twelve months I knew all about that. But nevertheless, for about half a second there, he was dead. 'Charity', though, that was the real killer. And without another word, I stood up and walked away.

Outside it was, of course, raining (come on, the whole world piss on me) and Aberdeen suddenly seemed a very bleak place. As I marched the mile or so home I started to wonder what to do next, but I just didn't know what to do next.

Back at the flat I made myself a coffee and tried to find some solace in the fact that, if nothing else, I still had the means of making a hot drink, and somewhere to go that was both warm and out of the rain. Oh, and I had a colour TV and a telephone. Being the combat-and-survivalist that I was, I went through the rubbish bin, dug out all my old cigarette butts and broke them down to re-roll. Alas, that source of tobacco wasn't going to last forever though, and neither was the coffee, tea, sugar and milk. As for food, there was absolutely nothing in the fridge, no cans in the cupboards, no peas in their pods, no bloody anything anywhere apart from a few sprouting potatoes in the vegetable rack – and I did find the standard half-pack of long-grain rice that you seem to get with all kitchens.

I used up the last of the money I had, and we're talking pennies here, when the milk ran out. By this time, although I had been in Aberdeen for less than a month, it was beginning to feel longer than my stay in Shepton Mallet.

I was keeping in touch with Carol by phoning her at her parents' house whenever she visited them, but the news from her end was no better than mine. We were way behind with the rent and the landlord wanted us out, so all she could think to do was move us back in with her mum and dad. The other good news was that I had completely gone and forgotten about the fact that I was still on probation and so had missed an appointment with my probation officer. Thankfully, I managed to sort out that situation with one phone call, but as for the house and losing it, I did the normal thing and left Carol to get on with it. Well, I had my own problems.

So there I was, sitting alone and broke in a flat in Scotland, and I couldn't help but think that I'd been better off when I was in prison. In fact, make that everyone had been better off when I was in prison. With nowhere to go and no money to go there with, I began to spend great chunks of time sitting on my own in the flat. I realised just how bad things were when my famous nicotine addiction pulled me from my chair one day and had me searching the streets of Aberdeen for dog-ends to break down and re-roll. In the past, when walking around London I'd had people come up bumming cigarettes off me on countless occasions, and yet when I had none I found I just couldn't stop complete strangers and ask if they had a smoke to spare – even if I could pick dog-ends up off the street. How's it go? Too proud to beg, too dumb to steal.

And then, just when it seemed that life couldn't possibly get any worse and I couldn't possibly get any lower, I developed a toothache of the type you remember for life. I couldn't find one thing even remotely medicinal in the flat, so, as I didn't have a penny to my name, all I could do was try and put up with it. Which of course I couldn't. In desperation I turned the whole place upside down looking for odd coins, and after searching absolutely everywhere I could think of I managed to come up with . . . nowhere near enough to buy any painkillers. But then I hit on a place I hadn't thought of before, a place that was to bring riches beyond my wildest fantasies. The washing machine. Or, to be more precise, inside the rubber bit that seals the door of the washing machine. Seventy pence I found, and before you could say 'soluble' I was out of the flat and off scoring aspirins. When I did get some I chewed them like they were sweets, and after about an hour my toothache was still there, but bearable to a level where at least it allowed me to get some sleep.

As I knew it would, the news soon came through from Carol that she had moved us out of the rented house and back in with her parents. On hearing this I guess I should have felt shame that I'd fucked up again, but by this time I was so defeated on all fronts that I didn't really care about anything. Of course, when Carol phoned I told her how desperate I was up in Aberdeen – and do you know what she did? The woman I'd deserted with a child, who had nothing in the world thanks to me? She sent me two pounds. I didn't even know it was coming, and when I opened the envelope it really did make me drop to my knees and want so much not to be me any more. *What* was I going to do?

The only thing I had left in my life was the telephone and the hope that one day it would ring and on the other end of the line would be a job offer. Though really I knew there was little or no hope of that.

And then, just when I was thinking once more that things couldn't possibly get any worse . . . I was right, for a change. Because along came some joy. And oh, what joy. In one ring of the phone all of my prayers were answered and I had myself a job offshore. After I put the receiver down I jumped up and down with delight, and if I'd been wearing any I would have swung my knickers in the air. I phoned Carol straight away to pass on the good news, and she, like me, was so happy that she could hardly contain herself. I would be starting work in five days' time and would work for thirty days straight, earning £80 a day. It was so perfect and so wonderful that it was hard to believe anything so right could happen to me. And it got even better almost immediately, because as soon as I'd phoned Carol I went down to the Social Security and explained that I'd just got a job but was still waiting for a giro, which I badly needed to prepare for my new employment. And all of a sudden they couldn't do enough for me. Once they had checked with the company that had offered me the job, right there and then they wrote me out a giro for £80 and stamped my file 'Closed'.

That night I went out on the town, got myself pissed and ended up going back to the flat with two girls I'd met in a nightclub. Neither of them was what you'd call a picture, I must admit, and the only reason I invited them back in the first place was because they had some hash on them. After a good session of smoking, one of them (the large one) made a move on me, and me being me as I was at the time, I took her into the bedroom and jumped aboard.

As I humped away in my drunken, out-of-it bliss, meanwhile, back home in England, my wife and my child slept in peace. The next morning I did feel bad about it, though, and I couldn't get rid of Jumbo-double-battered-sausage-and-large-chips here quick enough, with a promise that I'd phone her later in the day. (Would I fuck.) I'd also spent more money than I should have out on the piss, and if the rest was going to last me until I went offshore then I was going to have to go easy. But what the hell. At least I had a job now, and one that would clear all of our debts with the first pay cheque. Without a doubt, all of my prayers had been answered.

Though you know, sometimes, when God really wants to punish us, what he does is he answers our prayers.

Two days before I was due to go offshore, the phone rang again. This time it was to say that the contract had been cancelled and so I didn't have a job to go to any more. I would never have thought it possible, but once I'd put the phone down I was physically sick with the horror of what had just happened. Just like that, just as things finally looked as though they were going to work out, yet again the rug had been pulled from under me. I sat for hours, then, trying to put off for as long as I could the phone call I now had to make to pass on this devastating news to Carol. What had she ever done to deserve this? Married me. But then, what had even I ever done to deserve this?

Things now became even worse than they'd been before I was offered the job in the first place. Because I'd wasted most of my money going out drinking and womanising, I was soon flat broke again. And this time I couldn't even handle the thought of all the paperwork involved in going back to the Social.

So, totally defeated and with no other course of action left, I phoned Carol and worked the conversation round so that she was the one to ask me to please come home. I then packed my bags, walked to the railway station, climbed aboard the train to

England, and, with what I can only describe as my tail between my legs, prepared to return defeated to Carol and her family. But do you know, even then the bad luck didn't stop. There was to be one last stab in the guts for me on the journey home. Twenty minutes out of Aberdeen the inspector went to punch my ticket and noticed that it was out of date. I explained that I had no cash at all and asked if I could please send the money for the fare to British Rail after I got home. But he was having none of it and asked me to leave the train at the next stop, which was the station at fuck-knows-where in Scotland.

Up until that point I had thought that sitting in the flat in Aberdeen just after the news came through that I had no job after all would be the lowest point in my life, never to be beaten. But here I was suddenly sitting on a bench on a platform on a station in I didn't know where, totally at a loss as to what I was going to do. I didn't even have enough money to phone Carol and let her know that I wouldn't be on the train she was meeting. So I did the only thing I could. I laughed. Laughed like I hadn't in years. In fact, and I don't know if it's significant or not, but the last time I'd laughed so hard had been during by army basic training. If there had been anyone else on the platform at the time I would have stood a strong chance of being committed – which, come to think of it, might not have been such a bad thing. At least loonies of the certified kind get fed.

In the end, the only choice I had was to ride the trains back home hiding in the toilets. The worse that was likely to happen to me was that I'd be be thrown off at the next stop again, and so I figured that one way or another, eventually I'd make it home. I then made a reversed-charges call to my sister and got her to phone Carol and tell her that I'd been delayed. (No way, José, was I going to phone Carol's parents' house and reverse the charges.)

It wasn't until after I returned from Aberdeen that it finally dawned on me what I'd done by going there in the first place. Although initially my intentions had been good, or at least I thought they had, I'd left my wife and son to fend for themselves and in doing so had made them homeless again. In a stroke I had put us right back where we'd been on the day I was released from prison. Whilst in Aberdeen I'd wasted money that I should have sent home to my wife, and I'd even taken time out to sleep with another woman.

Though do you know what? When I stepped down from the train for the second time that year, not once did Carol or any member of her family ever beat me with what I had done by going away. (Mind you, at best they only knew a tenth of it.) They could have put me through a meat mincer and I couldn't have had too many complaints, but all they did was again welcome me back into the family fold.

On a brighter note, I was able to find some work back with my old employer almost straight away, and I guess the plan was for us to once more save up a deposit and start all over again. Now, though, I was even more head-bowed than I'd been when I was released from prison, and it got to the point where I just didn't want to be around anyone.

Then one day, more by chance than meaning, I came upon a new narcotic that was to change my life – one that was free of charge, got you off your face like you wouldn't believe, and was readily available by the pound no more than two hundred yards from my front door. Can you guess?

One Saturday morning, while rummaging through some of our still unpacked boxes from Aldershot, I came across a small pamphlet on the hallucinogenic mushrooms of the British Isles. And what a riveting read it was as well. So that evening I take the dog for a walk through the nearby fields and I'm looking at my feet all the way. By the time walkies are over I've picked a variety of about twenty little mushrooms, and back at home I compare them with the ones shown in the pamphlet. Unfortunately, not one is of the type I need to find. A couple of days later, though, I take the dog for another walk through the very same fields and there are thousands of them. Really thousands.

I picked about thirty in all, which was what the book said would make a reasonable dose, and giving it the old combat-

and-survive treatment I ate them raw as I went along. And fucking yuck!

About an hour later I was sitting at the dinner table with the rest of the family, happily listening to tales of everyone's day, when it hit me. I'd once before had a third of a microdot of acid, but that had been nothing compared to what thirty of these little pop-ups were now doing to me. Things just suddenly became totally unreal. The dinner table appeared to be a mile long, and every sound, be it speech or a fork scraping a plate, echoed and hung in the air far longer than sound normally did. I was just about on the verge of panic, realising that this was not the ideal place to be experiencing such things for the first time, when I happened to turn and look out of the window. The garden outside was the garden outside, and yet now when I looked I was quite simply overcome by the beauty it contained. It was like every living thing, from the tallest tree to the shortest blade of grass, was humming with life. And right away I knew that they always did – it was just that we never normally heard them. ('Cos of the noise pollution, man.)

From there on in I started munching the little mushrooms more than was good for anyone to and as a result was spending large parts of the day quite literally living in another dimension. And this may sound a bad comparison, but in one way tripping on mushrooms was pretty similar to life during battle, as in armed combat, in that when it was over I couldn't really explain to you how I'd felt during it, because I knew I could never truly remember. OK, yes, the grass turned blue, say, or a shell exploded over there, or the pattern on the wallpaper became liquid, or that corpse really didn't have a head . . . but how I truly felt inside at the time I couldn't come anywhere near to describing. (Though as far as the 'mind trips' of war are concerned, that's probably no bad thing, as I've often thought that all those soldiers who end up curled in a corner reliving every terrifying moment, their problem is one of not being able to let it go, forget the feelings at the time.)

For a change one night, and it was a change, I was left on my own in the house to look after our son while Carol and her parents went out. Having taken the excuse (woof, woof) for a walk earlier in the day, I'd picked about twenty omelettes' worth of mushrooms and once the baby boy was asleep I made myself a cup of tea with about seventy of them. Incidentally, the fact that my son was in the house and may at some point have needed me, and so I shouldn't have got off my face at all, didn't even cross my mind. Though hey! At least Hollywood would forgive me, because I was on mushroom drugs at the time and I don't do them any more.

Once the trip kicked in I began to reach levels of 'out of it' that even I wouldn't have thought possible and I really did start to get the whole boom-bang shampoo. First the wallpaper turned into waterfalls, with sound effects to match. Then one moment the room was the size of an aircraft hangar and you'd have had to take a bus just to get from one side of it to the other, and the next I was wondering how a giant like me was even able to squeeze into it. Every picture and photograph on the wall started turning into a TV set, and as for the 'real' TV set, well, one moment it was the marvel of the universe and the next a tool of Satan herself. I just thank fuck that it wasn't turned on at the time. Now because I know about drugs, or at least I thought I did, it wasn't too long before I decided that the best thing I could do would be to go and have a nice quiet lie down in the bedroom. So, with the lights off so as not to wake the baby-o, I lay down on my bed and went to places that I'd never been before.

Another grade A tip for you here (so you might like to grab a notepad and jot it down). Should you ever find yourself off your face on hallucinogenic drugs and you're not liking it very much, then here's what not to do. Do not go and lie down on your own in a quiet darkened room. And I'll tell you for why. Because if your mind is not occupied looking at anything or listening to anything, then with nowhere else to go, it goes inside you. If you do happen to be, say, the Dalai Lama or someone equally calm and blameless, then a good look inside yourself is probably a harmless, even an enjoyable, experience. Unfortunately, at the time I was hardly at peace with my inner self, and as I lay on my camp bed with my son asleep in the cot beside me, my mind started to run through the many failures of the life that was me.

Dwelling on what I was and where I was and all the things I'd done to make it that way, I was soon feeling close to suicidal. Demons filled my mind, and even before I tried to run I knew that I would never be able to rid myself of them. Thanks to me we had no money, we were in debt up to our earlobes, we were back living with Carol's parents – and that was only the physical side of it. As for me and my 'morals', and my almost complete, utter and total selfishness, changing that, changing me, it was never going to happen. And the demons kept coming, horrible face after horrible face. And I had no escape, ever, forever. For ever and ever. Amen. And I was so sorry . . .

But then, even though I was the last person on the planet to deserve one, what I can only describe as a miracle took place in my head. Because right there and then our Lord Jesus Christ came down from heaven and he saved me. Just as I was teetering on the emotional edge, feeling that I was no more than a piece of human scum, he saved me. Me, who had broken every single one of his commandments.

And then I was floating above a nighttime Jerusalem of two thousand years ago. Below me I saw a flat roof and sitting in a circle upon it, discussing the events of the past few fearful days, were the disciples. And then, suddenly, I understood something. I understood that from then on the rooftop to the present time, in all of its forms and all of its cathedrals, in all of its hymns and prayers, despite all of our human sins, the Word had spread and grown. Without really understanding anything, at that moment I understood it all. And 'it all' was that no matter what I had done in the past, even if I was unable to love myself, Jesus still loved me. Loved me for myself. Loved me so much that he had died for me.

(Incidentally, just in case you do feel like slamming the book shut at this point, a quick question for you. *Where* did you buy this book? Wasn't in one of them Christian bookshops, was it? Right. So no slamming.)

I went over to where my son slept, lifted him into my arms, and for the first time in I don't know how long I cried a little tear of pure joy. And can you believe it? You can still find people out there who'll tell you that drugs don't work.

Though here's the strange thing, and one that only goes to prove that the Lord does work in mysterious ways. The next morning, after the best night's sleep I'd had in years, I awoke a follower of Jesus Christ. 'Born again' I was. However, I didn't rush into breakfast rattling a tambourine and singing the joys of my conversion (a note for the board: suggestion for breakfast cereal brand name – 'Honey-nut roasted Kumbayahs'). The exact opposite, in fact. I kept it to myself.

However, I did suddenly turn into Mr Nice-and-Helpful, making myself useful in any way I could, and after a few days of this I could tell that Carol and her family were beginning to wonder what was going on. (Though they'd probably put it down to me getting hold of some sort of happy drug, I thought.)

Carol's mother was a deeply religious person herself and each Sunday she and Carol would go to the nearby village church. So, one bright Sunday morning (and that was another thing – I was up with the lark every day now) I asked if they'd mind if I joined them. (Eh-oop. Keep an eye on the collection plate!) As you know, I'd had a 'Road to the Parole Board'-type conversion while I was in prison, so when it came to the running order of the service and the bits where it was the congregation's turn to chant a few words, I was right on the ball.

A few days later I heard about a bible group that was meeting in one of the houses in the village, so on the appropriate evening I put on my smart clothes and slipped out of the house. When I got to the house where the meeting was, I was welcomed in with open arms, and once I had explained why I was there and gone through the bible group equivalent of AA's 'I am an alcoholic', we sat in a circle and, just like the disciples had done two thousand years ago (except that we had central heating and comfy chairs), we talked about Jesus. From there on in, if you were in the village on a Wednesday night and you were looking for Ken, then you'd find him at the bible group.

There of course came a point when I sat down with Carol and her mother and told them of my conversion, and although they were both pleased to hear what I had to say, I couldn't help but feel that they didn't quite believe it. Though of course, I understood. But as the days passed and my faith grew stronger and stronger and I became like Staffordshire's answer to Cliff Richard, even they began to believe that my faith was real. In church and at the bible group, I started holding my palms up to the sky whenever I prayed or sang, and in what spare time I did have I began writing gospel songs of my own. And now I'm going to put you through the first two verses and chorus of the first one that I ever penned. And I'll tell you for why. Because it shows what my religious conversion was really all about.

SELDOM

by Ken Lukowiak, aged 2 months

I seldom had a peaceful night
Seldom felt at ease
Seldom walked the path of righteous peace.
I seldom felt at one with life
And seldom heard you call.
Seldom seemed to be my guiding word.

Now I seldom have no place to go
And seldom feel alone.
I seldom have no one to share my joy.

I seldom feel I can't go on
And seldom hold no love.
Seldom still remains my guiding word.

So I thank you, Lord, for saving me

Because you saved me from myself.
You showed me right from wrong.
I found love for everyone else.
And I know I never lived before with love and harmony.

So, Thank you, Lord, praise you, Lord, for forgiving me.
  Thank you, Lord, praise you, Lord, for forgiving me.
  Thank you, Lord . . . (repeat until it's time for the HobNobs)

Yep, forgiveness. After everything I'd done, my problem had been one of not being able to forgive myself for what I had put others through. But now, because Jesus could still love me and forgive me, I could love and forgive myself.

So deep did my faith become that I started to attend the local church's confirmation group and put my name down for an adult baptism. Having been born a Jehovah's Witness, as a baby I had not been christened, because the followers of Jehovah God believe that baptism is something people should choose for themselves. Which is fair enough, I guess.

Another thing that was probably a major contributor to my conversion staying on line was the knowledge I already had of the bible, which again went back to my religious upbringing. When it comes to the Holy Bible and what's actually in it, your average ten-year-old Jehovah's Witness knows more about it than most of the world's archbishops. In fact, I'd go so far as to say that at the bible group I actually knew my bible better than most. On the whole, the rest of the group were pretty *au fait* with the Matthew, Mark, Luke and John bit, and even knew a little of Revelations and some of the things Paul had written, but as for the rest of it, and especially the Old Testament, they knew not a lot. But then, what did that matter when they knew the bottom line? Which was that Jesus loved them. Amen.

Eventually the great day of my baptism arrived, and would you believe it, the only church that had a full immersion pool (and I wanted the full monty) was the one on the housing estate near Wolverhampton that was built from the same brick as the houses, including the one we used to lived in.

As an event, if I say so myself, my baptism went very well. We had lots of guitars before, during and afterwards, and we sang our thanks and prayed our prayers of praise. But ... something strange had happened during my 'total immersion', which only I knew or, for that matter, cared about, but which had disturbed me very deeply and very instantly. My right hand didn't go under the water. And for the second or so that I was submerged, time stood still as I struggled to pull my hand below the waterline, wanting so much to cleanse it of its sins. For it was the hand I had once smoked dope with, raised glasses of alcohol with, wanked with, squeezed the trigger of my gun with and written out betting slips with. Whenever I had sinned, my right hand had always been there or thereabouts. The fact that it didn't go beneath the water left me with the uneasy feeling that I hadn't really been properly baptised, and if you'd asked me there and then if I wanted to do it all over again, I would have said yes please. As I said, though, no one else noticed and the celebration around me continued. So all I could do was what I always did when I faced a problem back then: pray my way out of it.

I carried on praying every day, and as the days passed gradually my prayers began to be answered. The first major one was finding somewhere to live that was not only nice and spacious but also cheap and within the village. Once again it was a house on a new estate, but this one was much smaller than the estate we'd lived on near Wolverhampton and was run by a housing association.

The joy the blessing of our new home brought I can't tell you, though strangely enough, the first time my faith was tested was just before we moved into it. Because the house was close to where Carol's parents lived, we had the opportunity of decorating it throughout and fitting new carpet before we moved in. So for some time I was working on the building site during the day and then on the house at night. Although it was of my own free will, by trying so hard to make up for all of my past wrongs, in the end I practically worked myself into the ground. When it came to getting carpet we just about managed to afford the cheapest in the shop, but I would have to fit it myself. I struggled for the best part of the night, and when it came to cutting the biggest piece, which was for the lounge, I cut it two metres short. I can't tell you how angry I got, and I started to use language that I hadn't used out loud in months. Then I stopped cursing and I said a prayer, asking my Lord for forgiveness, and after that I patched up the carpet as best I could.

A few days later we moved in and life became better than it had ever been. Well, for me anyway. And do you know what? It got even better, because not only had the Lord provided us with somewhere to live, he then provided the chance of a new job for me. It came one evening, the way they so often do, via the local paper. Advertised in it was a position as Youth Training Officer for a YTS scheme in the not too far away town of Walsall. The address to write to was a church and the person to write was a reverend. So what with me and my faith, I asked the Lord for some help and I sat down and composed a letter of application.

A few days later I got a reply and few days later still I was at the job interview. Unlike any of the times when I had applied for jobs in Aberdeen, I confessed immediately to my time in prison. Mind you, the way I saw it, who better to give the kids some straight talking about the dangers of drugs? Fortunately for me, the vicar, God bless him, seemed to think the same thing, and when I left the building some two hours later I had a definite feeling that I'd landed that job. Well, feel again, Ken, because after a few more days I received a letter thanking me for coming in but saying sorry, the job had been given to someone else. Luckily I now had my faith to fall back on and so this time I simply deemed the bad news to be God's will and carried on working at the building site.

And here's a nice little tale of the type that you *can* find endless amounts of in one of those Christian bookshops. It turned out that me not getting the job must have just been the Lord testing my faith again, because a couple of weeks after my rejection I received a phone call out of the blue enquiring if I was still interested in the position. Only that afternoon on the building site I'd been praying for another chance to change my occupation, and I hadn't been home from work two minutes before the phone rang and the Lord provided. The following week I started my new job as a training officer, and when I kissed my wife and son goodbye in the morning before setting off for Walsall, for the first time in my life I truly felt normal. Whatever that is.

Of course, there had been times before when life had almost got sorted out for me and each time I'd somehow managed to fuck things up (sorry Lord). But this time that wasn't going to happen, because this time I had my Lord and Saviour Jesus Christ to care for me every step of the way.

And my faith just grew and grew. I can recall that one night I was alone in the church with the vicar, a young guy only a few years older than myself who more than anyone had been responsible for my indoctrination into mainline C of E Christianity. I was telling him how deep my faith was and he said to me that I probably wouldn't always feel that way, that along the road my faith would be tested. I can recall looking at him and thinking: 'You are so wrong, my friend. My faith is now unshakable.' And I really did believe that. I couldn't even begin to imagine ever losing the faith in God that I held at that moment. But my friend the vicar persisted and told me that was the whole point. As far as Satan was concerned I was now a top priority target, because I had once been one of his finest (and who could argue with that?) and he would want his servant back.

The young vicar was proved right, because my faith didn't last. Though Satan, if you like, worked it out of me slowly, and looking back I can see that my fall from salvation first got under way when the great serpent lured me into a pub one Saturday morning while I was out and about shopping in Wolverhampton.

I'd gone into the pub for no more than a quiet pint – though when I noticed that they had a pool table it was an added bonus, because I like a game of pool, I do. Looking around me, it didn't take me too long to realise that the pub I had found myself in was what would have been described where I came from as a 'bikers' pub'. Lots of rough-looking types in leather, shooting pool, listening to loud rock music from the jukebox and all in all having what in their book went for a good time. But I knew it wasn't a 'good' time, because everyone in the pub bar me had obviously not yet given up the wicked ways of the world.

It didn't take me too long either to recognise the smell of burning hash, which was being rolled and smoked quite openly by half the occupants of the pub. When it became my turn to have a go on the pool table, I won a few games and ended up playing a more than cute little black girl – who wasn't a bad a little player either. She whooped me, and as this was 1985 and not many women were into pool back then, it was a surprise when a mere girl gave you a good run for your money. After we'd played I joined her and a couple of her friends at their table and found out a little about life in Wolverhampton. While they were talking, me and my one-time jailbird's brain began to scan the pub and soon took in the fact that there were at least three different individuals within it who were selling dope. Of course, I knew right away that what with me being a good Christian boy now, I shouldn't really have been in such a place. But there again, I reckoned that if Jesus had been alive today this would have been the sort of place he'd have been in, as these would have been the type of people he'd have needed to hang out with to guide them on to the straight and narrow. So I bought a round of drinks and I had a few more games of pool, and when my time ran out I said goodbye to my new friends and headed off home to my wife and son. Although I left the place still feeling all righteous, and even uplifted by the fact that I'd managed to talk to the young and misguided, I shouldn't have. Because the most significant thing to come out of me going into that pub was not that I'd presented myself as an example of a good Christian, but that I now knew just where to go if I wanted to score some dope. Not that I'd ever want to, of course.

The next chiselling away at my faith happened in the bible group meetings, which, now that we had a place of our own, were regularly being held in our house. For me the big thing about my new faith was that it was a tolerant one, and of course this spread largely from me having needed the tolerance of so many people all my life that I felt it only fair to give some back. Another reason, though, would have to be that the religion I'd been brought up with, the misguided one, tolerated absolutely no one and no thing. And yet strangely enough I found myself defending the Jehovah's Witnesses whenever the subject of other 'cults' was raised at the bible group. And that was the interesting thing, and something I had never witnessed in all of my years of sit-down-and-be-quiet obedience to Jehovah God: there were definite theological disagreements within the group. In fact, as the weeks passed I would say that you could quite easily have divided the fifteen or so regulars into three distinct Protestant wings, and that's something you could never have done down at the Kingdom Hall.

I found myself one night getting very annoyed with one of the bible group's most, shall we say, devoted members (who prayed for guidance each morning as to what clothes to wear that day) when she went off on one about a new all-Muslim school that was going to be opened in Wolverhampton. The bottom line of her Christian argument of love and faith and kindness and forgiveness was that if 'these' Muslims wanted to live here, then they should accept our Christian ways. If they couldn't, then they should be sent back to whence they came. No, well, I'm sorry, but I couldn't have that and I certainly wasn't having it in my own house – the end result of which was that the woman left and we both promised to pray for each other.

The following weekend, as if Satan really was planning it all, our estate was visited by a foursome of door-knocking Jehovah's Witnesses. When they climbed out of their car I was at the sink doing the washing up, and as they went from door to door

I happily followed their progress through the kitchen window. I then noticed that in a garden across the way, on his knees and obviously humbly praying to the Lord, was a member of our bible group. After he'd finished his prayers, he got to his knees and started to walk my way. When he reached our threshold I already had the door open and I invited him in for coffee. Refusing my offer, he asked instead if I'd like to join him on his knees out on the pavement so that we could pray while 'this evil' was among us. And make no mistake, those four followers of Satan, with their false bible and their lie-filled *Watchtower* magazines, they were evil.

Well, once again, I'm afraid I was not having that. My eldest sister was, and still is, a devout Jehovah's Witness, and she and her family may have been misguided, but no way in the world were they evil people. The exact opposite, in fact. So please go away. Interestingly enough (though not really, 'cos it's the same every time), when the four Jehovah's Witnesses reached my door that day and I invited them in to tell me all about it, as soon as they heard that I'd been brought up in the faith myself, they didn't want to talk about Jehovah God any more.

The next crack in my faith, and the one that caused the leak that was to burst the spiritual dam, was when I fell into temptation and had a few puffs on a joint. Wasn't my fault either, Lord. As you know, as you know everything, I was led astray. I went to have a few drinks after work with some of my new white-collar workmates and one of them, who was female and gorgeous to boot, invited everyone back for coffee afterwards, so I went along. Back at her place we all had a few more drinks, and when the joint got round to me, exactly like those German birds in that army drug abuse film, mein hostess started leaning over me, dangling her boobs in my face and urging me on. The long and short, not to mention tall and wide of which was that I got stoned.

I didn't get completely out of it, though, because when I felt it was time to leave I managed to do so without partaking of the fruits on offer. However, on the drive back I was so stoned that after driving for about twenty minutes I suddenly woke up and didn't have a clue where I was, and it then took me another hour to find my way home.

Once I'd had that joint, that was the beginning of the end really. I still tried to tell myself that having a toke wasn't that sinful, but I knew it was more than just the physical smoking of drugs. It was the lies that started again because of it. Naturally, when I got back home to Carol that night I said nothing to her about the smoke, and when, later the same week, I was invited back for another one, I didn't mention that either.

The next thing to start again was the gambling. Since the Lord had saved me I hadn't so much as bought a raffle ticket, but for some reason, just like that, having just passed a bookie's on the way home from work one afternoon, suddenly I was cutting across the traffic to pull into a parking space. When I got into the bookie's I said to myself that I was only going to lose a couple of quid and when I'd done that I'd go on home. Mind you, if I did win then I'd stay a bit longer. And do you know what? If there's one place on Earth where you can really witness the workings of Satan, it's in a bookie's. Someone walks into a betting shop for the first time, or a casino, come to that, doesn't even know how to write out a betting slip or place a chip on a table, and what happens? Ninety-nine times out of a hundred, they win. I tell you, if ever there was a foolproof gambling system, it would have to be going into a casino or a bookie's, picking out the first-timers and then following whatever they were betting on. And so the first time I go into a bookie's for months, I win.

And then that really was it. From there on, the loss of my faith was a mere formality. Only a matter of time. And once the faith was gone, everything else soon followed. With the money I'd won gambling, instead of, say, buying clothes for my child or maybe a present for my long-suffering wife, I went to the pub I'd discovered in Wolverhampton and scored myself some smoke of my own. When I did finally get back home again, lying that there had been a crisis at work, it wasn't very long before I was out again, walking the village to have a sneaky joint. The next time I went into the betting shop I of course lost all the money I'd won on my previous visit and more, and in no time I was a regular in the shop.

Because of my earlier disagreement with various members of the bible group it wasn't too hard to stop holding the meetings at our house, although for a while I did still go to them as they moved around the village. I also still went to church every Sunday, where I told myself on numerous occasions that I'd only suffered a slight backslide and would soon get back on the straight and narrow. But I never did. The simple truth was that I no longer believed. And I soon realised that I never really had, that all I'd been doing was pretending. And that bit of me that I've mentioned before, the bit that had travelled the world and lived for adventure, it just wasn't having it any more.

Almost as soon as I started to gamble and buy dope again, the money troubles started to build up and we fell behind with the rent, although Carol knew nothing about it. To make up the shortfall I went into the bank one afternoon and, on the strength of my regular salary payments, got a loan for £300. For a week or so things straightened themselves out, but eventually I wasted all of the loan and before long I was financially back in the position I'd been in before taking it out, only now with repayments to make.

The final act of my fall from grace came about one Saturday afternoon after I'd been playing rugby for the village team. After the game I got pissed to high heaven, and then, driving at speeds I should never have reached even if I'd been sober, I death-wished it home through the country lanes. My life flashed before my eyes when I lost control on a sharp bend and skidded across the road and into a ditch. I walked away from the wreckage with no more than a few shakes, but as for the car, it was a complete write-off, and how I was going to get it out of the ditch I didn't know. Eventually I got a friendly local farmer to tow the car back into the village for me, but after the local mechanic had looked at it he announced that it was good for no more than scrap. The thing that made the whole incident so ironic was that only the evening before I had given a lecture to teenagers in the village on the dangers of drink and drug abuse.

Then I was sent to Devon for a week to attend a training course for work, and it was while I was away from home that the game of deceit I'd been playing became well and truly up. The thing that did it was the post. Before going away to Devon, each morning I'd been able to intercept the postman and hide any letters from the bank or the housing association. While I was away, though, Carol got to the post first and then tons of it hit the fan. I got the news that all was not well when I phoned home one evening.

Carol had been walking around thinking everything was A-OK at last, but in the opening of a few envelopes her whole world had been shattered. She had known nothing of the loan I'd taken out, or the overdraft I'd built up at the bank, or the weeks we were behind with the rent. After the phone call home I had the rest of the week to worry about what awaited me on my return and to at least try and come up with some sort of excuse. Trouble was, by the time I did get back to the village I was so fed up to the core with myself and all my fuck-ups that I just couldn't be bothered to make any more excuses. The only excuse I could give was that it was just the way I was.

As for Carol and how she now felt after yet another set of letdowns, she was having no more of it. She wanted me to please go before I made any more of a mess of everyone's life. In response, all I could do was agree. I couldn't even find it in myself to plead for yet one more chance.

To be honest, I didn't really know what I was going to do next, it wasn't like I had the money to do anything, but – jammy git that I sometimes am – when I returned to work on the Monday and explained to my boss the vicar that Carol and I would be going our separate ways and so I would probably move to my dad's in Cornwall, he offered me a job in Devon on a new YTS scheme that he was setting up. As the position came with accommodation *and* the same rate of pay as I was already receiving, I just couldn't refuse. So once again, just like that, and through no one's fault but my own, my life took another major turn and off I went to live in Kingsteignton, Devon.

At weekends I drove up to the Midlands to see my son, and I guess every now and then I would even have a go at working my way back into Carol's affections, but this time she was adamant that we had reached the end. And who could blame her?

Eventually, as the months passed, I met another woman and, the way us boys so often are, was swept off my feet in a matter of minutes. After I'd gone, Carol applied for and got a job in London, and with me out of her life it was only a matter of months before she was up on her feet again and living the life she had always deserved but had never had a chance of getting while I was still on the scene. And life goes on.

Today, with what I can only describe as hurt and shame, I have to confess that I can't even remember when I last saw Carol, or, for that matter, our son. It must be at least ten years ago now, and even within myself I can't really work out how that came about. But it did, and it did because of me.

One day, though, I can't help but believe that there'll come a knock on my door, and just like I was always taught down at the Kingdom Hall of Jehovah's Witnesses, it will be my turn to stand and bear witness to the life that was (and still is) mine.

And all I can say in my defence is that I just didn't know how to love anyone. Like I'd never been taught. Although today I really do know how to hate me.

But please don't be concerned on my account, because I can always just roll another smoke to get over it.

After all, your Marijuana Time – they do say it's practically harmless.